Lucky S.O.B.

~

American without the Dream

A Biographic Memoir

By

Michael McNaney

ISBN: 979-8-218-92130-9

Table of Contents

This book is dedicated to my Father.
Tales of people he never really knew, yet affected greatly.

Foreword

When I see some celebrity I've heard of has written their memoirs, it seldom piques my interest. I'll think of what I know of that person, limited as it may be, and imagine what I know of them. I'll hold these imaginations up to my own experiences and compare flavors.

Usually, popular memoirs are from famous people, about famous people. Perhaps someone not so famous, but maybe had a very interesting or controversial chapter in their life everyone might like to know more about. Perhaps they accomplished something extraordinary, or something extraordinary happened to them. In the past decades of the 1900's, I'm sure we hear personal tales of childhoods wrought with hardship. The path leading to the ladder up was difficult, they were being held back or given a helping hand, the drama of love found, love lost.

I do read, yet have never actually read a memoir. The prospect of reading one has never intrigued me, I really don't know what goes on in there. I guess I've been too busy living my own life for one to catch my appeal. Unless there is some common thread between us, other people's sagas haven't interested me much. Though I would never dismiss anyone else's experience.

Experience is every person's spice of life. In our own minds, a fine blend of sour cream and Siracha. We all live such different lives here in America, some plain, some with sprinkles, some with chunks in the mix. Often, we don't have enough respect for other people and their experience, we tend to scoff, and why we do is rarely given second thought.

But I *do know* why I think this way....
Because I've been around, and I mean *Really around*.

- *Foreword*

I lived through times when our attitudes, morality, technology and social convention simply wasn't the same, the differences are actually quite stark.

I don't mean as in the old guy shaking his fist in defiance; *"Back in my day,"* or, *"kids used to have respect!"* Those being rose glasses situations. A conservative looking glass into our own individual past experience and the times we cherish most. Everyone has those better than now memories.

Everyone also has their sob story and their time of loss. These are merely part of our human experience, not necessarily something to write a book about. A person must go far beyond everyday situation to be set apart. They must beat the odds in a fashion the world has seldom seen, *And,* it needs to end well. If not for the person themselves, then for the environment in which they achieved and all those that follow.

We rarely see a popular memoir about an American who hasn't gained fame in one way or another. Yet, rather than memoirs from famous people, I lean towards biographies and documentaries. All kinds, individual, topical and situational, I love them, even search them out. An overall representation of time and situation. I especially like the ones which give perspective into the pain others have experienced and the conditions under which it was spurned. Big picture, Real life, Real tragedy, Real Love. *This* is my kind of looking glass.

In the past, when thinking of my own life and convolutes traversed, I've kept it all to myself. Being protected by modesty, it's easy to imagine those familiar with what constitutes a worthy memoir giving silent derisive scoffs. I think back to previous peoples enduring decades of oppression and toil as slaves. To those throughout the ages with lives so hard or violent, we today can't hold a candle to the pain they've been a part of, the suffering they've seen.

The type of pain a couple dollar bills won't ease.

Am I worthy?
Maybe not to stand in the halls of history, but has the entirety of my life been outrageous and interesting in the broader sense? Yes, immensely so. This book could be considered a confessional as well as biography or memoir.
Is confession worthy?

I've long since gone quiet on the subject, but I used to quip with my friends about experiences with my first wife. Maybe they knew her and were there for some of it and agreed. Perhaps they were late-comers shaking their head in disbelief then offering; I should write it all down.
I'd say; *"Yeah, one day I may sit down and give Steven King a run for his money."*

Yet that part of life was merely a chapter, not even an interesting one as far as I'm concerned. She actually helped in a sense, a tenderizer so what was to come wouldn't hurt so bad. A bit of respite from what had been. It may have been interesting, dramatic and even at times horrific, but in the grand scheme, not enough to claim as a life's defining hardship. For some other people in the mix, definitely so, but for myself, I try to blank it out. I certainly don't want to spend my remaining days hovering on that time in my life.

I've often thought perhaps I shouldn't say much about my past lest I become embarrassed. Maybe the statute of limitations hasn't quite run out on some of it.
Will I get a knock on the door? A visit from dark suits? Death threats? Exploding Candy-gram?

Setting a bad example is perhaps my deepest concern, yet I do realize those days are gone. The American experience has morphed so fast that most of what my life has consisted of can never be duplicated.

- *Foreword*

The advent of cameras everywhere, advancing technology, and instant everything, precludes anyone nowadays from being able to do, or get away with most of what filled my life. The technologies today are nothing but a sad replacement for what used to be actual life experience.

"My life was so hard, I had to twerk on Insta for tips," won't be able to hold anyone's attention in a future memoir. Everyone can do it, it seems everyone *is* doing it, even those who perhaps shouldn't.

The days of Daredevils, Outlaws, Cowboys and exploration are gone. Our attentions are now skewed more towards money grubbing and scrolling. The circumstances I've been involved in are thought of as todays fiction, and because of modern technologies, can no longer be experienced in the same way. This gives me a satisfaction, an inner feeling of confidence most people will never get to know.

In this book I open up and recount several tales I've never before spoken out loud. Many involving death, destruction and questionable moral compass. I was prompted to discuss many of them with my Grandfather in his last days. A man who lived 105 years and by virtue of being an American, had the same opportunity to experience more than even I can imagine. As we talked, I found myself judging his life as beyond the pale. In my eyes, a life of wasted opportunity, exactly the same way he was judging me. It turned out we were seeing each other from opposite ends of American culture.

I eventually came around to seeing us as what we really were, extreme opposites using the same playbook. Two people of the same family lineage, viewing and experiencing the same world in two completely different ways. Two people whose paths would never have crossed had he not been my Grandfather.

Foreword -

Throughout our lives, we each avoided contact with the likes of the other. Our satisfactions do not come from the same place. His defining lifelong ideal was to stifle his life, living for promises after, mine is to live a life of happiness till it ends.

I often muse to myself on how I got to where I am. Many doors opened easily, perhaps too easily. The beginning doesn't match this end, or any parts in the middle. From what we all know of our daily lives, this is not how it is supposed to work, yet it did. Given the indications of my childhood, many would guess my life would end in a fashion stereotypical of the path I was raised on; it will not.

The secret to my life's satisfaction *can* be had without the turmoil, drama and death, but it takes an introspection. Something which was thrust upon me, something I hope to spurn in the reader. Hopefully with a lighter touch than what I've pushed through.

Here, I hope to be able to help others think about where our lives are going. Hold this memoir up to their own and compare flavors. Maybe to think how we are raising our children, the consequences of our individual actions on one another and what drives us to how and why we do things.

If you have the stomach, please try to read this without judgement. This is actually a reveal of two American men, one of whom lived the extremes in the last decades of modern life that allowed it. The other, given the same opportunities, living his entire life devoted to God, immersed in religion and everything that entails.
Which will *you* judge as worthy?

I hope through reading this I can help *YOU* find a measure of satisfaction for yourself.

You, finding satisfaction through *me*, what a great ending to this memoir that would be.

As we live, challenged by many situations, our lives can be likened to a muse by Omar Khayyam. A muse, when first I read, proved and validated Mr. Khayyam's ability to convey broad meaning, with few words. Personally, I take it as both metaphor and invitation.

"The moving finger writes; and having writ, moves on. Nor all thy piety nor wit shall lure it back to cancel half a line. Nor all thy tears, wash out a word of it."

As snaps and creaks, and other odd sounds now follow me around; it's hard to imagine, yet easy to believe. I am now over sixty years old, an age I never imagined of myself. In today's environment, not particularly old. Yet, an age many who have known me, never thought I would see.

I'm not feeling old, not whining, that's not the point.
Have you ever throughout your life thought forward to how your life might be at a specific age? I have, different milestone years and ages.

From an early age, the year 2000 was an intrigue, I was to be 36, 2012-48, 2024-60. How will I have turned out? What will I be doing then? What will be the color my flying car? I have always thought to the future and how I would get there in one way or another. Yet, it is safe to say; Our imaginations rarely render the future as we eventually find it.

Strangely, I never imagined myself being sixty-one or over. For me, these were numbers on the other side of the hill. From that point on, I've assumed we can all just turn off at any moment, too old or weak to continue...

Let's see if I can get through this without keeling over.

I'm going to start-off closer to the end...

Lucky S.O.B.

Chapter One

In March of 2022 I found myself back in Des Moines.
I seem to have completed some sort of grand diaspora, yet I'd hate to put a limit on myself like that.

Many in my family thought I was nuts. Why on Earth would anyone do this to themselves? Why would I subject myself to the overbearing piety, ridicule... the endless judgement?

Since an all-encompassing change of mind washed over me several years earlier, sanity has been a topic breeched when I've made choices others were unsure of. I now make decisions from a different head space than most everyone else. What they were all thinking, giving me derisive looks, shaking their heads, casting their doubt, didn't bother me at all. I knew there was no-one in this family circle with any basis to draw like understanding from.

Though, I did have a few doubts of my own as we drove into town. This move felt different than others I'd made. As the page flipped to this next chapter, there was no familiar feeling of relief. The wide-open freshness I'd felt in the past when shaking off the ludd *(life's mud)* wasn't here this time.

It didn't help the weather was overcast, cold and muddy, a thin layer of dirty snow spotting the ground. Yet, as we drove into town, I could still feel the child-like familiarity this town has always held for me.

Still, for my arrival, I wish the day presented better.

Over the last decade, Gavin and I had become used to this, I could tell he wasn't bothered. We both had a confidence borne of familiarity. I knew just what to do and in what order, he knew I knew and was ready to hold up his end. First, I would get on my phone's map-app and look for State Parks. Next would be food banks, and when all that was settled, we'd look for rentals.

We started in Tucson, it was a two-week trip through Seattle to get here. Now, there was just enough money to rent an apartment and get through the next few weeks. It would take a little time to find a place and we most likely couldn't get in till the first of the month. So, as managed several times before, a tent pitched in a local State Park would do until it all came together.

We have spent a lot of time outdoors roughing it. A State Park was like the Marriot compared to some of the desert nethers and forests we'd visited in the past. Fully equipped for a camping stay, we had anything and everything needed for living outdoors. Camping doesn't bother us in the slightest.

A few days after getting settled in, I'd get a hold of Gramps and tell him we were here. Although previously mentioned during our last phone call, he wasn't really expecting us to come for an extended stay. I told him we were coming, but like everyone else in the family, he was incredulous as to the reasoning.

I told him Arizona was too much, it was time to leave.
I have always enjoyed Des Moines while visiting over the years, I thought I'd see how I liked it there, all true. I could see from his point of view though, he knew the family scoreboard. There was a reason for only getting an occasional call from family members, and he was just fine with that. He was on the path to salvation, we had our own path to wherever our sin was taking us.

For various reasons I myself am not quite sure of, and although no-one else in the family does, I feel a certain kinship to him. It's not heartfelt obligation as some might imagine, no, kinship is the right word. Over time, he alienated his children and most of his grandchildren with an overbearing religious attitude and was now living the results.

From the mid nineteen-fifties onward, my Grandfather shunned all secular entertainment. There was no smoking, drinking or foul language; no cards, gambling or dancing. Television and radio were for sports and news, nothing more. The only movies to watch would be Bible stories, and even then, he would pick them apart as not being true to the Bible. The only books he ever read besides his own industry publications were the Holy Bible and religious texts in exploration of the Bible.

His religious attitude was something to be wary of, yet skews of righteous indignation haven't been able to vex me for many years. Gavin and I are both conventional anomalies, we don't really fit in. Hard to reconcile with either secular or religious conventional thought.

To me, Gramps represented a challenge of sorts. He has been a conventionally minded person since childhood. His life has been completely controlled by, and lived within, the dogma of conservative Christian religion, borne within the expanding Capitalist mindset.

A mouthful at the very least, how do people of his ilk turn out? We all know of the effort religions take throughout our lives to control and recruit, what do they have for us when we are at the end of a life lived within all that?

I had hopes that being here with him would be a great learning experience and an enriching time of life for both of us.

Moving back to Des Moines wasn't an easy decision though. I was living a pseudo-decent life there in Tucson. Aside from the searing heat in the Summers, I could manage. Yet, hiding from sunlight and moving from one air-conditioned space to another wasn't fulfilling in any way, I felt stagnant.

I could move to Des Moines, get a fresh start and take care of my Grandfather, or I could let things unfold there in Tucson. If I let things progress as they inevitably would, I could see heartache was not far ahead.

I had a very nice girlfriend I'd come to realize was the kind of person I'd like to spend time with. Opinionated about the important things, soft, thoughtful, naive'. Not full of self-importance, not controlling, easy on the eyes, keeps up with me in wordplay and wit and would throw a few dry zingers at just the right time. Attributes I'd found pieces of in other women but not all at once. The problem was, she had children, one of which was still in school, and her Ex was across town. Although she loathed Tucson, she was committed to stay, at least a few more years.

On the other hand, I was living in a nice situation. I was the maintenance man for my landlord's properties, living in a nice mobile home within her gated and secure compound. Her husband died the year previous leaving two children. She trusted me implicitly and gave me advantage at every turn to make the most of the situation.

She was well-off, very good looking and throwing signals at me like a third base coach. I eventually would have given in and created a bad situation for myself. I did not want to leave my girlfriend and certainly did not want to hurt her. I also did not want to be a leather faced maintenance man stuck in Tucson for the rest of my life.

I... we, my girlfriend and I, had mused about leaving for a nicer place, settling into a peaceful loving life away from the mind-numbing heat and violence of Tucson. If I moved away to a nicer place and kept up with her, maybe one day this still had a chance. I hope so, *"If you Love, let it go..."*
You know; all-that. *Fingers crossed.*

The first part of the plan was together. Standard occurrence for me, within a few days we found the best deal on an apartment, in the best area we could have hoped for. There was really no doubt, I have always been charmed that way. Since the very first house I rented as a teen, great living situations seem to appear out of nowhere.

We would be able to move-in April first, yet the apartment was empty now. Not vacant, but not being lived in. A woman with a new baby was leasing there but was now living elsewhere getting help with her new child. All her belongings were in the apartment and we found she had no help to move. In exchange for our help moving her out, we would move-in early. Gavin and I were now Iowans.

Gramps and I had the same visits we'd become accustomed to over the years. An hour or so of small talk at his apartment, maybe lunch with the same. Then he'd go about his business I was no part of. For the first couple months, he was very suspicious and wary of my intent. He was often short with me and seemed irritated. Judging everything from my speech to reasonings with his self-righteous confidence.

One day, I was at home on the couch after a particularly harsh morning with him. Gavin was going to the store and I gave him some money to get something for me. I continued mulling over the morning's conversation, asking myself whether I should continue. If these *"going to hell"* type digs were going to continue, I might as well move-on and leave Gramps to his own devices.

After-all, part of my life's ideal was now to leave the negative behind, all of it, no matter what. It disturbed me a little I was seeing Gramps as a negative after all I'd previously thought.

Gavin soon came back and gave me my item and change. Not carrying coins anymore, I separate and save them for when they build up enough to pay for something. I also don't keep pennies newer than 1980.

I was filtering this change, and there were only two pennies face down in the lot. The first I flipped was not unusual, 1964, my birth year. One of the highest production years for pennies, many are still seen regularly in circulation. No surprise other than it was still a bit shiny, I appreciated that. The second made the hair stand-up on my neck. It was a wheatback penny, well-worn and flipped to reveal 1919, Grandpas birth year. The discussion with myself was now over. I taped the two pennies together and tucked them away.

In short time I invited myself to his church on Sunday, something he couldn't say no to, then we'd go out for lunch after. I manipulated the situation with my knowledge of his favorite subject.

He was impressed with my ability to turn directly to a passage in the Bible without looking at the table of contents. Also, that I could come up with not just popular everyday bible verses, but could discuss some of the deep-cuts he enjoyed. I let him know, this ability was partially of his doing. He was the driving religious force in my childhood. I have read and studied the Christian Bible several times over and it pretty much all started with him.

The first year I was in Des Moines Gramps was stand-offish. There were rules and sideways looks. I could come over after 11am, I needed to leave by two. One Sunday while eating lunch, he looked over at me with his matter-of-fact attitude.

"*You know I'm out of money, I'm down to Social Security now, never thought I'd live this long.*"

Offered with an intent stare; more accusation than comment.

I knew this was coming at some point so I dove right in...

"I'm not here for your money, I don't want anything. If that were the case, you'd already be feeling ill from the poison. I'm a pensioner too if that makes you feel any better. We might have to wash dishes for this meal. I'll wash, you dry."

He gave a little chuckle, "*Well, just so you know.*"

That first year I volunteered at the DSM Street Collective to keep busy, a homeless advocacy organization. My mechanical ability is as good as any, so I helped out in their bicycle shop and with any other help they needed from me. Also needing something to keep busy, Gavin jumped in and did the same.

Gavin and Gramps were a mystery to each other, so although he fully appreciated the old guy, Gavin didn't feel the need to hang around him as much as I did. He spent time on his bike exploring the town, hanging out at the Lake and playing pick-up volleyball. The girls were always attracted to him so the Collective gave a good reason to be busy when he needed a break from being popular.

Then came Gramps' 104th birthday.
His 103rd was shortly after we arrived a year earlier and he wanted nothing special, it passed without event. This year, he assumed was going to be the same, except this year I knew more of his church friends. His nephews and niece came from across the state. Church friends showed up separately and we all had a more traditional celebration.

Yet it was nothing like his 100th, my Sister coordinated that with over 50 people at a golf course clubhouse venue.

Complete with balloons, big history pictures on the walls and speeches. Friends and family came from all over, many of us flew in for that one. Those who never called, put their beef to the side and showed up. One hundred is a big deal, at the very least, a big celebration was expected. He made a grand entrance by insisting to show up by himself. Dozens of us were standing around waiting when Gramps drove up alone. He successfully showed us all; he was a 100-year-old wonder and fully capable.

Still, his hundredth was when I started to formulate the plan to move back to Des Moines. He was fine, but showing his age. His last wife was gone three years by then. One-hundred years old and all alone just didn't seem right.

It went unspoken, but I could tell he was happy to have a little extra attention on his 104th. A Chiropractor his entire working life and six-foot two, people looked up to him and gave him their attention. Being a 70-year resident of Des Moines, he was quite well-known and a right popular guy in his many church circles. Yet his generational friends and acquaintances were all long gone, he was missing the daily interaction with like minds.

With 104 came another driving test. Every couple year's after 75 in Iowa a person has to prove themselves to stay behind the wheel. Honestly, I think the testing is a little lax. He passed it easily at 100 and 102 and perhaps shouldn't have. This guy needed a lot of room to maneuver and his finesse for the controls was pretty much nil.

We talked about it at the next Sunday dinner. He didn't think he could pass the test this time. After a little muse on his life of driving and the different cars he'd owned throughout the years, he came out with it:

"It might be time I hung it up. My license is still good for 60 days after my birthday though so I'll keep at it for a while."

It would be a few more weeks before the town was safe again. Three weeks after his birthday I was with him the last time he drove; we nearly died. Several people went home that night with a wild story about some crazy old guy to tell at dinner. Two curbs, a median, taking a right in the middle of an intersection from the left turning lane, and smacking the pump isle at the gas station. It's a bit funny now, a complete Mr. Magoo adventure, but back then, I was a bit shaken-up.

I told him I'd buy a cap and be his chauffer. His insurance was outrageous because of his age, he was paying nearly three hundred per month for one ten-year old car.

We switched his car over to my insurance; I would now drive him anywhere he needed to go. This was the turning point, his attitude changed from thinking I was setting him up for a retirement home, to acceptance of what I was telling him all along, *"just here to help."*

He was thinking deeply about me being here. I could actually perceive the stairsteps we were taking towards acceptance. Each time before leaving his apartment, before shutting the door I would wish him good night and say "I love you." Mostly, his return would be a head nod or slight wave. Now, I was starting to get smiles with the nods, a *"you too,"* occasionally, and not long after starting to drive him, he even volunteered a *"Love you, see you later."* Them old dogs and their new tricks. This isn't something my Mother and Uncle were used to, apparently I was conjuring "small miracles."

He was having trouble with the small buttons on his ten-year old flip phone so I bought him a smart phone to make it easier to contact me. From this point on, I and all his friends would get three or four miss dials a day. Even with me putting icons on the front screen for all the things he needed, he never really figured that phone out. It gave him something to fiddle with when he was bored though.

He was very intrigued, it was the only piece of modern tech he ever owned other than a huge flat screen TV.

We would go to the store together but eventually he would make lists, give me money and I would go for him. Each time, he would try and give me ten dollars as payment but I always turned it down.

"It's part of the deal, no compensation needed. You can pay for dinner or coffee when we go out."

This never sat well with him, he always felt he needed to pay me for doing things for him. There was extra money, he always had a good bit left over each month, but money availability wasn't the issue. The issue was my altruistic attitude, this was off kilter for him.

I noticed his mental dependence on money as both a character reveal and an opportunity. I already knew it, this old dog was lacking another trick, I would make sure he understood, I expected nothing. When he would get indignant, my favorite prodding reminder would always quiet him down.

"What would Jesus do?"
"Yeah, well you aren't Jesus."
"But shouldn't we all try to be more like him?"
- Crickets -

This is an ideal I took-on back in 2013. I no longer accept money as compensation for casual work. I would really rather do everything for free. It's part of my "stick-it-to-convention," anti-establishment mentality. I am serious about this altruism stuff. Although I will admit, it has been a bane as well as a blessing. It frustrates most everyone, not just my Grandfather. Some people refuse this attitude and separate themselves from it. Unfortunately, those people I rarely see again.

Sorry for that, but I won't apologize for being this way, that's just silly on its face. I always feel a little sorry for those folks, what a terrible problem to have.

I've noticed these situational phenomena throughout my life, but in 2013 had time and reason to explore the idea. At that time, there was someone taking care of me at no cost and out of nothing more than the goodness of their heart. Back then I felt a twinge of guilt also. Since then, after much practice, I found Altruism can be a lifestyle.

When I perform services, fix things, make things, do things of any type for free, people take notice. I make good friends and am usually taken care of at a level equal to or greater than what I did for them. I don't have to ask, or plot, or connive. All I have to do is quash conventional greed training in favor of Altruism. It works out great, I love it.

It also worked out great in the case of my Grandfather. I don't need money from him, I get-by fine. The sums he offers up are paltry in comparison to the good feelings I have and the bonding we've accomplished simply by me not taking any compensation. I don't think he realized it at the time, but he came around.

Sometime at the end of June he started having health issues. He had good insurance so I took him to the hospital. I am aware of all the reasons and excuses hospitals have for their shortcomings, but that place treated him terribly. Luckily his issue was fixable and taken care of. On the way home we discussed it. I told him next time, for anything, I was taking him to the VA hospital.

Something else I knew, which apparently he had no idea of was; if he was in WW2, he had free full-coverage health insurance. He could have saved himself a lot of money and aggravation over the years.

The same recurring issue popped up a few weeks later, I took him to the VA and they treated him like a celebrity. People came in his room to visit and shake his hand. A WWII veteran over a hundred years old pulls a lot of weight at the VA, couldn't have been better.

Prodded by the doctors there, I started looking around for reasons to why he was having these issues. He started going downhill again and this time it seemed a bit worse.

There are no guarantees but I think he was having bachelor nutrition issues. I was buying him exactly the food he asked for but looking through it all and adding up the nutrition and caloric intake numbers, they didn't add up. I think his body was shutting down. He started having intestinal and renal issues.

I started making all his meals with this in mind but he slipped further. The VA had a special team come to his place and keep track of him, they did a great job. Thin as a rail his entire life, he was never more than a variance of five pounds from a lifelong weight of 180lbs. At 6-2", that's skinny, now he was 134lbs, skin covered bones. They thought he was on his way out. They recommended visits from VA Home Hospice team.

Until this point, I had merely been playing the part of a family helper he was familiar with. I'm sure I thought more of him than he of me. I had fond memories of him from my youth, he had none of that. Behind those eyes I could tell, he imagined God sent him a heathen he was familiar with to help him out. This was his kind of reasoning, very biblical, and who was I to say why I was prodded to move here. There are certainly other people in my family I would not do this for.

I stayed with him all day for over two months while he laid in bed. Now, we would start to talk like friends, I would start to hear his ideas, reasonings and laments.

Now, both of us would start to see who the other really was.

Lucky S.O.B.

Chapter Two

Gramps was generally in bed, but not incapacitated. He still moved about his bedroom. Sitting in his favorite mail reading chair. Still happily writing checks to Christian charities and paying the few remaining bills from his desk.

His issues at this time were weakness and restroom problems. He occasionally wandered out and watched a little TV at news time and meals, but most of his time was spent trying not to be completely tired of being tired. It got to a point he would sometimes call me into his room to help him turn over in bed, stand up and sit down.

At first, we pretended it was all normal. Just a little something like the flue or perhaps a malaise he would eventually snap out of. I went along with this feeling different, but what else to do? I played along.

One day, late in the afternoon he looked at me with a concerned face. I could tell there was something serious on his mind. He wanted me to do something he considered extremely personal for him.

"Mike, I need some skivvies, can you get me some?"

I was relieved it wasn't something that took brain power. We lightly discussed it, I did it, in the interest of modesty, nuff said. I got back later that day with the package.

Gramps and I had come to a place where there was nothing much to say to fill dead air so we took opportunities to make each other laugh, usually very dry and deadpan stuff.

I've always been good at making anyone laugh but generally most of what's funny about what he says is only humorous because he actually thinks it's funny. You understand by now, salvation isn't funny so he has very little experience.

I handed him the package and told him;
"I saw a guy selling underwear on the side of the road, he had your size so I got you a few. He said they weren't used but the package is open, so let me know. If they're used, I'll take them back and give him what-for."

He looked up at me, started to laugh, pitched forward, shook, coughed shaking his head then choked and couldn't catch his breath. All went still, he stopped breathing for at least 15 seconds. I thought that was it. I stood there blank.

Then, he just sat up like an animatron which just had its power turned on. He sat back, looked at me and felt his chest.
"oooh, I've got a pain... Oh, are these my underwear?"
He'd apparently forgotten the joke and that he'd just laughed so hard it took him off-line.
Or...
The joke was on me. I'm not sure he had the chops for that, but the possibility is titillating. That itself would have been a little humorous if I weren't still in shock. I was standing there slack jawed thinking about what I was going to say to the cops.

Keeping his nutrition issues in mind, I tried to swank up meal time a little bit. I would try and make food from his past or perhaps something he may have never tried.

Long story short: Whole milk, turkey and dressing, pie: Good. Pad Thai chicken, anything curry, foreign in name or just in general... cold, hot or not: Bad.

We settled on a rotation of standard Americanized foods. He felt a responsibility to the Iowa Pork council so they had to be included in a meaningful way.

The corn Farmers and the local Dairy also needed a place at the table. Pork loin, corn, potatoes, side salad, whole milk and pie, those were the *go-to* staples. When he would ask for food I myself won't eat, I'd just nod my head and hold my nose; liver and onions? *Oh my.*

I was curbing my embarrassment after serving him soup on a sunny day by ordering take-out to the door, when it just popped out of me:

"Hey, you know I've always been interested in your early days, you've never mentioned anything about when you were a kid."

I've asked many times in as many ways to see if there was anything out of the ordinary that happened in his life. Something he's done or been a part of which may have been special or above and beyond other than WW2, but his answer has always been the same; *"I've served the Lord."*
This time I was hoping to eek-out a little more than that.

"What was it like before sunlight? Did everyone have to carry around torches?"

He smiled and chortled a bit.
"Oh, no. Fire came much later."

"I see, Colonel Sanders was just a Private back then, so I guess cold raw chicken was the norm huh? feathers and all?"

"Yes, raw potatoes too. Chipped my tooth on one, see...."
He opened his mouth to bared gums.
I never knew he had an upper plate, I'd never before seen him without it, his display startled me and we both laughed.

"Well, what is it you you'd like to know? It's all still in here."

He tapped his head, I could see he would be happy to spend time and prove his memory.

"Tell me about your parents, I don't know much about them, I remember Great Grandpa a bit, but his wife not at all."

"Oh, well... it was standard stuff for the day. Both came to the country in their youth with their parents, late 1800s. From Germany, you know that. Came across from New York to Waterloo in a wagon, they already knew some people here. A few of my Uncles were already here in Iowa. My Dad was a trained tool and Die maker so he was able to get a pretty good job as long as they could understand him, he was also half deaf, you know that too I'm sure, it affected his speech a little. That made it harder for him but he was a good provider, we never went without food or shelter when I was young, I was born in 1919 you know, Pauline, my sister, you remember her don't you? she was born a few years earlier.

"What did they all do for work?"

" Well, by the time I was old enough to know anything, I remember we lived in a big house with others in the family, my Aunt and Uncles too. In Waterloo, that's where Pauline and I were born. I remember going back and visiting a lot after we moved but that house was replaced at some point and isn't there now. My earliest memories are from there. Mother's job was taking care of us and keeping things clean and straight at home. Women didn't work outside the home back then. My Dad worked at Chamberlain Machine works across town, not sure what he did before then but he was a tool and die maker.... I told you that.

In 1928 he finally saved up enough money to buy an acre of land outside town. After a short while, he also bought a very large chicken coop and had it moved to the land. We lived in that chicken coop for a year while he and my uncles were building our first house, the house is still there last I saw. The houses in that area were far apart back then, we were on the edge of town in the country.

Dad wanted to keep it that way so he bought the acre next door awhile later. The whole time we lived there until I left married, we had a Jersey Cow and a dozen Chickens on that acre next door with the old chicken Coop returned to its original use and a shelter for the Cow.
Is that ramble enough?"

"Wow, yeah, see, I never knew any of that, very interesting stuff. Lived in a Chicken Coop? wow. It's fun to imagine that time for me, it seems so innocent now."

"It does to me too, life was much simpler...."

He had been looking at his hands in his lap, now he looked up and over at me.

"It was just as hard to get by though, probably harder, we had no handouts, every man and boy worked. I was doing odd jobs for nickels. It was hard to get people to let you do something for them for as little as a nickel. Doesn't seem like much today but we were always on the lookout for an opportunity....
...And that nickel went in my Mothers apron. Every penny counted back then.

"I know what you mean, nickels and pennies still had buying power when I was a kid. Now, I usually pitch pennies into the parking lot before I get back in the car. The luck is worth more than the penny."

"The luck?"

"Yeah, *you know,* "Find a Penny on heads up and all day long you'll have good luck."

"But what if it doesn't land on heads?"

"If you find one like that, you're supposed to flip it over for the next guy. You hadn't heard that before? Mom taught me that, I assumed it was from you."

"She probably got that from her Mother, that sounds like something from Hazel. No, that must have come after pennies became worthless. When I was a kid, if you found a penny, that *was the luck. If your buddy was with you, you'd either fight over it for a week or go directly to the other side of town and find an ice cream or a soda to split."*

"Why the other side of town?"

"Because the shop keeper over there didn't know your parents. That penny should have gone in Mothers apron. Might get a couple licks for something like that."

"A couple licks? I never imagined that. On this side of the family I mean."

"Oh, not really. The threat was always there but the most what would happen was Mother would go get a switch from the backyard tree. I don't remember her ever using one. Dad was always very quiet. The look on his face was enough."

"So you weren't really ever hit?"

"Oh, no. Not that I remember. Closest I can think of was she was pretty mad for a while when that old car of mine was next to the house and we couldn't fix it. She wanted a separate garden there. I can't remember what happened to that car..."

"Hmm, lucky you I guess. I would have thought different of those days, certainly not my experience, but you skipped ahead, the car?"

"Well yeah. when I was 14, a friend and I went halves on a model T, it cost us $10 From a family friend down the road. We paid a little up front, then had .25c per week payments for a while. It started with the foot button for a few months but we had to push start it after that, then it just died. We drug it home from town and put it next to the house, it never got repaired.

Mother was not happy about that as I remember. I was back on my bike after that, pretty much till I left the house for College. ...but what do you mean by - "not my experience?"

"Oh, I was hit or threatened with harm all the time. Back then I imagined everyone was spanked or worse. My Father never held back. I got yanked, yelled at, hit or strictly punished for most of my childhood. Seems like it was till I was bigger than him he might have slowed down. He barely talked to us but was always ready with the board. He had a board like a bat he would use."

Gramps was looking intently at me.
"I didn't know that... hmmm, let's finish dinner."

His answer was deadpan, I was ready to continue but he shut it all down after dinner. It was time for his daily dose of news with desert. For a while I would sit there with him, but soon would have to leave the apartment. The television was always on so loud I was afraid of my own hearing loss, I'd start to get a headache. He didn't like it when I'd mute the commercials for small breaks in the din. After a while I started using ear plugs.

"What are we supposed to do? sit here and stare at each other during commercials?"

My Grandfather knew very little of his children or their families lives, any of them. It was clear when I was younger, he and my Father did not appreciate each other. I never remember Gramps in my childhood home and we rarely visited his home with my Father.

There was a time, Christmas day at their house, right after breakfast I committed an infraction and my Father stood me in the corner for the rest of the day. From that point on, he wasn't allowed back at their house. It wasn't much different at his own Mothers house except as far as he was allowed to go there was to sit us on the couch all day.

If needed, we would get our licks when we got home. His own Mother was tired of that stuff, but there was no-one to reel him in. She couldn't kick him out. His own Father was gone, died of lung cancer three months after I was born. From what I gleaned throughout my childhood, we all may have been fortunate in that respect. His Mother, Grandmother and Brother never had anything nice to say about ole' Bud.

My parents grew up in Des Moines, Iowa in the days of Bobby Socks and Drive-Inns, Poodle Skirts and Brylcreem. Two decades later there would be an infamous sitcom on television depicting the wholesomeness of those happy days. For the rest of their lives they would harken back to that time as being the best in human history.

Though, this is a theme isn't it?
There have been many television shows which pull their demographic from our childhood memories.

"The Walton's, Happy Days, The Goldberg's, The Wonder years...etc."

Many of us think like that, our Childhood was idyllic. I believe mainly because we had no bills to pay, drama at work or World meltdown issues to worry about. All we had to do was play. Strangely, I don't lament my childhood, but I've always been a cock-eyed optimist. Now, I see my childhood as the first obstacle I overcame. The lessons beat into me weren't the ones intended.

I think those of us with sketchy childhoods should really try and separate our memories though. Some folks have an over-all bad idea of their childhood, but even then, there are always a few individual memories that brighten eyes.

When thinking back on things outside of my childhood house, things are clear and bright. When I open the door to go in... it's darker in there.

I toured my childhood home the last time it was for sale. All I could see were the exact places in each room I was hit and punished. The realtor was perplexed as I lightly rubbed the wall where I was stood. Looking at the same spot I stared at for hours... even days. If I was to embellish my past, I'd make-up twists of good to place in the dark corners of each room, but I'm at a loss. I guess I'd need to know more about an idyllic childhood to be able to embellish mine.

My parents married in 1961. Then, within in a strictly conventional timeline, I was born in early 1964. They were High School sweethearts and by this time, my Father was out of a three-year hitch in the Airforce having been stationed in Morocco. He then came home to Iowa State University on the GI bill and worked with the Iowa State Highway Commission as a Draftsman for roads and bridges. My Mother graduated from a local Secretarial School. She worked a few jobs in the interim, but now, she would have children and take care of her family as all those before her had done.

When I was born, there was Vietnam to worry about. Kennedy was assassinated a few months earlier and Johnson was sure to sign that confounded equal rights bill. Life was being pushed forward very fast.

My first memories are very early. I thought they were from the house my parents lived in when I was born, above Grandpa's Chiropractic office. This was mentioned earlier in my stay, he thought it couldn't be from that house. Pieces of the memory include parts the yard and living room, they didn't match.

I could hear the ice cream man's bell from inside the house, he was on a big tricycle with a cooler box. I would toddle down the stoop and front walkway to give him a quarter. I can picture several angles of the yard and street. That was the key.

I called my mother later that day and mentioned it to her.

"That sounds like Mrs. Handy's house, but that can't be, you were very young then."

Gramps agreed, so we went to Mrs. Handy's old house and took a look. That was it, same house, same stoop and walkway, same corner lot. Mrs. Handy was a family friend and in 1966, as people did back then, she took a World tour, hers was of North Africa. My parents watched her house and stayed there free of charge six months while she was gone. This helped them save a down payment to buy their first home.

There are a couple other early memories, all before five years old, but the only other one I can completely put together and remember was maybe somewhere between three and four.

Standing on the passenger side front bench seat of a car holding on to the dashboard looking out the front window. I would be yelling GO! and my Father would say "sit down boy" and would "Pop" the clutch making the car lurch forward. I would be thrown back against the seat laughing hysterically as youngsters do. I'd get back up there and he'd do it again and again. That one's nice, it makes me smile.

Because of this kindness bestowed by Mrs. Handy, my parents were able to buy a house in 1966. This is the house I remember most from my childhood. It sold recently in 2025 for $200k. My Mothers says it cost them a little over $9000. Two years later, my Father would buy his first new car, a full-size, family 4-door Ford for $2700.

Our phone number was a "party-line." Several people on our side of the street had the same phone line. Households were separated only by the phone number, anyone else on that line could just pick up their phone and listen in on your call if they wanted.

Back then, some of the first things taught children were their address and phone number, I still remember that number.

Kids were commonly allowed to roam all over, so these were important things to teach. Neighbors and the community helped to raise and police children. There were houses with gold stars in the window. I was taught if you were lost or in trouble, I could knock on the door of one of those houses and that family would help get me home. Things were much different back then.

As I remember, the social aspects of my childhood were nearly the same as the 1940's short movie and television serial shorts; "The Little Rascals/Our Gang." I never saw one of those till I was much older, and because of the similarities to my own childhood thought nothing of the premise. Our ages and mischief were roughly the same. Nothing at all like today.

Rusty was my nemesis, Billy was my best friend, Joann and the Mitchell sisters lived across and up the street. There were many kids who lived around in the neighboring blocks. We would play in the ravines, tree climbing contests, ride our bikes everywhere we shouldn't, chase each other through everyone's back yard and drink from garden hoses hanging from anyone's outdoor spigot. As young as five years old I was out in the yard playing by myself. A time at six; I was two blocks away playing in a ravine with friends. At eight I was miles away on my bike regularly visiting a small store with a very large candy selection.
Yes, *much* different back then.

Most of the social aspects of my early childhood were standard trial and error learning situations. We got into harmless mischief, and as I mentioned, it was more like the little Rascals than anything else. There were a few nicer events that stand out, but none exceptional.

One that does stand out happened on a Halloween night, I guess it must have been around 1971.

There was an old stone house down the street around the corner from my house. Back then, the yard was overgrown and the house covered in bushes. An older house, probably one of the first in the area, and at that time must have been in a state of disrepair. All us kids were wary of that house...
a Witch lived there.

A gaggle of us kids were going around the neighborhood trick or treating. No need for chaperones back then, we were our own protectors, with nothing to be protected from... except maybe that Witch.

We had to pass that house on our way around the block. Billy, Rusty and me decided to stop and stare. The rest urged us to keep going but we stayed there while they carried on to the next house. The three of us were on the street at the mailbox ducked behind a ragged bush. The house was set back about eighty feet from the street, dark and ominous. Very scary stuff, except.... *the porch light was on.*

We hunkered down, betting and double-dog daring each other to go knock on the door. As always, Rusty got my ire up and I took the dare. A bitter sweet decision, I was scared, I could end up in the oven.
OR... as everyone knows, a house with the porch light on for Halloween certainly means there is candy behind that door.

I got to the door and looked back to the street, Rusty yelled out taunting; "*Go ahead chicken, KNOCK.*"

I grabbed the old door knocker and knocked; a ring holding a Lion's head. I almost ran when I heard an old ladies voice, *"just a minute"* from behind the big wooden door, but somehow, I stayed right there. A light came on in the foyer behind the door and as it opened, an old lady, hunched over, peered through the crack to see me.

The door opened wider. Looking through and behind her I shakily mentioned... "*Trick... or... treat.*" At that, she smiled wide and asked me what my trick was. Not understanding, I said what I was dressed as and she looked at me with bright eyes. This eased me a bit and I looked further past her into the foyer. There it was, against the wall... the Holy Grail of Candy.

Before then and since, I have only seen those in old stores. It's something they'd have in an old drug store, or now, at a place like the Cracker Barrel Restaurant. I haven't seen one of those in many years. A stand with rows of glass jars full of colored and flavored candy cane sticks. Each with the flavor on a tag behind and on the jar.

Who has a candy stand like that in their house?
A child luring Witch.

My eyes must have been very big. At that point I could have easily been ushered into the oven. She saw my delight and invited me in to take my choice.

Peering outside, she closed the door behind me.

"Where are your friends? Where are all the children? are you alone? I see kids out front walking by but none stop here."

She seemed very nice.
"They all think this is a Witch's house, are you a Witch?"
I guess I wasn't too clear on the finer points of Witches other than what I'd seen on the Wizard of Oz, this nice old lady did not look like that. Not quite a Glenda of the North either, maybe from the South?

A look of mirth came over her face, she bent over and slapped her knee laughing.
"Oh my, well I guess you'll just have to tell them won't you. Oh, you must be the bravest in the bunch. Here, pick three for yourself and take a few for your friends."

She pointed to the candy stand and pulled the window curtain next to the door aside to peer out.
"So there are other children?"

"They're behind the bush at the street."

She looked harder but couldn't see all the way out to the street for the darkness.
"Well you take them all some candy and tell them I'm a good Witch, any of you are welcome any time to come over and get a stick."
I was elated. I don't know how many I took, but it was at least a dozen.

When I got out to the bushes, Rusty and Billy were gone. They got scared when the door closed with me inside and ran back to Rusty's house to get his Dad. I headed that direction too and when I got around the corner saw them leading his Dad down the street.
He gave me a stern look. *"So I guess she's not really a Witch."*

"No, she's a nice old lady."

"What did you get? What kind of candy did she have?"
...was Rusty's greedy question.

I reached into my bag and pulled out one candy stick.
"She gave me this."
I kept all the candy sticks. The old lady was right, I *was* the bravest of the bunch, and Rusty gets nothin'.

Rusty and I also had the occasional dust-up. He was not well liked in the neighborhood, we included him when he showed up, but none of us ever knocked on his door to see if he could come out and play.

There *was* a short time when Rusty and I hung out together. I think it was in the last year my family lived there.

It's the only time I ever saw the inside of his house, It smelled weird in there. I followed him into his parent's room, we were going to smoke. He opened a dresser drawer to get a pack of cigarettes and in that drawer was a pile of sex toys.

He saw my eyes widen and he picked up a very large strap-on dildo and shook it giggling. Knowing all I know today, Rusty's parents were... stranger than most. That young, I had no idea of what a strap-on was and could certainly not imagine what it was used for. This episode and a couple lighter things were the only references to anything sexual I can remember from my early years.

Elementary School was just a few blocks away. I remember kindergarten there and a new girl coming into the classroom. She had long brown hair, a plaid dress to just above the knees and white Go-Go boots. *Maaaan,* her mom really knew how to dress her. That was the very moment I became aware. To this day, I'm still a sucker for long brown hair and Go-Go boots... *a plaid dress couldn't hurt.*

In first grade we were learning to read. They used a reading system with colored and numbered booklets of ever-increasing difficulty. I caught on very fast and was finished with the entire course before some in class made it through the first three. I guess one kid in particular was jealous of this and the attention I got from the teacher because of it.

Of-course in general terms it makes no difference, but in this case it lays out a baseline for me, he was a black kid. Seventy percent of the school were black kids. My family lived on the white neighborhood side of the school. Much to my Fathers chagrin, black folks were moving in on that side too. My Father did not appreciate that. He would tell people in conversation; *"Our neighborhood is turning black."*

Skin color was never an issue for me, I always remember accepting kids as kids. In that neighborhood, there were several black kids I played with without any thoughts of being separate or heeding any kind of racism. A side note to this being; these were also the hey-days of the Black Panthers, and Des Moines, Iowa was a particularly hot area for that movement. I understand there was a lot of racial tension in Des Moines in those days.

Anyway.... this kid would beat me up at recess quite often and call me names. Eventually I got tired of it and hit him back. I must have been better at it than him because soon, his brother in the 6th grade would come see me at lunch and smack me for hitting his little Brother.

One time, he told me not to do it again and gave me a particularly hard pounding. That emboldened the kid and one day soon after, he was in my face in class. I held back but after being pushed a couple times, I caved-in. I cocked him right in the lookers. That day at lunch his Brother showed up and beat me up pretty bad.
My Parents were not amused.

One thing led to another and I was put in a more advanced class, I remember it as fun. I was one of the best in class and was chosen to be in the peanut gallery on the afternoon local kids TV show, the "Floppy Show." Floppy was a puppet Dog that made wisecracks and introduced cartoons. There was a bleacher of kids on the stage called the peanut gallery. Floppy and the puppeteer would talk to the kids and ask them easy questions.

The fights did not stop because I changed classrooms though. I was telling my Mother I didn't want to go to School anymore and it wasn't long before they were driving me a couple miles away to a different School where I finished 2nd and then part of 3rd grade.

One other thing I remember about my first Elementary School is one of the Principles committing suicide there. He was found in the hallway in front of the office in his underwear. His twin Brother had been killed in Vietnam and it broke him.

Religion played a big part in my childhood. It was a mixed bag though, we tried-on a couple different brands of the Christian faith. In Des Moines, it was a non-denominational Christian. Later, we went to a Lutheran Church and when we moved South it was Southern Methodist.

None of these satisfied my Grandfather. He was always trying to steer us towards his brand of Christianity, which by-the-way, also morphed quite a bit over time. He was raised German Lutheran but in the late 1950's started exploring and looking around for other doctrines he found more to his taste. He finally settled on the Protestant Evangelical version of Christianity as his own. Years later, after going to Moody Bible College in the mid 80's, he also became a lay Minister. His donation to the community was to preach at the Des Moines Homeless Mission. I had to sit in front of him on Sunday preaching a couple times when young and all I can say about his style is that "preaching" was an apt term.

When seven and eight years old, to help steer me from the heathen ways, he offered to send me to Summer Bible Camp. Even though there was a chapel requirement three times a day, the two weeks per summer were fun and memorable.

Summer Camp activities back then were not tainted by safety restrictions. We canoed without wearing life preservers and shot real bows and arrows and .22 caliber rifles. There was biking and gas powered mini-bikes. Campfires with hotdogs and smores. A candy and snack canteen that opened at the same break time every day. And there was a girl's camp on the other side of the ravine we could wonder about. Those are some of my best childhood summer memories.

At the time, I had no questions about religion. It was what I was supposed to do and I followed along with honest intent. It was much later I realized the ins and outs of organized religion. As a kid, I honestly tried to believe and comply with everything I was told. My baptism at eight was a big deal and I was very nervous about it.

The last year of Summer Camp my Grandfather told one of the Camp Proctors to try and get me "saved." At that time, I guess he felt a responsibility to make sure his Grandchildren made it to heaven. To do that, you had to be saved. I learned all about it and was serious, I thought this would be something which would make my family happy and might change my home situation for the better.

One night during camp, the cabin proctor pulled me aside and we went and talked. He instructed me on how to do it... and I did. I asked Jesus into my heart and gave my soul to the Lord, denying Satan and all things evil.

When I did that, I had such an in-rush of feeling it made my head spin. It was an honest to goodness clean and fresh, wide awake feeling. I knew something good had to be going on.

I have since come to know, there actually was something going on and I now know what was happening. I had honestly let go of and accepted I wasn't in control. It was a denial of Ego and Id. A Kundalini effect, something real no matter which religion or non-religion gets you there. What's strange to me now is that all these factions imagine it is unique to their practice.

This opened my eyes, but the effects weren't exactly what everyone expected. I actually developed a more confident and uncaring demeanor. As I grew up and saw so many people confident in so many opposite factions and beliefs, I started on a comparative religion journey which would lead me away from organized religion rather than push me towards.

I felt none of it was right, but at the same time had no idea what was. I guess the correct term was agnostic.

By the time I was twelve years old, I followed along with my family under fear of my Fathers anger, but was confidently agnostic. At thirteen I was able to push away and wasn't required to go to church anymore. By that time, I was much bigger than him and rather than risking a taste of what he had given, I think he just thought I was incorrigibly doomed.

There was an Old Testament/New Testament situation going on not only in the religions I was subjected to, but also in my home. There was control, wrath, vengeance and a little benevolence thrown in for hope and good measure. I was just simply different than my Father imagined I should be. I always failed to nice, he considered that a weakness.

I was probably eight or nine, the house across the street was being rented by several college guys, mid-century types with girlfriends who came over. There were Barbeques in the back yard, Semi-quiet social parties which spilled over into the yard and street on occasion. I remember a car washing episode where everyone was in shorts and bikinis. Laughter, cigarettes, drinking, spraying each other with the hose and chasing each other around. They seemed to have a lot of fun over there. This was all very interesting stuff and us younger kids would sit by and watch, even wander over every now and then.

There was a good-sized boat beside the house with a cover on it and in the Summer when no-one was home, us kids would use it as a secret fort. One day Billy and I were doing just that and wandered into the back yard... then into the screened in porch.... then into the house, the back door was open. In there were all the things one might find in a bachelor pad, including Playboy Magazines, alcohol and cartons of cigarettes.

Billy and I made that a usual thing for a while. Once you've seen a playboy magazine, all bets are off. There was liquor and beer also and I remember trying some and thinking it was very nasty stuff. We'd sit around on the couch smoking Chesterfields and thumbing through the girly mags, we'd take them into the boat "Fort" also.

That's where the trouble came. They went to use the boat one weekend and found cigarette butts and missing magazines in there. The investigation led to Billy and me. My Fathers idea for punishment was his standard go-to, I got an ass whooping. But there was more this time, *I had been smoking*. This was a high-level sin in our house. His Father died just a few years earlier from smoking, he was extra nuts about smoking. As a smoking punishment / deterrent, he produced a huge circus cigar from somewhere and made me smoke it down till I turned blue and threw up.

Also at about eight or nine, some of us kids found a bunch of white tipped matches. The kind not sold in the US anymore, the kind which were self-lighting. You just drug the tip across anything that would snap the tip and it would lite. You could even do it with a fingernail if you could perfect the technique without burning yourself. That's what we were doing, getting our technique down. Then once they were lit, we would set little things on fire. Basically, playing with matches and fire.

All kids do that at some level when young, but not all of them did it in a neighbor's yard, behind a big Oak tree in the fall with leaves covering the yard. As one could guess, leaves caught fire. Billy ran but I stayed trying to put it out. I had no idea what to do and soon the whole yard was in flames, the house nearly caught also. Yelling for help, the neighbors and the Fire Department got there in time to put it out and save the day... but not my butt.

Back to frothing ass-whooping time, and this time we'll add a fire deterrent. My Father made me strike a match, then held my fingers together as the match burnt down to the tips of my fingers. Several times he did that. Since then and till this day, the tip of my left index finger is numb with very little feeling.

One of the milder forms of punishment he would employ was to ignore you, completely acting like you weren't there. He'd then walk away or leave the house. If I got on his nerves too much, he'd stand me in the corner. You'd get to stand against the wall in the corner for an hour at a time, up to and including weeks, no sitting.

My Mother rarely had anything to say, but this did not sit well with his own Mother. Grandma McNaney was a very sweet lady. When I was young she would baby sit me, I have very nice memories of her. I even remember her second wedding, I was there in 1968. My Great Grandmother, "Mi-Mi," kept me quiet with her standard offering, a half a stick of Wrigley's spearmint gum. She'd keep me busy filling in the "O's and "D's with a pencil in an old church bulletin.

Grandma McNaney won the game, she re-married a very nice man. From that point on, he was considered my Grandpa. From that point on, they were always referred to as Grandma and Grandpa Gill. He made good money and she lived real nice from then on.

We rarely went to my Father's Brother, my Uncles house. He wouldn't have my Fathers attitude stuff at all. Being of two opposite characters, my Dad emulated his Father and Uncle Steve, his Mom. Because of this, we rarely got to go see or play with our cousins even though they only lived about ten miles away. I can only ever remember visiting their house four or five times the entire time I was young, they never came to our house that I remember.

My Father started hitting me fairly young. The earliest I can recall was an incident when I was about six years old. I knocked over a can of paint on the garage floor and it went everywhere. He picked me up by the arm and smacked me in circles with his other hand all the time yelling.

When young, I can clearly remember being yanked by the arm and being told *"Now say you're sorry."*
Anything I did, perceived as wrong, I had to say sorry for. It was much later when I actually learned the conditions of being sorry. To my Father, like many things, being sorry was merely a social platitude. You didn't have to be it, you just had to say it.

To this day, no-one can ever remember my Father ever saying he was sorry about anything. I cannot remember my Father ever in my life telling me he Loved me. My Mother either, until much later in life after she accepted the example I gave her.

Don't get me wrong though, I was well taken care of. I got the same thing they got as they grew up, *"three hots and a cot,"* to them, that was love. I only got hugs from my parents in public as a conventional display. I would hug and kiss my siblings all the time when we were young. I was different, it unsettled my Father. I naturally expected something he had no idea of. I was a little, walking, talking admonishment. I imagine he took as a failing judgement of something he never thought twice about.... until I came along.

I've often thought perhaps I was resented in my Father's eyes from the start. Being the first born, my given middle name is my Mother's Father's first name, not his own, at that time, terminally ill Father's name. I really don't know, but I can see that sticking in the craw of a man like my Father.

Eventually he lightly came around to a softer way of thinking but it was too late for my brother, sister and I.

His second wife's kids got a different brand of my Father, he evolved a little. He entered into that relationship pretending he'd been a bit softer all along and it was *us* that didn't appreciate him. I guess that's the way it goes, glad I could help.

Years later, he tried to treat my son the same way he treated me and I lit into him. I imagine he was never taught about life, as many people aren't, as I wasn't, as my siblings weren't. This wasn't something to overtly teach. A person had to bounce off each experience themselves and reap either the negative consequence or positive benefit. The only actual lesson was the example to connive till you got ahead.

Yet, I've always known since very young, blame won't help anything, it just is, as it was. Even considering my childhood and my Fathers part in it, I lay no real blame. He was following examples given him in the convention of his time. I learned long ago and very young, there are no bad examples. Something can be learned from every occasion. What people call bad examples are mostly just things to never do again and people to put behind you. It is up to us to realize this and act accordingly. Good examples heeded are their own reward aren't they?

There was a time when we visited much later in life with some of his friends present and a few old family stories came up. I was in my late 30's living in Seattle, I hadn't seen him in several years. He recognized during the tales I didn't make him look bad and left out a few things which might have. A little later I asked myself why I was there and just left the gathering. Before he left town, he confronted me without saying anything negative, but wanted to know why I just left early and he hadn't heard from me or been around since. I told him that for me, his stay was over.

He acted hurt, I then laid it out for him;

"That reminiscing was a good reminder for me. It reminded me that if you want to be treated like my Father, that's fine, just come up with five things you did to me and my Brother and Sister when we were growing up and say you're sorry for them. That should be pretty easy since there are hundreds."

I knew he would never do that. His response was one so predictable I nearly felt like Johnny Carson's "Karnak the Mystical," holding an envelope to my head.

"I think I did a great job raising you, look how you turned out... you're a much better Father than I was. Things have turned out great for you."

I won't respond to backhanded compliments, I walked away. I wouldn't see him or talk to him for another eight years, but his wife did call me and invite me to his 60th birthday party.

"Mike, it would be great if you-all would make up, we'd love to see you here, I'm asking everyone to bring pictures and give a little story about a good time from the past they can remember. Are there any old pictures or family movies?"

In turn, I had to shortly lay it out for her. She really hadn't heard or known anything about my Father's life before her except what little I'm sure he told her from his point of view.

"Shirley, there isn't any such thing. I'd rather not remember anything from back then and he certainly wouldn't want me relaying any of what I do remember in a crowd. I won't be there, but thank you for asking."

Shirley is a nice enough lady but was a conventional Southern wife. She takes care of her man and does what she's told, a perfect mate for my Father. She was his secretary when my Mother and Father were divorced and previously came from a very typical country marriage.

Hard to imagine, but my Father was a big step up for her. She was living in a trailer with her kids, bowing to a physically abusive husband before she got divorced. Family rumor has-it; my Father had to sign a prenuptial agreement that he would never hit her or her children.

As I think of this, after writing all of this down, I realize that I don't hold my Father responsible for my direction and never really have. I've never used him as an excuse or played the child abuse card. Somehow, I've risen above my Fathers uselessly inflated, easily bruised ego lashing out at those around him. Somehow, I have mitigated his example and things turned out acceptably well for me.

I'm sure that clinically, some would say I'm a case, but more so, I hold him guilty for my Brothers life. Held back in later years, legally threatened with jail time, he dealt my brother a heavy psychological hand. Punishment switched from overtly physical to psychological. My brother has spent his life in a never-ending turmoil. He has emulated his Fathers mental insecurity with his own relationships and children and gone much further than his Father ever did. Truly, the cycle continues.

Although my box of crosses is heavy, this may actually be my heaviest burden. Even though he would vehemently deny it, I deeply love my Brother, I lament he has never been taught about, or realized real love. It hurts me that I can't help him.

My Mother was, as she was raised also, except there was education and ease in her past. She attributes her previous attitude to that of German stoicism. The same attitudes that enabled the Nazi's. She stood by and watched a lot of stuff happen to her kids, and only said something a couple times as far as I can remember. This is a big sticking point for my Brother. I can see that, I just wish it didn't weigh so heavily on him.

She took care of us and reminded us that if we didn't fly right, our Father would be home soon to straighten us out. She didn't know any better, she married out of convention and to get away from her increasingly stifling, over-religious family life. Breaking loose in later years, she ended up with a little fun in her life. She woke up a bit to the world with subsequent relationships and I think feels a remorse for the past. None of us can do anything about the past except to be better people now and in the future. I still see her quite often and we get along fine.

I know there had to be good family memories to remember from my early childhood but strangely I don't remember many. I don't remember Love, or happiness or security. I know there was a level of security, that is obviously so, but my Mother and Father were more distant caretakers than nurturing parents.

Like myself in later years, my Father was emulating his own childhood without thought as to its relevance. I did the same, except I flipped to an overly loving attitude for my children, trying to compensate for my own lack. As you will read, that didn't work well. Primarily because I had no training or positive attention given to me as a youngster. I had no directly positive or nurturing examples of relationships to follow.

Intentions are all we have, I'm sure intentions were always skewed to the good side, we don't know what we don't know. Yet the examples of previous generations were still being perpetuated. I see several places in my early life where there was a fork in the road. It's interesting for me to think about how the life I have now, was the chosen road then.

Lucky S.O.B.

Chapter Three

Over the course of a month or two, Gramps languished in his apartment, mostly in his bedroom as his malaise held on. I would come make breakfast, leave for errands, then back for lunch. A minimum of 6 hours a day, leaving after dinner at four as he previously asked. He had both morning and evening devotional practices which were personal to him and he valued his privacy.

One afternoon we were talking about my bicycle leaning against the dining room wall. Discussing old and new, reasons for riding and my thoughts on the subject when he sent me to the garage to find a box. In that box were old pictures, and in those pictures was one of him on his new bike back in 1931.

There are a few pictures of my Grandfather and his family from back then. They owned a Brownie camera, a luxury item not everyone had. He dug through the box, handing me sepia and black and white pictures with fancy trim. I'd never seen any of them and was quite intent looking through the pile, ready with questions when he came up with it.

"Here it is...
What kind of bike do you think this is? I can't remember the make. I got that for my eleventh birthday, the picture is the day after I got it. Mom and dad asked me what I wanted for my Birthday and gave me three choices. A pair of socks, a bar of soap or a new bike."

I looked up at him and could see he crafted that quip just for me. He had a twinkle and a slight grin as he handed me the pic.

The picture was of a proud young man wearing a skally cap and knickers, straddling what was then called a motobike. A style fashioned after the motorcycles of the day. His wasn't fully adorned but that big smile said more than any I'd seen on him in a long while. I held the picture up to his face level.

"Sure this is you? this kid is much better looking."
He chortled a bit.
"I'll have you know, people used to say I look like some movie star they've seen. I've never broken any mirrors."

Having rarely gone to the movies in his entire life, he couldn't pick any names out of the air but I knew what he was talking about. It was true, back in the 50's and 60's he and Gregory Peck were supposed ringers. My Mom had mentioned it before. Not only did they look similar, Gramps and he even shared mannerisms and speaking inflection. It stood out a little as this was the only time he had *ever* mentioned *anything* secular like that.

"Can't remember which, but we ordered it from either the Monkey Wards or Sears catalog. I ran home from school every day, it took over a month for it to arrive. Back then, you had to mail your money in to the company, that took extra time.
I got home from school one day, and there it was in a crate on the porch with my name on it.

I had to wait two days till Saturday for my Dad and Uncles to uncrate and put it together. That picture was after Church the next day.

I went everywhere on that bike. I even rode back to Waterloo a few times to play with some old friends there. I would give them rides on the handlebars. I had that bike at least until I was seventeen. I used to ride it to my first real job in town as a busboy at a Restaurant there. Can't remember what ever happened to it..."

"So your first real job was a busboy at seventeen?"

"Yes, before that it was all odd jobs, most all the real jobs were taken and held on-to like the gospel. Nearly every kid in town was available for odd jobs. We'd clear fields, top corn, paint, rake, whatever was to be done that would get us a nickel or two. Those would go to Mother and she would make change giving back a penny for each nickel. Make no mistake though, a penny was enough to get a soda or Ice cream cone. If you ever saved up a Quarter, you had your choice of all kinds of stuff."

Gramps was one of seven kids in his graduating class. He went to a small local school, not much more than a few rooms which held combined grade levels at the same time. They combined locally with other schools in Waterloo and Cedar Falls for sports and he liked Basketball. He said the rules and play was nothing like today, but because he was the tallest in school, he was one of the best. In his senior year, collectively, all three combined schools gave him a partial Basketball scholarship to Creighton University in Nebraska.

"I liked Basketball but it just wasn't something I was real good at, I only lasted a year. Came back home to Cedar Heights and started looking for a job. That was '37, not a real good time to get a job, but my Father thought I should go try at the packing plant outside of town. I went there and sat in their employment office for a few days. There were at least 60 other people waiting around every day to see if their name would be called. There was a window closed with a wooden shutter. It would open every now and then and a guy was there calling out names to be interviewed. When he called my name, first thing he asked was who my Father was. When I told him, he called me in back and I started work the next day."

"What was the pay back then?"

"I seem to remember I started out at .37c an hour. No complaining about that in those days. A job kept you busy, out of trouble and food on the table."

It seemed my Grandfather and his family were lucky in many respects. None had any issues through the 1919 pandemic. None were called to service in World War One and each had and kept, a paying job through the depression.

Here and now, Gramps was sliding, I was staying in touch with a VA assistance team who recommended he officially be put on full Home Hospice Care. An extremely experienced Doctor and team of hospice professionals each came once a week on different days to check on him, advise me and make sure he was comfortable.

They loaded his apartment with all the geriatric appliances and furniture anyone could need. They tried, but he would not let them replace his bed with an adjustable hospital bed. He was already using a walker and to him, this other stuff was like them telling him he was dying. One would imagine he could figure this out, but he was still stubbornly incredulous to what seemed painfully obvious. I was there full-time now, sleeping on the couch.

After his last wife died, he moved to a one-bedroom apartment in the same secured building. Although quite nice, it was pretty small. One night while reading in the living room I could hear him talking. He was having a conversation with God.

..."How much longer God? I pray to be by your side. What is there left for me to do? Please let me know... anything.
... What?... Whats that!
Oh, I've had enough of you. Get Behind Me Satan!

There was more... I have thought about this spontaneous eavesdropping moment many times from several angles.

Then, each angle has a dogleg or two. Happenstance or purposeful? It's hard not to place myself in the conundrum somehow. After-all, he knew I was out there sitting in the corner chair. Yet, it was not the only time I'd caught snippets. His twice daily devotionals were open conversations with God.

This is an interesting aspect of being here at this time in my Grandfathers life. Without the answer from the previous question, there are others here I was slowly getting the answers to. After a true lifetime of devotion, what does the end of life hold for mind, body and our closely held life ideals? I was seeing his belief from many angles.

Being with him as much as I was, *Everyone* commented on what a blessing it was for him to have lived this long. He would always nod with a smile. At home, his attitude was a bit different. There were a few weeks he had an open wound, aching leg issue and he got serious with me.

"I Just feel like I'm falling apart, have been for many years. As I think about it, at 92 would have been a good year. I think that was my last good year. Seems it all started then. Betty started going down-hill, I started getting sick every year, now this..."

"That was a long time ago Gramps, you're not saying you've been suffering since then are you?"

"No, not suffering, just that's when everything took a turn. That's when I shoulda took up taking the train."

Huh? what's that?"

"The two best ways to go. In your sleep, or train wreck. Next thing you know, you're at the gates..."

He snuck one in.

"Well, you've tried your best, look how long you drove..."

It might have been taken as disrespect, so I never asked him, but did wonder what he really thought about the obvious opposite. I have wondered if he thought he was left here for a reason, or perhaps left behind, or being punished... or any number of perceived reasons God might leave the old human body of the staunchest of his believers to painfully wither with unusually long age. Was his age a kindness or bane?

In mid-August he truly became bed-ridden, he could hardly sit up in bed by himself. I helped him sit up and stand and get on his walker to the toilet. I brought him his meals, served on a bedside table appliance supplied by the VA.

It had been quite a while since we talked in depth about anything. He was sleeping a lot, and when awake wanted to keep with his previous schedule of going through the mail. There were phone calls to friends, which were very frustrating and time consuming considering his hands and fingers were now not much use. There was both kinds of television programming *(Religious & News)* and of course meals.

One particularly lucid day he had me order pizza to the door.

"Mike, I've been wanting to tell you, I'm sorry you got hit when younger. I didn't know then but maybe I should have. I also wanted you to know, even though I rarely say anything about your Grandmother, I loved Hazel very much. Betty and her were two different people, that's all. Hazel took care of us all very well, no one could ask for more.

You know; we met back when I was working at Rath packing, it was 1938. She was going to secretarial school in town at the University and was boarding in an open room at the house next door. We got married in the fall of '39."

I gave Gramps a grin and a little arm shake.

"That's right, I heard you work fast. You and Betty only went steady for 8 months wasn't it?"
He got a bashful look.

"Oh, something like that. You've got to make a choice and get on with it I guess. Hazel and I were married a couple years saving money when your Mom came along. We were happy, I got my Draft Notice a few months before she was born though. If we ever did have any "ifs," it was over religion. Her and I weren't compatible that way you know. My family was Lutheran and hers was Methodist. Though, I have always credited her for moving me towards the Lord. The Lutheran faith is just not for me. It didn't take hold right away of-course, it took a while."

"When did you change your path that way?"

"It started at her Church before I went off in the Navy. We would trade off going to each other's Church. The week before I went off to basic, her church had a "Come to Jesus" event for all the new draftees heading off to war. A deacon there took me aside and counseled me on accepting Jesus into my heart. I figured it couldn't hurt considering my circumstances.

At that moment, I gave myself whole heartedly to the Lord and prayed that if he kept me safe through the war, I would devote my life to his service.
Did you know all that Mike?
That's the first time I came to the Lord."

He nodded his head with a satisfied look.

"No-I-did-not. So that is when you switched from being Lutheran? How did your family take it?"

"No, no, that didn't happen till much later..."

The pizza arrived, TV on, conversation over.

Listening to this new material got me thinking about my previous memories of him. I took a few days and tried to remember anything and everything throughout the years. Turns out there are only a few dozen at best. All positive, or at least not actually negative.

I'm sure he does remember some other points of my childhood if prodded, but truly, we rarely saw each other. More so I remember snippets of my time at his house with my Uncle. Avoiding his gaze as we looked for ways to cure our boredom.

When it came to my Uncle, we saw each other so seldom growing up, when we did come together, there was usually some sort of debauchery at hand. I mostly remember Pot, shop-lifting, a little beer... Grand Theft-Auto...

Our ages were four years apart, so as we grew up, I looked up to him, and also bothered him. I told Gramps a few tamer stories about us two together. Not that I couldn't, I just wouldn't tell him any of the wilder ones. Any true tale of bad behavior told to my Grandfather could only serve to validate another depth of Hell we must all renounce and climb out of.

There is really no good reason to relay any of my negative childhood experiences to him I can think of. I am more than certain he wasn't let-in on any of it as it was happening for reasons of modesty and embarrassment. These were still the days of "nobody needs to know your business." Even within the family, what everyone else was doing came strictly at holiday get togethers and in measured quantities.

For one reason or another, in 1973 my parents broke the mold. I think here is where it started. My parent's choices spurned in me the scourge of wanderlust. It had to be from somewhere, for some reason, and it seems easy to say this family move to Illinois set the standard.

Most people stay close to where they were born until they die. Many never stray far from home or even care what's out there in the World to see.

We even had precedent in our family. Grandma and Grandpa Gill had retired to Arkansas. They built a house there, left Iowa behind and seemed quite comfortable. I was sent there on a bus to visit them for a month here and there in the summers. It was set in my mind that it was OK to move around and take up where you left off and to create a new life. It worked out well and somewhat easy for my Grandparents and my family seemed to take it in stride as we left Iowa for Illinois.

My Father got a job with a sewer inspection company in Rockford, Illinois. We initially lived in an apartment complex while looking for a house. There was a construction site next to the apartment complex where us kids would play. We would all get our pillows from home and take turns being rolled down a hill inside big wooden cable spools. I broke my arm jumping my bike over a mound of dirt. On the other side was the hole, soon to be a basement from where the mound of dirt had come. This was the second time I broke the same arm, in the same place. My first bike, the red bomber was also a casualty, it died. It would put up with no more abuse.

The house we next moved into was where I took a turn towards the wild side. There was where I eventually started smoking Pot in the fifth grade and getting into heavy mischief.

There aren't many black folks in my Rockford memories. They played a defining role in my young life in Des Moines but here, we lived in a "whiter" side of town. I'm pretty sure that was on the criteria list for our new house.

I don't remember much from the 4th grade except an IQ test the entire class took. I was given different work than the other kids afterward.

My Mother likes to remind me it was a pretty high score. I don't put much value on those things. As you will come to read, I got much smarter and a whole lot *"stupider"* in an alternating fashion. I've come to think it is the examples we accept which drive us to excel or digress.

I've known plenty of really intelligent people who have done very stupid things. If I happen to know a little more than you about something, I'll be glad to help you along and I hope you'll do the same for me if I fall short. Where does *that* land on the IQ meter?

My first friend there was a kid named Bandu, he wasn't very popular at school. Very smart and strange, he made up weird names for all the kids and would use only those names when talking about, or to them. I was "Frog," for some reason. His Father was Punjab Indian and his Mother German, they were Jehovah Witnesses. To me, the only thing being a Jehovah's Witness meant was no playing on Saturday. Bandu was a strange kid but very happy and likable. Any time I went to his house, his Mother was cooking something that smelled great. After school, we'd watch Bat Man and share a peanut butter sandwich while his Mother cooked dinner.

My first "girlfriend" was in the 6th grade. A Black Girl with straightened hair in pigtails, she always wore a dress. I think she liked me because I was the only one that ever talked to her. I'm pretty sure my parents weren't aware of this because I don't remember anything from them about it. I'm sure my Father would have had something to say if he'd known.

We'd pass notes and talk during recess. Like that old song "Spiders and Snakes," most of our Love was just touching smiles. It didn't go over well, I was made fun of quite a bit and the only other black kids in the grade took it personally. I was big for my age and there was nothing they could do about it. All they got was a "shut up or I'll pound ya" attitude.

One of them told me if I didn't stop, he was going to tell his cousin who went to a different school and this Cousin would come over and *kick-my-ass*. Yeah, sure, All talk...

Then, one day as I was leaving out the front doors of the school there was a crowd. Standing there waiting for me was this kid's Cousin; it wasn't all-talk. It seemed everyone knew about this happening but me, and the bets were against me. This kid looked like a miniature Bull, smaller than me, but a fire plug.

We exchanged a few heated words, then since it was obvious it was going to happen anyway, I hit him directly in the face and pushed him over the patio railing. He came back immediately and we continued. I was landing heavy ones but he wasn't fazed. His shake-offs were just giving me a few seconds to think about my escape. I turned again and was grabbed from behind by the School Principle. The only damage I took was the clean hit he got while the principle was holding me. *Fuckers.*

There were plenty of experiences from Rockford which were nicer, at least, no more fights. The Summers were what I remember most, the Winters were cold and snowy. Back in those days, if you lived anywhere near school, you walked or rode your bike. That's how I mostly got to school from the first through the 6th grade. Even in Des Moines as a small kid, I walked to school after being shown how to get there.

In Des Moines it was only two blocks away, in Rockford it was a bit more than a mile. The walk was pretty much a straight shot. In the Winters, similar to the tired nonsense I constantly heard as a child, I truly did walk a mile to school in knee deep snow uphill both ways. The street going there was a steep hill going down to a thoroughfare road, then a steep hill up another several blocks to the school.

We lived very close to a park and in the Winters the City would make a skating rink from the baseball field.

I got a hockey stick and a pair of skates for my tenth birthday and spent all my free time there with neighbor kids playing pick-up hockey. I also started playing City League football.

Through the City football league, I met several kids my age who lived in the same area of town. The practice field was a couple miles or more from my house and I had to ride my bike there. If I had a flat tire, I had to walk, no rides, ever. None of the guys on my team went to my Elementary School but several would be there with me at my Jr. High School. I was the biggest kid on the team and had to actually diet to make the 140lb. weight limit.

Alan was a friend on the team and lived close to the field. He suggested we play the sleeping over at each other's house game one weekend. We tried to hitch a ride to Chicago to see a Cubs game, I was eleven. We got a ride after a few minutes of hitching. The guy was smooth about it and asked us a lot of questions including where we lived. He rode around a while then dropped us off in front of the park across from my house.

"You kids are too young to be hitching rides, don't make me go tell your parents."
I'm sure that would have been another terrible ass kicking.

As I got older, this is how I gauged my time and events. I would think to myself the level of ass-kicking I may get for each infraction and whether it was worth it. I had become desensitized. Apparently, at that time I thought most of what I did was worth it in some way.

My Father became a professional at whooping us kids, especially my Brother and I. I can only imagine his Father was a good teacher. He made a special board out of hardwood, it had a handle and all. Like a miniature bat except flat, it was kept on top of the refrigerator.

When the time came, you could volunteer to bend over, take it from his lap while he held you down, or get chased around while getting smacked wherever it landed, your choice. As I grew, I learned on the fly being chased helped my adrenaline absorb a lot of the pain.

There was a time he chased me around and nearly beat me to death with that board. I went to the hospital bleeding with contusions all over me and the police were called. Back then, there wasn't a whole legal system devoted to people who beat their wives and kids, it was simply called discipline. He did end up with a police record for that one though.

Visiting friends of my parents, I was playing with others in the house as children do and spotted a small semi-automatic pistol lying on a dresser unattended. I had it out of its holster standing in front of the bedroom window looking at the gun when I heard my Mom calling my name. With no time to put it back where I found it across the room, I quickly hid it away in my pants as to not get caught.

Unfortunately, she was coming to find me for the trip home and I was ushered outside to the car before I could put it back. The car trip home was torturous, we weren't home ten minutes before the phone was answered and the gun was soon found. A short time later I was in the hospital. Not from the gun itself but from the beat down I got from my Father when he found I was the one who had taken it.

In retrospect of that event, if that would have happened with my son and myself in the same manner, I would have handled the situation a bit differently, and also probably would have had one less friend. After-all, leaving a loaded pistol lying out in the open with a house full of young children is not very smart from any angle of excuse.

Because of that episode, my Mom likes to describe him as a "documented abuser." He was also adept at both mental and physical tortures. Here in Rockford is where he fine-tuned his skills. My Brother and Sister were not immune, although my Sister didn't get near the same. She unfortunately did see it all played out on her brothers.

Everything wasn't bad about my Father. I'm sure he had a couple good attributes. There were times when he wasn't yelling or hitting, times when we did things as a family. But it seems even within these times, I can only remember the negative aspects. That's what negativity does, it overshadows the good. I have to work hard thinking of good family memories from my childhood. I don't have many of my Father, although I'm sure there are a few that could be prodded out.

He encouraged me to build models. There was a complex balsa wood airplane model we started together. I finished by myself after it sat for months. I made a lot of plastic car models by myself. He encouraged me in a Beer Can Collecting hobby I started. He didn't drink beer, but as a salesman, would still bring me back cans from his travels all over the US. One time he even took the effort to go to an old dump somewhere in Connecticut and dig out some real old ones. Hmmm, it actually feels good to remember the good side.

On the City football team, I also met a friend named Adam. He was a thick burley kid with long curly brown hair, he seemed cooler and was fun to hang around with. Mostly what we did was ride our bikes around to different places to shoplift and smoke pot. His Brother made a trip to Mexico in the Spring with a friend and brought back a lot of Mexican souvenirs, ponchos, hats, paintings, furniture, etc. I was at Adams house the day his Brother got back. Deep in the back of the truck was an old trunk, and that trunk was *FULL* of Pot.

It was a couple days later, Adam showed up with what would today be called Mexican Brick weed. From that point on, he always had some on him and would sell it by the ounce for $20. I would mow lawns in the neighborhood to buy it.

I kept my pot and paraphernalia in an old book I'd hollowed out for that purpose. Later when older, my Mother told me she knew about that book and would sneak a hit every now and then. She was wiley that way, she also occasionally smoked cigarettes behind my Fathers back when he was traveling on sales trips.

The pot situation lasted through the summer, I even planted a few seeds next to the house and they grew well. I was the one doing the yard work in my family so they got a couple feet high before I pulled them up and tried to smoke them. A first failed attempt at growing pot.

In the spring and early summer of 1976, I took a step up, more of a ramp actually. I had free roam and no accountability, a practice for what was coming later.

Something that still makes me smile and stands out about that time, really of no consequence, was that after trying endlessly for two years, I finally won a contest on the local Rock-and-Roll radio station, it would be the first of many. To win, you had to be the right caller, *I was*. Next you had to say the "phrase that pays," *and I did*.

There used to be a practice of radio stations holding contests for prizes like swag, concert tickets etc. Not sure if it's a thing anymore but all radio stations used to hold contests back then. It occupied a good portion of my life while filling the voids, up into my thirties actually.

The radio station was two blocks from my elementary school, the towers were beacons I always looked at with wonder.

I'd pedal by the building on my bike wondering what went on in there for me to hear it on the radio. It was easy to ride my bike to go pick up my winnings, and a thrill to actually go inside to get them. There were pictures of the DJ's, gold records and awards all over the wall. The Receptionist congratulated me and pulled all the prizes from a big metal locker behind her desk. Being the Spring of 1976, the prize package was tinged towards the Bicentennial and quite extensive. I can remember all the prizes so clearly. I had that t-shirt long into the future.

That summer, we went to visit my Father's side Grandparents in Arkansas for the 1976 4th of July Bicentennial Celebration. We went to Branson for the fireworks show, then to Silver Dollar City. I always had a great time down there.

My Grandparents and Uncle came to visit that Fall for Thanksgiving. Chris came with Hash and I had pot. My room was in the basement and we did the same things there we'd done previously in my grandparent's basement when I visited there. Watched TV, played music and got high. There was only one video game back then, PONG, and I didn't have it.

As one can imagine, boredom was heavy in those days so Chris stepped it up a notch. He went upstairs and came back with his Dad's *(Grandpas)* car keys. We snuck out the basement window and went for a ride around Rockford. I remember it as a very cold ride with smoking manhole covers.

When they went home, he left a book behind, Abby Hoffman's, "Steal This Book." I poured through that book. If you aren't familiar with Abby Hoffman or that book, he was a counter culture "Hippy." Kind of a long haired, tie-dyed communisto, truly a flash in the pan. The book was a long dissertation on the evils of Capitalism and Government control and gave step-by-step instructions on how to; *"stick-it-to-the-man."* I tried out many of them and remember a few that worked.

From the book; Quarter *(.25c)* gumballs for a penny, phone calls from a payphone for a nickel, free pinball machine credits and one I would later take to heart about growing your own pot.

That fall was the last season in Rockford. I started the 7th grade at a new school. I met a friend Derek on the bus going to school, he got on at the same corner as me. His Mom dropped him there on her way to work. We used to skip classes and get high under the bridge in front of the school. I visited his house a couple times, his parents were very strict with him.

He said it was because his brother was in jail and they didn't want him to turn out like his brother. I'm not sure I remember what his brother was in the slam for, but his parents plan wasn't working, Derek was a young wild one. Not long before my family moved South, he and I burglarized a house just to do it, I followed along not realizing what was going on at first. It was the home of someone he knew. Somehow, we got caught and I remember sitting in the Police department with my Mom. My Father was out of town on business. I was let go with no repercussions since we were leaving town.
When my Father got back.... *Whew.*

Once again, reinforcing the ideals of the Gypsy, we picked up and took flight to an unknown land. This change would be a one-hundred-eighty-degree turn from all previous experience. Earlier, Iowa to Illinois wasn't such a big deal, I mingled with all the same types of people. In Rockford, there were very few black folks in my circles. I never thought of black and white folks in any socially separate fashion, that was soon to change. In Georgia, black folks would outnumber the whites by far, and it seemed the white folks spent a lot of energy worrying about and trying to control that.

There were other glaring differences.
Up North, all the black folks I ever knew talked like me and seemed to be at the same intellectual level as myself.

In Georgia it was quite different, everyone I met talked slow and strangely. Many thought as slow as they talked. Some of the black folks were hard to understand and even the white folks talked at a strange pace and tone. It was something to get used to, but really, I don't think I ever actually did. I learned to emulate them so I could fit in... but inside, I was always different. Luckily, none of it permanently stuck.

It may have turned out different had my family stayed in the North, but there in the South I think is where I irretrievably lost most of my respect for my Father. He seemed to really like it there and took to the white southern ways easily. To me, as they say down there; he was "like a pig in mud." But I'm sure to him, it was a more comfortable new life.

Here is where I consciously noticed the differences in thought, attitude and perspective between us.

Lucky S.O.B.

Chapter Four

Grandpa seemed interested in the parsed and mostly mundane tales of my youth. He would ask questions which would spurn a tangent and we'd go from there. After we had a break and hadn't spoken for a while, he would be the one to ask a question from the past and start it back up again. Our chats became a lost entertainment, a serial drama on the radio sort of break in the day.

Up until this point, Grandpa was catching up on my youth and I on his. Probably because this all comes from my perspective, but it seems his youth was solely church and family oriented with a few semi-interesting anecdotes evenly spaced out. He didn't have any hobbies to speak of and free time between working odd jobs was a premium. Whereas, while I listened to myself talk and answer questions, mine seemed a bit looser, and graphic. I had more of a social aspect to my childhood he didn't have. City mouse, country mouse? The differences in era and religious control?

We came to talk about times when he, Grandma and Chris came down to Georgia for a visit. From here, I would have to take an even lighter approach. My youth from here on was tumultuous. I was rearranging memories to present softer out of respect for my Grandfather's sensibilities. Truly, it is probably more in my head than anywhere else. I don't think long-gone circumstance would matter much to him, but at this point, why give him something to feel negative about?

As we talked, although I write them here, when talking with him, I would leave out events and circumstances that were/are either immoral or illegal.

I wouldn't mention questionable choices or even go very far into introspection of any of the events. He would get a milder version of most all that would come, sanitized for both our protection, his sensibilities, my embarrassment.

In Georgia, our first house was out in the country a few miles outside a small town by the name of Ochlocknee. We were renting from a farmer at a crossroads far out in the country. Across the road from our house was a barn storage area aside a livestock pen. Looking past and through the barns, you could see John Bulloch's newer house better than a mile away.

John Bullock was a cock-sure country farmer with a rifle and shotgun on a rack in the back window of his large pick-up truck. There was a big cowboy style revolver on the dash in plain sight. This was not unusual back then in the country or anywhere else in the South. I eventually adopted a version of this style also. These weapons he had in the truck were ones specifically for the farm truck and stayed there at all times.

Brutus, the Farm's American bulldog roamed the land and stood guard at his house at night. He eventually took to me because when I was bored, I would go across the road with a little .22 single shot rifle and shoot rats in the barn. He would retrieve the rats and take them somewhere. A very scary and ugly dog, there were many fights under his collar with who knows what kind of animals. He was very scarred up with knots and lesions on his head.

It was seven miles to the small town of Ochlocknee, nothing more than a spot on the road. A few dozen houses and one old gas station. So "Kuntry-bass-akwards," at that time, the city limits sign and the water tower had the name of the town spelled differently. It was 26 miles from Ochlocknee to Thomasville, a big small town of twenty thousand or so. That's where my 7th grade middle school was and I caught the school bus every morning out front of my house.

On the bus, I usually sat next to a kid who lived a half mile down the road, a black boy named Nylon Johnson. In the mornings, his cornrowed hair glistened and smelled of bacon grease. His family were share croppers on the Bulloch's land and lived in an old dilapidated shack. There were quilts and blankets on the walls as insulation. If not for those, you could see right through the house's clap board siding to the outside. Once, we went inside his house to ask his mom if I could stay for dinner, the house smelled like a big fart. His mom was cleaning chitterlings for dinner. A tub of chitterlings was a bit cheaper uncleaned. I don't remember how I got out of that, but I *did not* stay for dinner.

I turned thirteen in '77 and think back on a few things like being on the School football team. Taking a few licks in the Principles office as Corporal punishment for lighting a string of fireworks on campus during a "bathroom break." I was quite popular there as the new kid. I spoke with a Northern "accent" and had a different attitude than the Southern kids. Several girls liked me but I was quickly absorbing the Southern ways and would soon assimilate as a typical Southern boy.

I was driving a car since about then. I don't exactly remember, it may have been as young as twelve. Of-course I wasn't supposed to be driving that young, but no-one knew.

I probably first got the idea from my Uncle. Thinking about it, I sure had some balls back then. It seems I had the nerve to do most anything, and considering what you shouldn't do, actually did most everything. By the time I left South Georgia, nearly every Sheriff Deputy in the County either knew me, or knew of me. Most of the run-ins had hell raisin' and cars involved. These were also some of the better reasons which eventually urged me to leave.

When out in *"Old-Knock-knee,"* I used to take my parent's car in the middle of the night and go to parties.

Sometimes I'd take one and go pick up a friend to ride around and get high. Sometimes just by myself. My parents had two cars then. One was a '74 Ford which would one day be my first car. The other, a '77 Plymouth, my Fathers leased business car. I even took Mr. Bulloch's old Army Jeep in the barn across the road several times.

Our house was older and had hardwood floors. When you walked down the hall, the floor creaked and snapped. In the middle of the night it was a loud enough noise to wake my parents. Their bedroom door was often opened a crack. I kept their door and my bedroom door's hinges oiled so they made no noise opening and shutting.

I would wait till I heard heavy breathing and snoring from their room. Then slowly creep down the hall in a pre-determined fashion, tight against the wall so as not to get creaking from the floor. I'd specter into their room and lift the keys off the dresser, repeating this process upon my return. It's amazing I never got caught. I probably did that better than 30 times.

One would think being out in the country and going back and forth would present a problem for gas, but the Bulloch's Farm machinery Barn across the road had two 500-gallon fuel tanks. One was diesel and the other regular gas. There was a hand pump and nozzle next to each that was never locked, free gas. A couple years after we'd gone from that house, I drove out there to fill up my car a couple times when money was short.

There was a time when I was fifteen, it was my parent's anniversary weekend. They both took Friday off and were gone to Tallahassee. They would be back sometime late, hopefully before midnight Saturday they said. I was alone at the house, my Sister and Brother were staying with friends somewhere.

I was on a learner's permit and wasn't supposed to be driving the car alone. But screw that, *learner's permit?...pfft.*

I'd been taking and driving the car in the middle of the night for a couple years, it was like second nature to me. Getting across the County at breakneck speed, I was fading and drifting before those terms were thought up. Dirt roads were nothing, and when the Georgia clay got wet, the knobby snow tires my Father brought with us to the South, gripped real good making it even more fun.

Strangely enough, we lived out there in the country from 76' through 1979. "The Dukes of Hazard" wouldn't debut on television until the fall of 1979. In those years, I had bushy blonde hair just like John Schneider (*Bo Duke*) in that show and I *WAS* Bo Duke before Bo Duke was ever a thing. About a year later, a few of my friends put two-and-two together and I got the nickname Bo-D. I never liked that nickname, or that show.

It was Saturday before sundown, I was heading home for supper to be there to straighten-up before my parents got home. I'd been at a friend's house, and as was typical for me in those days, had stuff in the car I couldn't get caught with. I was 15 years old, high as a kite, carrying drugs and on the road in my parent's car, Illegal in several ways. And of course, time was always of the essence, I was probably cruising at standard velocity, about 80mph.

Problem was, the speed limit in those days was 55mph. As a young buck would do, I didn't slow down when approaching a known speed radar hazard to see if there was a cop there. I passed "speed trap road" and *dammit*, there was a county cop in the shadows behind the trees. His lights immediately came on, I quickly made the decision; I gunned it.

Several reasons came together all at once as to why I would not stop.

ONE: I had a quarter pound of marijuana on the passenger seat next to me.

TWO: If you get caught going twenty mph over the speed limit, they could impound your car.
THREE: My Father would certainly beat me near to death.
All probable and likely consequences.

Building speed, it was only three miles to a dirt road turn-off where I thought to lose him. I knew the roads out there like the back of my hand. The big Ford's speedo was bouncing at 125; wide open. I had a good lead on him, but with a much bigger engine, he'd catch up with me soon enough. There was a saying in those days *"Whatever you were doing, disappear fast. You can't outrun the Motorola."*

Coming up to the dirt road, he was about a half mile behind me, closing fast. At this point I hit the brakes hard and slowed down fast. I had randomly practiced this type of maneuver several times for fun. About 50 yards before the turn I reached down and grabbed the emergency brake release, let off the brakes and jammed on the emergency brake. The car fishtailed left and fishtailed right. As it went left again, I was compensating with the steering wheel. Letting the E-brake go, the car was sliding sideways at a 90-degree angle, I jammed the gas and shot straight onto the dirt road.

The rear went down into the ditch slightly but momentum, the snow tires and good counter steering got the car back up on the road. I gunned it again and was off. I'd made the turn like a good Bo should.

Looking in the rearview mirror, there were red lights bouncing through clouds of dust as the deputy made the turn. Stepping on the gas, I concentrated on the road and stopped looking back. I was blindly sliding sideways around curves and taking side roads which went the opposite way I was really going.

I cut through an abandon farm and ended up on the road to my house. Apparently, I'd lost him.

I got home, hosed the car off and parked it in the exact spot it was when my parents left.

My parents got home late, they were sleeping late. At around 8AM Sunday morning there came a pounding on the front door, my Father answered it. There were a half dozen Sheriff cars outside in the yard. Somehow, the Deputy either recognized the car from his patrol of the County or saw the license number before I made the turn. Either way, he was in the hospital bruised up after hitting that deep Georgia ditch, rolling his cruiser trying to make the turn off the freeway. Playin' his part in that week's episode, *Roscoe P. Coltrane*.

I spent 3 days in jail, then a week in Thomas County RYDC (*Regional Youth Development Center*). My Father thought it prudent to teach a deeper lesson and wouldn't allow me back in the house so I ended up at the Orphanage in Thomasville, these were traffic offenses, I hadn't done enough for the State to put me in jail, somehow this was deemed the answer. I was only there a few weeks before I rectified *that* situation.

The kids in the orphanage were wild. The whole place was dingy white, quite a bleak place. There were several kids there my age and I became friends with one in particular. He was a mild-mannered kid with a crazy streak. During afternoon free time, I would sneak off to the convenience store and get sodas, chips, candy bars etc. Things only given out for good behavior at the orphanage. Then one day he suggested we sneak off to his last Foster Home. The next time the opportunity arose, we took it.

When we got there nobody was home, but he went around back and soon opened the front door. Not there to steal anything, just hang out, we ate and smoked. Soon he came out of a back room with a .38 special revolver, jumping around pretending he was shooting someone.

He said he hoped he could use it on his Father, I was a little nervous.

We headed back and he brought the gun with us. When we got back, we were able to get onto the grounds easy enough and went into one of the abandon buildings. He hid the gun on a ledge in the basement. There was another kid watching us, I saw him watching through a window and didn't mention it. I thought it better for that gun to be found.

It *was* soon found and we both got in a heap of trouble. I'd finally done enough for the State to send me to the Georgia State YDC in Augusta for youthful offenders. By the time I got back home five months later, the rumor mill had been turning, I was legend in Thomas County amongst my derelict peers and their parents. *I was trouble*, bad company, and couldn't deny it. Every cop and Sheriff in the area knew me or knew of me. Not a real good position to be in. This wasn't Hazard County and I wasn't really an actor on TV.

Augusta YDC (*Youth Development Center)* was a State institution for first time minor offenders. Specifically for kids under eighteen, which for one reason or another, couldn't go home or were sentenced to more time than the regional County facilities were allowed to keep them.

Nothing more than a big University-like Campus with dorms, there were no fences or walls. Teens were housed in open rooms in groups of twenty, it was actually pretty decent there, no locking cells like in the County facilities. There was a separate lockdown building with cells for anyone who got out of hand. The mix of kids was split nearly even between blacks and whites and there was a hierarchy involved. I tried to stay out of the way and neutral but it wasn't easy. Black or white, it was still animal country and if you seemed weak in any way you would be picked on by either group.

Being larger than many but quietly not asserting myself got me picked on by a couple larger guys in the black group. One time I was smacked and hit while the guy danced around me begging to fight. I knew better though, there weren't enough white kids of sand to help me. If I started up and looked to be winning, all the black kids would have jumped in and most likely beat me pretty bad.

A day or so after that incident, I was sitting in the locker room on a wide shelf reading. The door was closed and in walked the assumed leader of the white kid's faction. He was taller than me, built well and had long curly blonde hair. He hadn't been around when the black kid was taunting me. He copped an attitude for some reason and started calling me a names and smacking me. *That was it.*

The door was closed and we were in there alone. I grabbed him by his hair and banged his head against the wall. His long hair made it easy to control him. He was dazed so I held him down and explained how I saw the situation. When let go, he stayed on the floor and crawled out of the room. From that point on, he kept people off me.

I only had a five-month stint. Most of my time was spent reading, trying to stay in the background. I bided my time, eventually sent home to try again.

I mentioned I'd taken the family car in the middle of the night a few times, quite a lot actually. One night a friend and I were just driving the backroads through the County smoking pot and we came upon a lot of cars parked on the side of the road. There was a glowing coming from upon ahead off into the woods. I slowed down as we came to the cars and could see a few guys between the cars ahead. They had white robes in their hands. They rubber necked at us, and us at them.

The road split-off to the right up ahead and as we passed, you could see a clearing up that road a piece with a huge bonfire and at least a hundred KKK members in robes standing around drinking beer. Gawking, I almost ran into a car on the side. A couple guys yelled at me to stop but I kept going and was soon down the road and gone.

I didn't know what to think. My friend said he knew a neighbor in the Klan and thought everyone on his home road was probably in it too. I have often wondered what was going on that night and if it was just a typical outing for them or what. That's the only time I ran into anything like that but it made a lasting impression. After that I always thought to myself whether the white men I came across in my County were in the Klan. Many of them openly disliked black folks.

Most of these midnight car outings were mundane if that word can even be used in cases like this, but three specific late-night car adventures come to mind....

I don't remember my exact age concerning this particular event. It happened before I was sent to Augusta for the Sheriff chasing me and Orphanage incident, probably 14-15 years old.

My friend Sherman and I heard from other friends there were big parties in the woods out in a location off the highway on the way to Ochlocknee. There was a parallel dirt road fading in and out of sight through the trees from the highway. It used to be the main road before they put in the new black-top highway. On that road was an old Steel Bridge. When people referred to that area, they would say, "Down by the Old Steel Bridge," or other more long-term residents called it the Confederate bridge.

Beyond, was all low-land swampy woods back country where factions of adults and youth would go "Boggin" and have big parties around pallet and tire bonfires.

A notorious area rife with drugs, alcohol and rowdiness. After a while it was posted by the County as off-limits. Patrolled by County Sheriffs with occasional drive-byes in the evenings on the weekends.

One Friday at school we were talking about it and I told Sherman if he wanted to, I'd pick him up at midnight and we'd go see what was happening down there. He didn't believe I'd show up, but I did.

I already tested it out and knew how to get it running, I'd been out riding around several times. About 11:30 that night I snuck out of the house, went across the road and started up Mr. Bullochs old Army Jeep. The key was always in it. A favorite toy of his, the WW2 Jeep had a roll cage and a more modern V8 motor driveline.

It had a roll cage added and still had an original WW2 machine gun mount in the back. He even had an original machine gun that worked for it. I once watched him and a couple other guys shooting birds out of an old dead tree in the pig field with it. The pigs ate every one of those dead birds, there must have been a couple hundred.

Anyway... the Machine gun was not kept on the Jeep.
I drove it over to the gas pump, topped off the tank, then headed to Sherman's house. When I knocked on his window, he was wide eyed and surprised to see me.

When we got there, a couple fires could be seen back in the woods so we headed back. We checked them out and got out to talk to folks. We were soon offered a beer so we stood around the fire and made new friends.

A few cars had come and gone, passed-by without incident, but one slowed down and had three lights. There was a spotlight shining into the woods.

Then from the other direction came the same. Then a couple more. Sheriff cruisers were coming from different directions, everyone ran to their cars, *time to get gone*.

Sherman and I did the same. We jumped into the Jeep and got in line behind several other cars and trucks heading towards the road. The Sheriffs had the trail blocked off and were screening and ticketing people as they left.

A couple Deputies were walking down the line of cars and Sherman was scared to death. His Dad was a pretty violent guy and roughed him up quite a bit. He was sure to get a terrible beating when brought home by the cops. We were under-age driving a stolen vehicle, drunk. His and my Dad would probably take turns on us.

I put my seat belt on (*lap belts only*) and told Sherman to do the same. *"Come-on, do it man, I'm going to try something."*
I slowly started to pull off the trail into the weeds. The Deputies saw and started running towards the Jeep yelling with their hands up. I switched on the headlamps and KC-Highliters on the roll cage then gave it the gas. From there the Jeep tore through the woods toward the road. A couple cruisers moved to intercept me and sirens blipped on, I heard call-outs on the loud speakers from their cruisers. I was dodging trees, grinding bushes and snapping saplings.

When I got to the road, a cruiser looked like it was going to ram me, I swerved and saw another coming from the other side. Sherman was yelling at me *"just stop, it's over man."*
But I didn't.

I flipped the Jeep around back into the woods for about 40 yards, got behind the cruiser and headed towards the spot where they were screening the cars. There, Deputies had their pistols drawn, others had shotguns.

The Jeep was rigged to spot-hunt deer at night, my lights had everyone blinded. I swung wide then turned hard into the opposite ditch. Over the top there was 50 yards of brush, grass, limbs and stumps till an impossibly steep rise to the main Highway above.

I got stuck moving forward for a second and had to back up to take a different angle. It was then when three Deputies ran up to the Jeep. One grabbed Sherman's arm and tried to pull him out, but he was buckled in. One reached across and tried to shut off the Jeep but I pushed him away, and one was up on the rear bumper holding onto the roll cage.

I jammed the gas, heading for the climb to the Highway. One Deputy was still on the back but all he could do was yell and hold on. When we started the steep climb at about 20mph, he was soon pitched off.

The Jeep was at a very steep up angle, I thought we were going to tip over backwards, but each time we almost did, the front seemed to find traction and we kept climbing. As we got closer to the top, the dirt was looser and we started to slow up so I gave it all the gas it would take, I couldn't chance missing a downshift. Throwing up rooster tails, we popped over the top with the front of the Jeep in the air. It being only a two-lane highway, we bounced a couple times almost going over the other side and down again. I jammed on the brakes without taking it out of gear and the motor stalled.

It took about a two-minutes to gain composure, get it started again, do a three point turn around and head down the highway. We could hear yelling, hooting, horns blaring and see headlights flashing from below. Sherman was jumping up and down hooting and screaming. I felt like Superman. We hooted and yelled all the way back to his house. There was no way they could catch us, every spare Deputy in that part of the County was down there.

The Jeep was a farm vehicle, no license plates for them to see. I got the Jeep back to the Barn and was in bed by 4am.

A week later, my Mom picked me up from school. We stopped in Ochlocknee to get gas and while at the pump, Mr. Bulloch pulled up beside us in his pickup. There were the normal greetings and small talk, then he looked at me, and asked my Mom;
"By the way, you haven't heard anything going on at the barns at night have you? I'm pretty sure someone was out in my Jeep last weekend. I haven't had it out in a while and there were leaves and twigs stuck under it like it had been out in the woods."
Both my Mom and I said no, shook our heads and promised to keep an eye out.

Then, maybe a year later, I must have been 16, driving legally before I lost my license for too many tickets. I was stopped for speeding and the Deputy recognized me from the Jeep situation. I think he was the Deputy who tried to pull Sherman out of the Jeep. I denied any knowledge of the incident but he called another Deputy who was also there. That guy couldn't ID me, so after sitting on the side of the road, sweating it out for an hour, I drove away.

That incident was an unsolved County mystery and the thing legends were made of. It went down in the annals of Thomas County lore. I swore Sherman to secrecy. He agreed since he thought there would definitely be jail time and chain-gang consequences. The deputy who fell off the back of the Jeep spent time in the hospital. That was just one in several handfuls of illegal experience for which I never got caught.

Another time, we planned a big blowout party at a friend's house. He was a bit older and his parents were footing his half of the rent on a house out in the country. He and his roommate had parties all the time.

Sherman came to my house after school and was going to stay the weekend with me, so at least I didn't have to go get him. We were to pick up several people for the party but there wasn't enough room in just one car. That night we took *BOTH* my parent's cars. He drove the Satellite, I was in the Ford.

When it was time to get back to my house, we were both shit-faced and decided to race each other back. We would take separate ways of nearly equal distance. Late at night there would be no cars out in the country so we could haul-ass.

I got back to Ochlocknee in record time. I opened it up and ran every stop sign. I knew for sure I beat him, so I pulled into the old church parking lot facing the road, turned the lights off and sat there waiting. In a few minutes there were headlights coming down the road. As they got closer, I could tell it was him, he wasn't going fast at all, pretty much the 55mph limit. There was another car about a half mile behind him so as he passed, I turned on the lights, started up and got out on the road behind him.

I flashed my lights at him letting him know it was me and I'd beaten him. When I looked in my rearview mirror, that car that was way behind, was all of a sudden close behind me and moving real fast. The lights went on, it was a County Deputy.

Reacting immediately, I turned left on the street I was about to pass. I skirted the ditch and sped up. The Deputy missed the turn and had to stop and back-up to continue. I started darting down streets blindly and within a minute, didn't know which way was which. I could see the cruiser lights bouncing off every tree and window of every house. There was no siren but my window was open and I could hear the carburetor on the cruiser sucking air loudly. I ended up at a dead end, stopped abruptly, threw the car into park and jumped out. The car didn't make it completely into park and slowly came to stop lightly smacking a tree.

Darting in and out of bushes, I froze still in the tall grass of a ditch. The cruiser passed me slowly looking around with its spot light. I could hear the radio and the Deputy talking. He made a circle around the block and then back close to where I was hiding.

In short time I came to the only realization available, I had to give-it-up. After-all, the family car was right there and I wasn't home, what was the obvious conclusion? I stood up, crawled out of the ditch and was immediately lit with the spot light. The Deputy got out of his car with gun drawn, put me on the ground and cuffed me. He then pulled me to my feet, leaned me against his car and asked all the obvious questions to which I spilled all the beans. I also told him my Father was going to literally beat me up. It was true, that is exactly what was coming. I was teary eyed and resigned to my fate.

To my surprise, he uncuffed me and told me what was next. He would follow me home and we would face my Father with this story to see how much was true.

None of this was going as I expected. I got in my car and the Deputy followed me home. The whole way there, the only thing I can remember thinking was that at least there would be a law officer there to keep my Father from killing me.

We pulled into the driveway and there sat the Satellite, parked exactly where it was when we left earlier in the evening. Our headlights were lighting up the house so I expected all the house lights to come on and my Father to appear.... but he didn't. I shut off my lights and the Deputy did also.

I got out and went over to the cruiser. "See, there's the car." He got out and went over and felt the hood, it was hot as it should have been.
"Where's your friend?"

"I don't know," was all I could say. The Deputy took out his flashlight and looked all around the yard. I was loud whispering for Sherman to come out but he didn't.

The Deputy came over to me and gave me another tongue lashing.

"... and when you next see your friend, I recommend you tell him all of this too."

Huh? I was lost.

The Deputy then looked at me pointing his finger.

"You're going to have a hard-enough time explaining that bent front bumper. If I ever catch you out like this again, I'm going to go knock on the door and tell your Dad. Never again boy, do you understand?"

I was dumb struck. All I could do was nod and say "thank you" over and over.

He got back in his cruiser, backed out of the driveway before turning on his headlights and slowly drove away.

I was drunk, under age, stolen family car, no license, evading the law.

Let-go scot-free.

"You are one Fucking Lucky Son of a Bitch."

I could hear Sherman but couldn't see him. He was above on a Pecan tree limb hanging over the driveway. There listening to the whole thing as it unfolded. I parked the Ford in its place while Sherman shimmied down the tree. We sat in the back yard behind the shed and smoked a joint discussing the whole thing. All Sherman could say was;

"I can't fucking believe it, you are one lucky son of a bitch," again and again.

The sun was coming up so we started chopping wood. That would be a good cover for us to be outside this early. My Father liked Sherman. When he was around, I did my chores.

The bumper of the car was slightly skewed after tapping the tree. Sherman and I both jumped up and down on it together and it helped. These were "five mile an hour" bumpers, quite flimsy actually. My Father didn't notice it till a few days later, and in that time, the car had been in town twice on shopping trips. In the end, he accepted it was probably hit in the parking lot of the shopping center in town by another car.... and *"some son of a bitch just left without leaving a note or anything. Dammit!"*

Well, that's two. The third one was the last time I ever took my parents car. I got caught... *kinda.*

This one was not so much about car theft... *hmmm*, come to think of it that way... it actually was, but much more than that really, for sure it was a definite turning point. Circumstances are lost to memory, but this time it was a friend named Ricky who was with me.

It was a rainy night in Georgia and we were on our way back from a night of carousing. He was staying the night at my house and somehow, we got the car stuck in the ditch... in front of my house. It was very muddy, we tried to get it out of the mud for an hour but only served to get it stuck deeper. I can't remember all the reasoning, but getting caught was not an option, so we took the other car and ran away from home.

Ricky had a car but he was on restriction from it. His Dad bought him an old police cruiser at the county auction for his 16th birthday, it was quite cool, an old cop car. All white, poverty caps, certified calibration, and it would smoke the tires clean off. The very reason he was on restriction from it, another ticket for laying-drag in town, smokin' the weenies.

We went to his house to get his things. We left my Father's Satellite at his house and took Ricky's car.

It was much cooler to us, and it somehow came to me that both of my family's cars being used this way was a bit too much disrespect, even for me. Colorado sounded good to us. At the gas station we got a road map and plotted a course, North through Atlanta.

By the time we got to Atlanta the next day we were tired, out of gas, out of energy and out of money. We spent the night at a bowling alley, then walked around downtown Atlanta the following day. By evening we were at the Omni complex. It was relatively new at that time and quite an attraction. That night I slept in a window well in a hallway of the Omni high-rise condo complex.

We decided to car prowl for money to get more gas so the next night we went through every unlocked car in the parking garage. I tried the door on a sweet black 76' Grand Prix SJ and found it open. While I was going through the car, like I've seen in the movies, the keys were above the visor.

Next thing you know, I'm driving through the garage looking for Ricky. It had a full tank and a good amount of treasure sprinkled throughout. Back at his car we gathered our things and he left his Dad a note for when they found his car. If I ever knew, I don't now know what that note said. In the end, Ricky's parents were a lot different than mine.

In the bowling alley parking lot, we completely went through the Grand Prix. It obviously belonged to someone with money.... and guns.... and kinks. There were high end trinkets throughout. Several guns and ammo in the trunk and a bag with photographic equipment. Also, a Polaroid camera bag with many pictures of a naked woman in the woods posing.

From there we dined and dashed and took advantage of a small blip in time where they let you fill your gas tank before going inside to pay.

All fill-ups ended with us leaving without paying. This was the beginning of self-serve gas. There were no debit cards then or outdoors payment. It was cash or an actual credit card used inside. Before then, someone always came out and filled your car for you. It went from all full service to a full serve and a self-serve Island, to what we have today being all self-serve.

Since we were heading basically in that direction, I had the bright idea of going to Rockford, Illinois where I used to live. We could visit my old stomping grounds, find some of my old friends and maybe some pot.

Ricky thought that sounded good so we headed up through Tennessee then into Kentucky. I don't remember the exact time of year this all happened but there was snow on the ground. I specifically remember Paducah, Kentucky.

We stopped in Paducah low on gas. We would fill up in the morning and hit the road again. We were driving around seeing the sights and went through a neighborhood. Ricky was driving, I was playing with the Polaroid camera we found in the trunk. Looking through pictures of some naked woman in the woods. I'm not sure she was into it, her expression struck me as odd.

As we were driving down the street, there was a girl sitting on the steps of a porch up ahead. I had Ricky stop in front of the house, rolled the window down and pretended to take a picture of her with the camera. I motioned for her to come over, she was hesitant but did. A little older than us, she walked up to the car confidently.

I handed her a pic of the naked lady leaning against a tree and coyly pretended it was the one I just took. She saw it and her face changed expression several times, finally settling on a smile and a wry laugh.
"Who the hell is this? and what the hell are you doing?"

We started laughing, then talking, and before we knew it, she invited us in for dinner. She was bored in Paducah and we were just what she needed right then. She was very intrigued that we were runaways in a stolen car.

Her Mother was huge, never moved off the sofa and kept calling her crazy. She called the girl over and you could hear her loudly insist she tell us to leave. The girl was having none of it and just sassed back. Mom finally gave up and engaged us with a little conversation.

That night we slept in the back room, nothing more than an enclosed porch, it was pretty cold. The next morning, she made us a little breakfast and coffee and asked if she could go with us. Sure, why not? None of us were thinking straight, just a bunch of kids.

We took her to a house where her sister was so she could talk to her and get some money. We waited in the car, someone peeked out the window blinds a few times. In about fifteen minutes she came back out to the car and told us she wasn't coming. We said our goodbyes and headed to a gas station.

We made it to Rockford and looked up my old friend Derek, he was surprised to see us. It was very snowy and slick in Rockford and none of us had any experience driving in snow so we took it easy. Derek got us some pot and we decided to go to a City Park close by. We parked and got high and talked of old times.

Soon Derek talked us into letting him drive the car around the park, what could that hurt? He drove around and we kept the joints going. We got to the top of a hill, and as we started down, the car lost traction. Derek actually knew nothing about driving, he jammed on the brakes and kept them on, all the time flailing the steering wheel around to try and steer straight.

We started spinning in circles as we descended the hill and at the bottom, the road swerved left. We weren't going to be making that turn.

There were pilings along the edge as a guard to keep cars from going over the edge of the road and down the hill further and into a field. We took out two pilings, the car flipped over once landing back on the wheels and kept sliding down into the field. After everything settled, none of us was hurt. The car still ran but one of the pilings skewed a front tire so the front wheels ended up Pidgeon-toed. It was stuck there in the field about 20 yards from the road.

We flagged down a car and he took me to a phone. I called a tow truck, and when it arrived he was able to get a cable down and pull the car back up onto the road. Problem was, we didn't have any money to pay for the tow truck, he was pretty mad. All we had was a little less than twenty dollars left so we made him a trade of what money we had and a pistol out of the trunk. He wasn't happy about it but accepted and didn't call the cops.

The car was messed up but still drove. We headed towards Derek's house but couldn't really go there. We made it to a mall not far from his house and parked the car. We were pretty hungry and there was a Bishops Cafeteria in the parking lot area. We agreed, we'd go in to eat, then dash out the door.

We ate, but the dash didn't quite work. We agreed to all walk towards the cashier and then hit it out the door but Derek went to the bathroom then dashed out leaving us at the table. We tried to get out but the manager grabbed me. I don't remember just how it went, but the ending was that Derek's Dad had to come and pay the bill. Ricky and I ended up back at the car and our parents now had an idea of where we were. It started snowing.

Ricky and I headed out of town with the car crunched up and the front-end wobbling terribly. By the time we got to the Madison, Wisconsin area, one of the front tires blew out and we were stranded on the road in the snow.

There was some sort of company not far away so we gathered our stuff and walked over there, it was a cheese factory. There was a guy going in who let us in to call a tow truck and warm up. While we were in there, we tried several lockers in the break room and one had car keys hanging in it. We made our way back to the parking lot and after a few minutes found the car, an old rattletrap Camaro.

We hit the road but were seen taking the car, the County Sheriff was behind us within 10 minutes. That car barely ran and it was snowing. Busted.

The Deputies really enjoyed hearing about our adventure. They were pretty interested in what was in the trunk of the Gran Prix also. After a day, Ricky's parents drove there and picked him up, I never saw him again. My Dad wouldn't come get me so the State of Georgia flew me home a week later and I was put in the County RYDC again.

My Mom came to visit and signed a smoking chit, she also brought some cigarettes. I would be in there a while and kids could smoke back then at 16 if their parents signed a note saying it was ok. About half the kids there would take a smoke break once every three hours. Nothing better to do sitting in the can but look forward to smoking a cigarette.

The guy we stole the car from in Wisconsin didn't press charges, the guy we stole the car from in Atlanta wouldn't press charges. There was no-one else to answer to for anything but disappointment. The Judge put me under a type of house arrest, I had to answer to my Father for 90 days and report back.

Surprisingly, my Father let me back home, but I had to account for every second of every day. He enjoyed that, completely legal heavy-handed control. He put a padlock on the outside of my bedroom door to lock me in at night and nailed the windows shut from the outside. My parents recently bought a property in Thomasville and were building a house, I was to help with that.

For a month or so things went Ok, my Father even bought me a stereo as incentive and payment for helping with the new house in Thomasville on the weekends. I would come home from school to the house in Ochlocknee, get high and lay in my bed with eyes closed and headphones on. My Mom was worried, I had become quiet and withdrawn. For some reason this made her insist I go to psychiatric counseling. I couldn't tell her I was just getting high and jamming, trying to stay out of trouble like I was asked, for the first time ever. Yeah, I admit, that was strange behavior from me. My Father didn't approve of the counseling situation but went along since it was part of my "rehabilitation."

About two weeks before the 90 days was up; I'd been out with friends and got high but couldn't come home that way so I ended up late to curfew.

My Father tore into me demanding to know where I was. After a while, I got cocky and told him;
"Next time I'll take a typewriter with me and write it all down."

He snapped and came unglued, he came after me like a Banshee. Grabbing me by the neck, he put me on the floor, pinned me down yelling in my face. After I was able to get up, he got right back in my face yelling and I saw red. I popped him right between the eyes so hard it knocked him backwards and he stumbled over. I ran out with nothing, slept in the weeds that night and made it to a friend's house the next day.

My Mom called around and found me. A day later a Sheriff came to pick me up. My Father of-course called the court and reported the incident. I wouldn't be allowed back in the house. Consequently, I was sent to Milledgeville YDC.

Milledgeville, Georgia YDC had been the Georgia State youth offender facility since the 1930's. There is where they sent repeat offender youth and hard cases. It was quite a bit different than Augusta. It was regimented and had a twelve-foot fence with barbed wire all the way around. Armed guards making rounds and all the inmates wore the same clothes with numbers and all. There were many "kids" there who would by law, only be let go at twenty-one, "lifers." It had what they called cottages which were big stone and brick houses with an open dorm and basement. In the early days, the proctors of each Cottage actually lived in a residence in the building. Twenty teens per building, one proctor, get out of line and you got solitary in a different building. You did what you were told, when you were told, no lip, stay in line.

I was given nine months and was actually "reformed" when I left after eleven. It wasn't the place, or the guards, or the teaching or anything institutional that performed the reformation. It was the inmates.

There was no way I would ever go back into a jail like that again. Most of the "kids" there were incorrigibles for one reason or another, I'm sure most of them got out when their time was done and either found their way to the State pens or died of something they brought on themselves. At least 80% of the inmates were black. There were angry kids everywhere. Fights in the Cafeteria, in lines of kids being marching to and fro, pretty much everywhere. Most all the white kids kept in the background to avoid trouble, I got my share of trouble. There were a couple kids there I tried to stay away from.

If not for the employees and guards being used to these conditions, I would have been in a couple knock-down-drag-outs. Fighting got everyone involved two or three days in solitary. Blood sausage, stale bread and tepid water.

In the Cottage I was assigned we had a couple choice examples. John Stocke and Alton Simmons were "lifer" killers. John beat a man to death in a fight and Alton pushed a guy in front of a bus on purpose. They sort of ran the cottage when the proctors weren't looking or weren't around. John ran on fear, Alton on crazy.

John was a very dark black boy with not an ounce of fat on him, he was as cut as any person I've ever seen. Always loud and angry, when he threatened you, he meant it. He hurt several guys in front of others while I was there and then asked if anyone else wanted any. Alton was a thin light skinned black kid with a fat head who would come up behind a person and choke them or hit them over the head when they weren't aware. You didn't turn your back on him if he thought you were wrong. We all saw his ire on several occasions. Both would do these things to other inmates, then spend time in solitary and be back in a few days to a week.

We had to clean and mop every day as part of the routine. All the materials, buckets and mops were in the basement. One time we were down there getting things together and Alton was acting up. I had a mop roller bucket full of hot water and pine oil and was climbing the stairs at the head of the line. Alton was two behind me with a mop and kept jabbing me in the ass with the handle. A couple steps from the top, the handle nearly went up my butt.

I turned and threw the whole bucket of steaming pine water on him, jumped on him and started pounding. I was tearing at his face and ripped one of his eyelids nearly off.

The guard hit the alarm and went to pull me off him, then the others started in on me. I broke loose running up the stairs and into the main room. The others were right behind and a brawl got about two minutes of play before ten guards rushed in wearing masks and sprayed everyone.

After Alton got out of the infirmary, they put him in a cell next to me. There was nothing between us but bars. He was so stupid, crazy and vicious, I could goad him into trying to grab me and he'd hurt himself on the bars. Half his face was bandaged, he could barely see. His head smacking the bars a few times made him madder. He kept trying till all he was doing was tearing his face open on the bars. They dragged him out of there frothing mad. Word was, he was sent to the State mental Hospital. I don't really know, I never saw him again.

John Stocke did not like that.
Especially being it was an average white boy who got the best of Alton. At every turn for the next month he threatened me. I made sure I was always close to the proctor and rarely slept. We were all in an open dorm with the beds laid out together and the night watchman was in a crow's nest. He couldn't get down in time to help anyone. All he had was an alarm switch so my sleeping was reserved for the main room when John wasn't around.

The day was coming, and it finally got there. There was a special occasion and we were going to the auditorium to see a movie. On the way there, John offered me a few choice threats in line. They put our cottage in the mezzanine. I was in the front row in an end seat and John was three seats from me.

Our guard was in a chair three rows back on the end behind me. The lights went down and it wasn't a few minutes before John was talking more smack.

After a while I just gave him a stern look...

"Hey John, why don't you just shut the hell up, everybody is getting tired of it."

He jumped up and over two guys, grabbed my arm and threw what would have been a murder blow had it landed. I pulled my head back and he missed. He had thrust so hard, his body laid right across me. I stood up and pushed his body off me. I hadn't tried to, it was just a reaction, but John Stocke went right over the balcony. It was about 30 feet to the seats below and he somehow landed on laps of guys sitting down there with no one else getting hurt too bad.

John wasn't hurt one bit. We could all hear him yelling and thrashing, trying to get back up the stairs to me. He was subdued, cuffed and taken out. We never saw him again.
I spent three days in solitary.

There were other tough guys there, but I never got any more trouble from anyone. It was dark in that theater, I offered nothing, they-all imagined much.

When I finally got out of Milledgeville, I was sent home on a bus. A couple other kids were on their way home also. The bus had to go through Atlanta for me to transfer South and there was a lay-over.

This other guy and I were chatting with a black lady on the bus who was real nice, she was very interested that we just got out of Milledgeville. *"Oh, you probably lookin' then huh?"*

She knew we were under age but suggested we go with her to, as she put it; "*a koo pace I knows.*"

It has been said; *you can take the dog out of the fight....*

The other guy I was with had the same layover and we both had a couple hours to waste so we went with her. We paid for the cab with our exit allotment.

The address was a dilapidated house in a questionable part of town. She had been away and was back visiting friends and family for a while. The family business was an Illegal bar in the house, copper collection, a liquor still in back and whatever grift they could get away with.

The main floor of the house was nothing more than a big room with couches along the walls. A console stereo with a selection of records on top, two refrigerators, a short hall to the bathroom and the kitchen, open and sparse. When we showed up, everyone recognized her and greeted her with hugs and exclamations, all the time giving us sideways looks. She explained the situation and a drunk old geezer showed us to a refrigerator.
"Well alrights then, whatch ya'll young bucks havin?"

He opened the door revealing a selection of beers inside. We both chose a Miller High Life for $1ea. This at a time when a 6-pack of Miller was about $1.69 at a 7-11.

There was music playing and the geezer grabbed our lady friend and started grooving, she played along while we looked around.

The kitchen door to the back yard was open. A couple guys were tending a fire in a 55-gallon drum used for burning the insulation off loops of stolen copper wire stuffed inside. There was a garage with a stack coming out of the roof smoking. I asked about the smoke and the Lady of the house brought out a bottle of clear liquid;
"Well maybe you want a taste, its fire I'm tellin' ya."
The still was in the garage, .75c a shot.

We hung out for about an hour, the guy with me got a shot, I didn't. Soon after, we said our goodbyes and left. I don't remember how we got back to the bus station, but we made the bus on time. Soon I was back home in Thomasville.

Lucky S.O.B.

Chapter Five

*"You know, I have never believed in divorce. If two can start it up, they can work it through and finish. But I can't say I was sorry when I heard your Mother divorced your Father. And from what I'm hearing, it could have been sooner.
Well, what's done....*

*You know we weren't a real close family to tell all our business, but you'd think I would have heard some of that.
An Orphanage!! Oh, my."*

Gramps had his eyes closed and was lightly shaking his head.

"What a time you had, I would have helped if I'd known."

"Oh, Grampa, there's no point. Thank You, but if you did that, things would have turned out different. And everything turned out just fine didn't it?
We'll just agree not to do any of that again, hows that?

I have to say, those days are a mystery to me too. I don't think back on it much, no use in it. It's good for me to think it through and keep it all compartmentalized in its place. Don't worry, none of this stuff bothers me. I've gone over it all, and put it all behind. It's fun every now and then to share stories. What were you doing at those ages?"

*"I have to admire that Mike, that's fine, just fine.
Well, I don't have anything to match you with. I did it for a while, but smoking cigarettes never appealed to me. I never had an opportunity for any real mischief I guess. Why don't you keep going and I'll jump in when I hear something I know about?"*

As he talked right then, I realized, his attitude lately was a bit softer from us spending so much time together. I was realizing I hadn't heard anything negative from him in quite a while...

When home from Milledgeville, I went back to High School. We now lived in the new house in Thomasville, a house my Dad only got to live in for a short while. He wasn't there, my Mom had divorced him. After a little while, she got a new car and I was given the old Ford as my first car.

Although very plain and not cool at all for a teenager, that car will always be a fond memory for me. I had the same girlfriend all through my teen years in Thomasville. I had many other interests and girls weren't a main focus for me, I've never been girl crazy. Yet sometime during my sixteenth year, my girlfriend and I lost our virginity in the front seat of that car, sitting in the front yard of my house. Summer nights in the pecan orchard at the fairgrounds, in the middle of deserted dirt roads far out in the country. We gave that car a workout.

Cars were a big deal when I was a teenager. The muscle cars of the 60's and seventies were very popular and always readily available fairly cheap. Back then they were merely used cars. Many of the kids I knew had cars which today are worth a lot of money and make people car crazy. Many of those same cars also met their end in our hands.

The nearest drag strip was outside Tallahassee, Fl., about 50 miles away. That was a bit too far for us so we had our own un-official drag strip out South of town a little closer on Highway 59, the Miccosukee Road. Everyone raced there. Sometimes even in broad daylight on the weekends.

It was a barren strip of two-lane black top stretching flat for about two miles. Right in the middle of the stretch was the Florida State line.

The idea was that if the cops came from the Florida side, everyone would run into Georgia. If they came from the Georgia side you run into Florida. Being in Georgia, we always raced heading South into Florida, the cops never came.

I went there several times to watch. I never had anything good to race but a couple of us would match up our family cars occasionally. We never raced for more than $10 or so, but others there would put up $100, even more. Some of these guys were serious and would even trailer their cars there. Steve Shroot and the Elin Brothers were the top dogs with their Camaro vs. Road Runner rivalry. Both cars were basically drag cars and were so wild they couldn't easily be driven on the street. I remember the rivalry but not which one was best.

I do remember some black guys there regularly who had a new Kawasaki KZ900 motorcycle they would routinely put up against cars. They would spot car length head starts depending on what you had and they only raced for large money. They spotted the Elin's Camaro six car lengths one time and got beat by two. As I remember, that was a $500 bet, quite a bit of money in those days.

I did ride with a guy during a race once, can't remember his name. A classmate I was partying with was in a heated argument with some guy that owned a 60's Camaro. This friend of mine had a Brother in the Army with a 71' Dodge Demon and he swore it would send the Camaro to the body shop for a new set of doors. The argument rose to the level of prove-it, shut-up or take an ass kicking. Problem was, his Brother joined the Army and was off to wear camouflage. But... the car was in his Mothers back yard.

Soooo... Later that night we went to his Mother's house. He took the keys to the car when she fell asleep. Then we pushed it out of the weeds grown around it and down the driveway to the street before starting the motor.

We got it going and ended up on Miccosukee Road about 2am. There was a small crowd and a fifty-dollar bet. I was in the passenger seat and when the race started, the Demon's front lifted up to where I couldn't see the road ahead.
We were ahead to start with, then at about the half-way point he started gaining and kept going till we won by just a bit. When my friend let off the gas there was a loud pop sound and the car swerved hard left. Brakes jammed on, we hit the soft shoulder, slid down into the very deep ditch and flipped on the cars side. We slid backwards into a concrete culvert. I got a ride home with someone else. I know that sounds a little like the movie "American Graffiti," but its true.

My first car being the old family car, wasn't very cool, so I wasn't satisfied with it. It filled the gaps before I was licensed and socially immersed but I was saving and always had my eyes open. Soon I saw a truck on the used car lot across the street from the school next to McDonalds where I was working. It was a 79' Ford F-150 Ranger short bed in a striking Black over Red color. It was a trade-in, barely one year old with high miles and a four-speed manual transmission behind a V8.

I traded the LTD on the Ranger and wound up with my first monthly payments, $69 per month. That was easy since I was still living at home and my McDonalds job was netting me about $140 every two weeks. That truck made me quite popular in town. It was clean and good looking, the newest vehicle anyone in my crowd had.

There was a cruise scene in Thomasville when I was a teenager. On Friday and Saturday nights, kids would drive up and down the main drag showing off and making noise. The route was from McDonalds where I worked in front of the County high school towards town to another burger joint named Chandlers. Chandlers would let you park there as long as you bought food, the place was always packed.

A 7-11 was across the street from Chandlers and one night a couple friends and myself were standing out front when an old Chevy pick-up came barreling into the lot. It wasn't stopping fast enough and soon jumped the curb in front of the store smacking me in the leg, knocking me to the ground.

The driver was Danny-Joe Brown of Molly Hatchet fame, he was drunk as hell. I knew him by sight but not personally. He had a girlfriend/wife in nearby Boston, Ga. My girlfriend occasionally babysat for them. He jumped out of the truck ignoring us in front and ran into the store. A few minutes later he came out with a case of beer, got back in his truck and tore off without a word.

I didn't go to the hospital then, I just had a bruised leg and limped around for a month. But much later in life after an x-ray for other reasons, a small cracked bone stich area was noticed there on my femur. Effin' Danny-Joe Brown busted my leg.

I'd been working at McDonald's for over a year, there were pay raises a nickel and dime at a time and I'd made "Grill Chief." I had the run of the place, I was making $3.35 an hour and the attitude was; I should be thankful. The next step up was assistant manager, I didn't really want to do that. I saw how much time it took and the pains in the ass these people put up with. Besides, the current lead assistant manager was a nasty woman who got her entitlement from the managers bed, and *HE* didn't even seem to like her very much. I could barely put up with her condescension only interacting with her occasionally, I certainly wouldn't volunteer for more.

I'd been working at McDonalds for quite a while when one day a store meeting was called. Inventory came up short and they wanted to get to the bottom of it. Of-course nobody knew anything. After a week, another surprise inventory was taken and it came up short again. Time to call in the lie detector company.

We went through two rounds in a week. After the last round, the next day, the lead Assistant Manager fired me. *Hmffph*. It wasn't me. That Bitch, I almost decided to tell on her "secret" boyfriend manager, that's who it was. But that would have meant she would end up with his job, I couldn't have that.

We were Rock-and Roll forever back then, specifically Southern Rock. My friends and I would routinely go to college auditoriums and see bands on their way up. I saw the Atlanta Rhythm section dozens of times. Lynyrd Skynyrd, Molly Hatchet, Double Trouble, Allman Brothers, 38 Special, Marshall Tucker.... You name the band, if they were anywhere within a 200-mile radius, I was at their concerts in the late 70's early 80's. Tickets back then were pretty cheap too, $15 was the most I can ever remember paying for a local concert, usually it was eight or ten. But then, there was a big one coming up, Rock-and-Roll Marathon 1981 in Dothan, Alabama.

A week before, several of us got together and planned it out at Buzz Sawyers house. I don't remember his real name, or even if his last name was really Sawyer. It occurs to me it was most likely a mix of him regularly being called Buzz because he was always high, and Tom Sawyer because that was his favorite Rush Song. He always had it blasting, air drumming / guitaring it everywhere.

The cost of this one was going to be quite a stretch for each of us. The tickets were high, $35, so we all needed to scrape that together. Not everyone in my crowd could afford the $80 we figured each of us would need for the entire trip, so being Pecan season, one of the guys mentioned an orchard he knew was being shook that week.

When pecans are ready to be harvested, they come out with a machine that grabs the trees and shakes them. Pecans coat the ground, then they are vacuumed or back then, just plain picked up by share croppers.

They shook the trees one day, then pick-up the next. Not the first time we did this, we did it every year. We'd go to the orchards in the middle of the night and get pecans then go sell them at a broker the next day in another county.

Five of us got in my truck with over a dozen five-gallon buckets. We went to an orchard we knew was just shaken that day, then I drove down into the ditch, up the other side and into the grove. Everybody jumped out and drug buckets across the ground scraping pecans into them until they were full. As I remember, a five-gallon bucket full of Stuarts back then was worth about $30. We ended up with enough money for all our needs including food.

There were seven of us going so we borrowed one of the guys brother's car big enough for all of us to fit in, a 1967 Chrysler Newport four door. This was one of the cars which helped coin the phrase "Land Yacht." The cost for the car rental was a bag of pot up front and a full tank of gas when we got back. Back then, pot was a lot cheaper and a lot weaker than it is today. We typically sat around with our own supply and "matched" joints with each other till we were "baked." Gas was around .50c per gallon, cigarettes, .55c a pack.

The trip there was typical. By the time we got there and entered the auditorium, we were all hammered. I got up on someone's shoulders, climbing into the big Marshall Stack speakers stacked three high. My hair was being blown forward as I sat on the edge jamming air drums and guitar. I was soon pulled out by security staff, but had garnered concert cred that would be remembered.

It was a long rowdy all day and night concert. Normally we would have all stayed there sleeping in the car till morning, but the car had to be back for this guy's brother to go to work in the morning so we hit the road, it was raining.

I was one of the four sitting in the back seat. My friend Buster was on my right and Buzz on my left sitting against the driver side rear door. We were all still messed up of-course and it was raining fairly hard. It was a bit chilly and I was asking to turn the heater up a notch.

I was leaning forward talking to someone in the front seat, looking out the front window at the road and watching the wipers trying to keep up. We were flying, at least 80mph, standard velocity. The driver was talking and looked to the right at the front passenger. The road swung left and the bald tires we were riding on kept going straight. The driver tried to veer left but we spun off the road. The car went down into the deep Georgia ditch, catapulted, flipped several times, all the while skidding through a fence, then into the field and ended wrapped around an old Live Oak tree.

Six of us survived. All of us were cut up and bruised pretty bad, one had a broken arm. Buzz was impaled by the rear window regulator and died right there. Buster and I tried to pull him out but it was stuck in him pretty deep.

Buster and I were dropped off at his Dad's house by one of the other guys parents that came to get him. The next weekend we had a blowout party in the woods by the Steel Bridge in remembrance of Buzz.

There were at least a hundred people there, we played Rush all night. The cops stopped by thinking they were going to roust us, but when they heard of the occasion, they let us be with a promise of no problems. I don't remember hardly ever talking of that night again after that. You know how songs from the past take you back to a time and place? This is what Rush's song "Tom Sawyer" brings back to me.

My truck was not easy on gas but I found the same situation in Thomasville for free gas I'd had in Ochlocknee.

There was an unlocked handpump and nozzle at a machinery storage not far from my house. The back gate never had a lock on it because to get there you had to go through a separate locked gate up front. They never figured anyone would drive through the woods behind the lot but that's what I did, I filled up many times.

Down the street from our house in Thomasville there was a wide path that left the road and crossed the spillway separating the fishing pond and Horseshoe Lake. Back then, the Lake was surrounded by woods. I would jump the curb, drive down the path, across the spillway and up the path on the other side through the woods about 100 yards and it came out right behind that machinery storage.

After I'd emptied that tank several times, I showed up one night to a lock on the pump handle. I guess they figured it out. Back in those days there was no such thing as cameras for video recording. If you wanted to catch someone doing something, you had to watch a live camera feed or be there to watch in person. When I saw that lock on the pump, it raised my cackles. I thought for sure there was someone there to catch me, but there wasn't. I went back several more times by foot to see if the pump was locked, it always was.

I never told anyone about that pump, it was my secret. But one time when I was particularly short on money and my friends and I wanted gas to carouse, I told a friend of mine if we had a way to cut a lock, we could have all the gas we needed. He called his brother, who eventually called another, and soon we had a bolt cutter, six cars and several gas cans to fill up. My friend and I went in the back way in my truck, we snapped the lock and filled up my truck and two five-gallon gas cans. I then went to the front gate and snapped the lock there. I flashed my lights to the waiting line across the road.

We left out the back way and went to his place where everyone soon showed up and we all had a big party. It was Friday night, and by Sunday noon, that tank was empty. I never went back or even looked in that direction again. That was the last of the free gas.

I was still in High School, pretty sure it was the eleventh grade. My Father was living in a trailer park on the edge of town. I had a photography class in school and we were all were given cameras to take home as practice for lighting and composition.

My siblings and I didn't see our Father much after he left the house. But for one reason or another, this weekend I had the school camera and we saw him at his place. Photography was a topic my Father lightly indulged in throughout previous years although he never got too involved. He had a great camera kit he bought at the PX when in the service in Morocco.

He was interested in my camera project so was helping me and offered a hand held light meter to use from his camera kit. I took it and used it, and of-course was supposed to give it back when finished.

Well, in the course of a week I couldn't find the light meter and he was incensed. I looked everywhere and couldn't figure where I'd lost it. He had a yelling match with my Mom about it.

Within two weeks there comes a knock on the door asking for me, it's some guy in a suit I'd never seen before. I'd been served, my Father was suing me for the loss of his light meter.

The court appearance was just the Judge, my Father and I sitting together at the Judge's desk. He asked the conditions of the situation and we both told our sides. Mine was simply that it disappeared, lame, but it was true. The judged admonished him for being such a vindictive and petty person with his son, he recommended counseling. I got a payment schedule to pay the court ten dollars per week until payed off

Later... I was long out of the house and living on my own when my Mother and siblings moved from that house. I helped them pack things in a truck. The light meter was behind my Brothers dresser. *Yeah*, Good Times...

I quit High School in the eleventh grade, bored stiff and high most of the time. I went next door to Thomas Area Tech and applied for a GED diploma. I barely studied for it, then took the test in January of what would have been my senior year. It was super easy, I passed in the top tier. I then applied for an automotive course at the Tech School. I went there about 3 months before quitting that also.

After I got my GED then quit the Tech School, I took a job at Sunnyland Foods. Sunnyland was a very large employer in the County. It was a pork slaughterhouse/processor that killed upwards of 3000 hogs per day. I worked there for a little short of two years, first in the Bacon House, then in the cooler area of the warehouse.

Before I started working there, Sunnyland made a name for itself by being a union busting enterprise. There were riots and car explosions and houses set on fire. Many people in town recalled tales of those days in the mid 1970's.

When I worked there it was an "open shop," I never joined the union. I was just 17, and with overtime, was making more than anyone I knew. A 3-$400 per week take home check was enough for a whole family to live on back then. I wasted most of it on things I can't even remember. I was out of the family house with no hope of going back, I did have rent and a few household bills. Crazy though, my rent in that house was $150 per month. It was a one bedroom living area above a two-car garage on a lot next to the owner's house.

I got my friend Buster a job at the slaughterhouse but he didn't keep it very long.

We went to work at four in the morning together. He didn't have a car at the time. One morning he said he knew a shorter way past a friend's house. He needed to pick something up from him and we should go that way. We went that way, it *was* shorter. I dropped him off and sat on the street waiting. He came back a bit later holding a brown paper sack with something in it.

A day later he presented me with a stereo set for my truck, a very high-end Alpine unit. Those were scarce and unseen in our neck of the woods. High quality car audio was a new thing at that time and hadn't made it to South Georgia just yet. He said he got it from that friend as a present for me for helping him out.

A few days later Buster ended up in County jail again on a 6-month stint after violating his last parole. He'd been caught with a bag of pot... at work.

I continued using that route to go to work and about a week later was having flat tire issues. While going through that neighborhood I was nearly riding on the rim so I pulled over and parked. I wasn't far from work and didn't want to be late so I hoofed it down the street. No further than a block, the cops showed up. They thought I was car prowling, there had been a few cars broken into a few weeks earlier. My truck was seen early in the morning here before.

It quickly came together in my head.

I went downtown, missing work that day. Luckily, I hadn't put that stereo in my truck yet, I was going to get new speakers with my next check and put it all in together. The Detective who questioned me had my file and it was a thick one, he didn't believe anything I said but they had nothing to really hold me on so I was let go.
Fuckin' Buster

It wasn't long after that, a few months maybe, I was on my way to my girlfriend's house in Metcalf, South of Thomasville. I'd been at another friend's house North of town and was on a stretch of open road when I saw a hitch hiker ahead. As I got closer, I saw it was my old friend Buster. I pulled over, he got in and we caught up. He said his Dad was tired of him and kicked him out. Right now, he was on the way to his Mom's house. That was convenient since his Mom lived just a mile or so before the cut-off I had to take to go to my girlfriend's house.

I took a direct route through town but Buster didn't like that and recommended going around. It was faster through town so that's the way I went. Back then Thomasville was pretty small and easy to get around in. He was a bit hyper so we smoked a joint. When we got close to the center of town there was a slow line of traffic, road work was being done ahead. Weaving around, I could see orange cones, work trucks and guys in striped suites. They had a chain gang doing the hard stuff, typical in those days.

As we get close and pass by the work, Buster decides he's hot and gets stuck taking off his shirt. He drops something on the floorboard and spends some time rooting around down there looking for it. We pass through the roadwork area, on our way.

We drive and smoke and catch-up, then I drop him off at his Mom's house. I get back out on the road, get up to speed and see a cop coming up fast behind me. I mean *real* fast, he was wide open. I slowed a bit and was thinking he must be on his way somewhere. I had the right-side tires on the fog line as he passed me, then looked in my rearview again and there was another so close I couldn't see the front of his car. I looked forward and the one that passed me slid sideways and was blocking the road. More cops were coming from the front. Rearview mirror, more cops from the rear. I stopped.

Cop cars pulled up beside. Cops were all out on the highway pointing their pistols and shotguns at me yelling for me to get out of the truck.
WHAT THE FUCK !!! was all I could come up with at the time.

I was pulled from the truck and tackled to the ground. I had four cops holding me down, one cuffing me and a couple others yelling *"Where's Morris!!? Where's Morris!!?"*

Fuckin' Buster, real name Alvin Morris, had escaped the chain gang four days ago and was spotted in my truck as we passed the road work. My truck was good looking and got attention. I told them where I dropped him and both of us made the evening news that night. I got a camera shot being cuffed and put in the back of a cruiser, he was filmed being drug out from under his Mother's mobile home by Police Dogs.

I was in a cell at the Thomas County Jail. Through the window I saw them tow my truck in and drop it in the yard. They brought Buster in and he acted surprised I was there.

As they led him down the hall, he yelled *"I'M SORRY MAN, I'LL TELL THEM THE WHOLE THING, YOU DIDNT DO ANYTHING!!"*

I was let-go the next day. Given my keys, I drove out of there.

Side notes to this story are that my Mom was the secretary to the owner of the TV station that got all the film footage and was able to get my name taken out of the story. I was just a "suspect" seen being put in a cruiser. Also, there was stuff in my truck which should have kept me in jail but they never actually searched my truck for some reason.

Much later when Buster got out, he looked me up and begged a place to stay. I was wary and didn't really want him there but told him he could sleep on the couch till he found somewhere else. A week later my Landlord from next door came over and asked if I had seen anyone creeping around their place.

Someone crawled in through the dog-door and went through their things, only a small amount of cash was missing.

Buster had come up with a few dollars the other day after being broke so I knew it was him. He wouldn't admit it so I resigned. A week after that, his Dad showed up and Buster asked if *HE* could stay there for a few weeks till he found a place for both of them. What could I say? His Dad was a good enough guy and put up with me at his place several times. He would sleep on a fold-up Army cot in the living room.

A short time after that, I was tired of them both mooching. I was making good money and they knew it. Every day when I got home the place was a complete mess and there was no food. Then one day while I was getting ready for work, Buster came out of the bathroom. He had just gone in there to pee before I went in to do my morning routine.

I went in and saw that he pee'd all over the toilet, seat and floor, then just walked away.
That was it.
When I yelled at him about it, he took my bath towel and tried to wipe it up. I freaked out.

With nothing I could do, I gathered all my valuables, told them not to be there when I got home and went to work. I fully expected the house to be in cinders when I got back but I'll bet his Dad kept things even. I never saw either one of them again although I always had my eye out for clues of Buster re-appearing. This could be looked at from a couple different angles, I prefer the lessons learned angle.

Being so close to Florida and the Gulf of Mexico, spring breaks were a regular vacation event. Everyone that could, would. Favorite places were Jacksonville, Carrabelle Beach and Panama City Beach.

It must have been 1980 or '81, four of us pooled our money, jammed into my truck and got a hotel room at the Fountain Bleu Hotel on Panama City Beach. The whole place was lit with teenagers everywhere. During the day, a couple of us rented motorcycles and drove all over. We were told explicitly not to ride on the beach and not to take the bikes into the town;
"Do not go over the bridge into town."
We skewed that to mean not to do anything crazy on the other side of the bridge but it actually meant those motorcycles were not allowed by ordnance in the town of Panama City.

The first day, I wrecked one of them riding wheelies down the beach and had to pay $150 for repairs. Two days later we tried again but had to rent from another company. I was banned from that rental place. Then of course a couple of us went over the bridge to a restaurant for lunch and got fined $80 each. The bikes were impounded and we had to pay the impound fee to the rental place also.

The day before we were to leave, the entire Hotel seemed to be having a multi-level party. Every door was open and a couple of us were going all over the Hotel meeting everyone and drinking in every room. By 10pm I was completely wasted and could barely walk, I headed back to our room. There, I opened the fridge and drank "Kool-Aid" directly from a pitcher. I did not know it at the time, but that was a batch of "Hunch-Punch." "Spody-Odie," in some parts of the Country. Grain alcohol mixed with Hi-C and Orange Juice. I blacked out and apparently vomited all over everything. Everyone's clothes, both beds, in shoes, *everything.*

I barely remembered being put in the bed of my truck the next morning with everyone's soiled belongings, they were all pretty mad at me. I had a hangover for four days solid, I'm pretty sure I almost died of alcohol poisoning.

I attribute that episode as the reasoning for why my body doesn't like to drink very much. To this day I despise the feeling of being alcohol drunk.

I had a casual friend named Mark. I can't remember why, but him and I were together a lot at parties in the woods down by the Old Steel Bridge. It might have been that he lived close to there and knew the locals because I remember his Brother had a big tire "Bog-Monster" truck. We and dozens of others would be in the deep back woods areas past the bridge in an area that seldom dried up. After a good rain there would be swamp and deep mud holes for weeks.

The Hell hole was made at the bottom of a hill and was used for boggin' contests. This place was a big valley of sorts with mud flats, holes and raised bush islands. There would be weekend get-togethers out there and folks would bring their trucks to splash around in the mud. Favorite past-times were chaining trucks together back-to-back and seeing which could pull which the furthest dragging the other. Those boys would even hold these contests in-town on asphalt parking lots.

The big contest was getting through the Hell-Hole. It was the deepest, gnarliest mud hole in the bog. At times it was 10 feet deep. Only the biggest tire trucks could ever get through and they'd have to get a big head start run and nearly float through it at high speed, kicking mud and water 30 feet in the air. A tractor was always there with long lengths of chain to pull trucks out of the bog that got stuck.

One weekend Mark and I were there with a large group. It hadn't rained in a while so the bog was easier for smaller trucks. My truck was two-wheel drive and had no business in the mud but we were all high and talking smack. One guy got stuck, I thought because he drove poorly and I chided him by saying; *"Even I could get through there in my 2WD truck."*

One thing led to another and I was challenged to get through "Hell-hole" in my two-wheel drive Ford F150 Ranger.
The water was down and *(much bigger 4x4)* trucks had gone through it that day seemingly easily. It seemed to be only three feet deep or so at the edges at the time. When everyone put up money to see me try, the pool was over $50. *It was on.* I thought I'd just get a good run at it, hit the edge and speed through on momentum. I was wrong.

Even though I had Off-Road knobby truck tires on it at the time, I only made it half the way through, slid toward a large pool area and started to sink. The more I spun the rear tires, the deeper it sank. Everyone was laughing and yelling and I had to climb out the sun-roof (*I had an after-market sun-roof installed in that truck*).

I got out and had to swim in the mud back to the edge and take my medicine. I also had to go back out there with the chains, dive under the mud and hook them to my truck so the tractor could pull it out. The mud and water were up to the door handles of the truck. It took weeks to clean it all up and there was still muck in the crannies till that truck was gone. It never got completely cleaned out.

After working a year at Sunnyland in the Bacon House, I transferred to the cold storage warehouse. I worked under an old grizzled manager who was a drunken bigot. He carried a half pint in the pocket of his long, white cooler coat and could be seen taking swigs all day. I called him sir once and he told me I wasn't a nigger so I didn't have to call him sir. He made the black guys call him sir though and they always did all the dirty work and crap jobs.

In there, the job was pretty easy and my pay went up. I also had access to the executive cooler. There is where they kept choice cuts and product for the company hierarchy.

This operation was pork only, but the main company also owned chicken and beef slaughterhouses and occasionally we would get a truck in from them with product to be put in the Executive cooler. The keys were hanging in the managers booth and it was easy to snag them and go fill a bag with whatever you wanted. Several of us on the docks would do it. My favorite was individually brown-paper wrapped New York Strip Steaks. Those, and stolen sausage were my staples.

Even though there was a guard shack and controlled access with searches of suspicious people and vehicles, a lot of product left through those gates hidden in the legs and arms of freezer suites and coats on their way home for the evening.

One Thanksgiving eve, the assistant dock manager had me help him do the evening cleanup, a job usually done by the black guys. I didn't know what the deal was at the time, but it turned out later, I was being tested and indoctrinated into the home-boys club.

We filled garbage cans and boxes with product and put them in the back of a big dump garbage truck at one of the bays. The truck would then be put in the parking lot and, emptied after the Holiday. When we left that night, we went to the truck in the parking lot with our cars and unloaded all the stuff. I took part in a few big Bar-B-ques but never knew where most of that stuff ended up. There was too much and it happened too often to be filling just one-or-two family freezers.

Occasionally I would walk around and see how a slaughter house operated. The Bacon House was at the far end of the lot, I never had time to roam when I worked there. I'll refrain from any descriptions of slaughterhouse operation. It is enough to say that by any human standard, it is a gut wrenching and soulless operation. The first time I walked through the kill and separation areas was also the last.

One thing I *will* mention which has always been stuck in my head is; I would take breaks and go sit on the intake pen railing. There were a couple very large pens, in the mornings they would be full. Trucks would come in all through the night and drop off hogs. Trucks trickled in during the day also. One time while on a break, sitting on a rail, I watched a truck back up to the receiving pen. A worker came out and opened the gate, the driver got out and opened up the back of the trailer. Not one hog would get out. They were stuffed in there so tight they couldn't move, they were on top of one another, but not one would exit that trailer.

It must have been a standard occurrence, the truck driver casually opened up a compartment and pulled out a prod. He climbed up to the top of the trailer and opened a hatch on top at the very front of the trailer. There, he electrically cattle prodded the hogs on the top tier which caused a stampede rearward and down the ramps till hogs started popping out the back of the trailer. A horrendous and disgusting site.

I have hardly eaten pork since that day. Something else which also sickened me about that place was the smell of pork grease as they made pork rinds or *"cracklins"* for local sale (*fried pig skin*). I can't stand the smell of Pork grease now, it sickens me to this day. There was also the everlasting smell of blood and death which held in the air like a fog which never dispersed. I am absolutely sure it's the same at all slaughterhouses for every type of animal but I can't bring myself to be full-on vegetarian. I will go without meat a week or two on occasion.

Most of the trouble I ever got into was because my friends and I were bored. Thomasville was small and there wasn't much to do besides drink, get high and raise one kind of hell or another. We were sitting around a friend's house one weekday night, most likely drinking beer and matching joints.

One of the guys mentioned his brother went to Tallahassee the week before and went to a bar in the city. They had a stage, and a pool room, and most intriguing of all was that his brother was under-age. I remember this specifically because I was 18 and grandfathered into the drinking age in Georgia when it changed to 19 but a few of my friends weren't. This kept us all from going out to local bars together.

Even I, being of age, never went into bars, mostly we just bought alcohol and had private parties. Back then in the South you rarely got carded if you even looked remotely of age. I was buying beer at Jax State Line Liquors (*on the highway to Tallahassee*) since I was sixteen and able to drive there.

I'd gone to a local bar once in down-town Thomasville when I first turned 18. I ended up drunk walking the streets, puking on the police station steps, then spending the night in the drunk-tank inside. That soured me on bars at that time.

Tallahassee is less than an hour drive from Thomasville, an easy drive, so we all decided we would go to that bar on Friday night and check it out.

We met, we drove, we got there around 9pm. There were two full cars of us. The place was pretty big, I think it was called the City of Night.

We settled into the atmosphere, a lot of people were there. Pitchers of beer and pool, we had a pretty good time. One thing a couple of us made mention of was that there weren't many girls there, a regular sausage fest. A little after midnight a few of us were blitzed and tired of pool, we started looking to get everyone together for the trip home. Some of the guys we were playing pool with insisted we stay a little longer. There was a stage show at 1am that lasted till last-call. We ended up staying.

When the girl came out in a costume and started singing on stage, we all took double takes and started looking sideways at each other.
That was a man.

I don't know exactly when the others realized, but for me it was right then, *this was a gay bar*. None of us had any experience with gay people past calling each other fags as put-downs for fun. Nobody I'm thinking except maybe the guy whose brother came here and recommended this place to us. Some of the guys got upset and ran out. I stood there for a little while looking around, watching the stage act and taking it all in. To me, it was humorous, we all got into this situation and none of us had a clue till now, what a bunch of Gomers.

After a few minutes one of the guys grabbed my arm and begged me to go before we got left behind. All of a sudden, I could tell as I looked around, yeah, I see it now. There were effeminate looking guys standing around. Outside at the entrance a very tall, thin guy in drag was complaining about something to a cop... in a man's voice.
We all went home and swore not to tell anyone. Who were we gonna tell? We *ALL* went there.
To me, it was like a Carol Burnette skit gone right.

That was my first experience with gay people, it would not be my last. Much later I learned the term homophobic. For some reason, by nature, I was not homophobic. I was definitely straight but it has never seemed to bother me like it does many people. *What do I care?*

I've mentioned I spent a lot of time down at the steel bridge parties. That party area in the woods afforded enough space for different factions of rednecks to have their own bonfires and music and not bother each other. At those times, in one Friday or Saturday night there may be four or five different parties going on in the woods within a thirty to forty-acre area.

Commonly present were Bikers, Street Racers, Stoners, KKK... You name the horde of vice and they were down there in the woods somewhere near the old steel bridge. Stumbling around a bonfire inebriated, waiting for "Free Bird" to make the rotation on a wailing car stereo.

One of these Saturday evenings I was asked to take a girl home who was drunk and late for curfew. When I returned forty-five minutes later, a friend was being beat up and cut with a knife next to the campfire. I could see, guns were present. I could see him on the ground with someone standing over him holding a knife to his neck, there was blood on his clothes. Everyone else there with us previously was now gone, and in their place, was a large group of long-haired scruffy types drunkenly mulling around urging on this one-sided attack.

When I saw what was going on with my friend, I quickly ran back to the truck and retrieved my M1 carbine rifle from the gun rack behind the bench seat of my truck. I yelled and sprayed bullets in the air. Everybody started running and as they tore-off, I riddled their escape vehicles. I was able to disperse the assault, not get hit by returned pistol fire and got him to the hospital.

We found out later it was a biker gang that did that deed, and in biker fashion, retribution was at first considered with high explosives I had access to at that time. This put me very deep into a situation I was not comfortable in, it was going too far. There was a choice to be made so I took the high road and opted out of any further involvement. He was mad I wouldn't help him get back at them. That was the end of our friendship.

In 1981/82 I was looking around myself, thinking about my life, thinking... I'd had enough. I was constantly looking for ways to get out of the red-neck lifestyle I was attached to.

In 82', I was eighteen, in June I tried to enlist in the Navy.

I stopped smoking pot a few months earlier and told the recruiter about my juvenile "mis-steps." He thought he could get me a waiver if it wasn't too bad but we had to go down to the police station and get a copy of my police record, I had to ok and sign for it. The recruiter and I were at the watch window waiting when from down the hall there came heckling.

"In here again McNaney? I hope it's something to keep you in for a good long time!"

I didn't recognize who it was at first, just some cop in a uniform. It was the detective I last talked to who was a real ball buster, but now, for some reason, he was in a regular police uniform. He came down the hallway, I looked at the recruiter. He told the officer I was enlisting in the Navy and we were just here to get my records.

"I wouldn't have him in MY military, you can't turn your back on him."

I immediately came back with something about that being from a guy demoted from Detective to meter maid and he blew up. It must have been true, he reached out and yanked my arm behind my back, drug me down the hall, opened the front doors and threw me down the stairs.

Through the glass doors I could see the recruiter talking to the officer whose arms were flailing. A few minutes later he came out with my records in his hand. He would look them over and give me a call. I never heard from him again.

I spent another few months in Thomasville. In that time, I'd gotten dead sick of my job at the slaughterhouse. Right after my nineteenth birthday I quit. I didn't know what I would do next but I couldn't do that anymore. I'd made all that money but had nothing to show for it. I even used my truck as collateral for another loan my mother co-signed for. No one ever taught me anything about money management.

I was close to default so the truck was turned in before it affected my Mothers credit. I previously bought an old Dodge Charger with issues for $400 as a project car so I fixed and drove it.

A short time later, that car burnt to the ground at a stoplight after something under the dash caught fire. Probably the under-dash FM converter and 8-track tape player wiring. Its big motor was then put into a 73' Road Runner I bought from a repair shop. It had been abandoned there with its own motor dead. The Road Runner was $300. I used to have a picture of me in front of it at my girlfriend's house in Metcalf, Georgia. It was also a long, straight road to her place from Thomasville, I got several tickets on that road. That's where I went on the Roadrunner's shakedown run after installing the big motor. I got it up to 140 on the cars 150mph speedo before it began to shake badly and I was forced to slow down.

My Mother moved to Tampa Florida that Spring with her new beau Chuck. I got a job at the Coats and Clarks thread mill in town. A more boring, dead-end job there has never been. I quit after three weeks.

My girlfriend and I were on-and-off. She would show up occasionally to see if my attitude had changed, it had not. The last time she came over, she brought a kitten with her. Looking back, I consider her similar to Ellie-May Clampet on the Beverly Hillbillies. She grew-up in the far-off country, loved all sorts of animals and had many as pets.

This time when she came over, we talked a little and this kitten she brought with her wasn't feeling well. It crapped thin feces all over my living room carpet and I flipped out. I made sure she knew that was the end of us right there. Thomasville and everything about southern Georgia was weighing heavily on my nerves. Unfortunately, at that moment I took it out on her.

I kicked around till my money was almost out then got a job as a short order cook at the Omelet Shop on the highway. There, I was driven crazy by the inebriants, the cigarette smoke and the jukebox. That place still haunts me. If I ever hear that corn-pone tune about Charlotte in her swing just a *swangin'* it again, I swear, I'll go on a rampage.

There at the Omelet shop was the last time and place I saw my girlfriend. Her and her new boyfriend came in to eat. I don't think she knew I was working there, at least her face didn't show it. We looked at each other a couple times, but that was it. We had both given up on each other.

There was a morning I remember quite well.
I was getting ready for my day and was looking in a full-length mirror hanging on the back of my bedroom door. There I was, dressed as a southern man. I think what bothered me most was the big belt buckle and ruddy cap.
A feeling of disgust came over me... *you fucking redneck.*

Here is where I started using my new word; Ludd. Stuck in the mud, not being able to advance, tied down to unpleasant circumstance. Walking through the mud of life. Mud that sticks to your boots making your feet heavy and hard to walk or even move.
I needed to free myself from the Ludd, life's mud.

I decided right there, as my Mother had, I would get the hell out of that hick town and move to Tampa. I needed to evolve, I felt hemmed in, like I was losing something. I felt helpless, worthless and stale. I had to go, anything was better than ending up forever in Thomasville.

Lucky S.O.B.

Chapter Six

"I do remember something about you getting in a bit of trouble when you were young, something to do with cars. I was never told the extent of things. I'm sorry you had to go through that. Your Brother had some problems back then too didn't he? Betty and I went to visit him in a Minnesota jail a few times."

"Yes, he followed me by a few years though. His issues were all through the late 80s and the 90s."

"How is he anyway? I haven't heard from him since those days. What is he doing now?"

"Oh, he's fine I guess. Has a landscape business in Tampa. He doesn't respond to anyone anymore. I'm not sure what his problem is, que sera' I guess.

You know, before I left the house there in Thomasville, Grandma Hazel came down by herself for a visit. Then, I remember she went to Maryland to see Aunt Modell. She was painting in the garage and we had a pretty good time. It was at New Years, she stayed with us that night while Mom and Dad went out. She made us all paper hats and we cut up paper for confetti, we were all dancing around, a fun memory. Seems it wasn't but a few months after she left, she died. I always wondered if that trip was planned as a goodbye. Did she already know she was soon to pass?"

"Well, she had a cancer you know. There was a treatment and she got better for a while, that's when she decided to go visit everyone. When she got back, the doctors found it was back and worse, she went downhill pretty fast. She died in 1981, at 61 years old. That was a very hard time for us all.

I doubled down on my church life, that's when I went and finished my studies at Moody Bible Institute. I got ordained and became what they call a Lay Minister."

"I remember the call Mom got. I was downstairs and could see her at the desk chair up the stairs. She started wailing. It was the first time I ever saw her cry like that, the only time actually, that stuff is hard. The thought of it preys on me too."

"So true, but it's God's plan Mike, knowing that, and that you will see them again in Heaven helps to console us. As long as we know Jesus, we never die...."

It was at this point Gramps saw an opening and continued on by expounding on the goods of redemption and the evils all around us the Devil temps us with. I had questions I knew he didn't know the answers to, but have heard all of this many, many times. At each break in the conversation I tried to lightly steer away. Throughout my time with him I always avoided religious confrontation. There were things I was aware of that were not included in his surety of the damned. This guy had pastored many churches as a substitute throughout the 1980's and 90's. He even had his own church for a couple years after their pastor left. He was a temp at first but it went on awhile as they looked around for another permanent pastor.

He held his ground on religion. I felt no need to create any kind of stir, I know for absolute sure, nothing I had to say on the subject would be anything he would want to hear. What would be the point of introducing other angles of thought?
He picked up on my diversions, got short and lightly huffy.

"Why don't you go to the store and get us some ice cream, you can tell me a little more when you get back..."

Does anyone know how hard it is to find Butter Brickle?
Apparently, he did.

When I first got to Tampa, I was nineteen. I stayed at my Mom's place with my siblings and Chuck. It was a three-bedroom apartment in Temple Terrace, I slept on the couch. There are a few things that stick with me about this place.

My Mom and Chuck were looking for a house. I was on an extended vacation spending the first few weeks there pretending to look for a job but spending most of my time with the single Moms at the pool. Two of them eventually talked me into "helping them out" with incidental chores at their apartments.

One had an XKE Jaguar convertible she took from her ex-husband. She said the Jag was his favorite thing in the world. She caught him cheating on her with some girl in it, so she made sure she got it in the divorce. We would drive out to the causeway at night and hang out in the parking areas at the beach. She liked having sex on it in every way possible. I'd take pictures of her naked spread out on it, then she would send the pictures to her ex with a note, asking him who he thought was taking the pictures and telling him how much, and just how, she was enjoying the car. At the apartment complex, he would stand outside in the parking lot and they would scream at each other through an open window.
WHO IS IT DIANE !! I'LL KILL HIM !!

After a couple weeks, Chuck asked me to help him deliver some stuff for his job on a Saturday. He would pay me quite a bit. He worked at a company that made PVC outdoor furniture and irrigation parts. We filled a big box truck with a lot of stuff and packed it in randomly.

About an hour away, we unloaded into a big storage garage. We then went to lunch where he gave me four hundred dollars and said we could do this every couple weeks if I would help him. I took that trip with him twice more. I'm sure he was stealing this stuff and selling it.

I'm also sure I was made an unwitting *(at first)* accomplice to ensure my mouth would stay shut.

In these same weeks, a friend from Thomasville came down to visit, he stayed at an old strip motel. He was thinking about leaving T-ville also and wanted to look around Tampa.

We were having dinner at the house one evening, my Brother and Sister weren't there. We'd finished and my friend and I were out on the patio looking out over the apartment complex grounds. My Mother was in the kitchen washing dishes and Chuck popped through the sliding glass door to tell me, my Mother wanted to see me. I went back in and my Mother was standing with her back to me, I smelled pot.
I asked her what she wanted, then she turned around and handed me a joint. Holding her last breath in, she spit out all the smoke at me laughing at my surprised face. Chuck and my friend were in on it and were laughing also.

This is how I found out my Mother had been corrupted by the world. This wouldn't be the end of it either. I understand while in Tampa with Chuck and his friends, she also had her share of Cocaine and wild parties. I'm glad she got to have experience with a different side of life. It didn't stick to her. A few years later when her and Chuck parted ways, she left all that behind.

These were pretty nice apartments we were all living in and the parking lot had some very nice cars. Chuck talked my Mom into buying a 280Z Datsun. I occasionally had to drive my sister to her boyfriend's house and got to know his sister. She asked me to take her to her prom and we went in the 280Z. Chuck did not like that, he was getting tired of me. Actually, getting tired of all of us, my Mom's kids that is.

I initially got a job at a Hess gas station working through the night. I enrolled in a local Community College taking Computer science courses.

The school lasted just a couple months. Fortran and Cobol programming language was exceedingly boring and I could not stand it. I maintained the job at Hess but was fired after my till came up short $20 one morning. They thought I stole it but I had actually been taken-in that night by a grifter quick-change ruse at the payment window.

At about the second month, I found a job at Ethan Allen Carriage House on Dale Mabry Blvd. I was paying a share of rent and saving to get my own place. I was there at my Mom and Chucks apartment for a little shy of three months.

One day I was sitting on the couch mesmerized by MTV. It was a new phenomenon which had the same kind of hold on youth back then as social media does today. I was sitting there and in came Chuck and my Mom. Chuck was upset and wanted to know how long I had been there. He'd been calling the house and got no answer. There was a message he thought I would have taken had I been answering. He was half-drunk as always and it sounded sketchy so I glazed over. I'd heard the phone ring but there was an answering machine in their bedroom, since it wasn't my phone, I let it go to message. He was pissed.

He was ranting and my sister chimed in. I gave him a smart aleck answer and she was giving him shit and he snapped. He grabbed her around the neck and put her against the wall.
I jumped up and tried to calm him down;
"That's enough Chuck, leave her alone."

I pulled back on his shoulder and he looked at me spewing a bunch of threats, then went back to throttling her. I then grabbed him around the neck with my arm and threw him to the floor. *It was on.*

He was bigger than me, a very thick guy, burly, quite strong and had about eighty pounds on me. He had me off the ground against the wall by my neck shaking me and I let loose.

I beat him within an inch of his life. At some time in the middle I even grabbed a dining room chair and hit him over the head. He would not go down.

He was covered in blood, both of us were, his blood. He stood there and screamed like a madman and I told him that was enough, *stop*. He wouldn't.
He came at me again and we ended up on the couch. I struggled to get on top and let loose with some intense pounding. His face ended up torn wide open, it was horrific. I jumped up shouting at him... *ENOUGH !!*

By this time, my Mom, Sister and Brother had already exited out the front door of the apartment and down the stairs. He ran staggering and screaming through the front door. The crowd which had gathered outside at the bottom of the stairs gasped and screamed at what they saw.

I looked around the apartment, there was blood everywhere, literally splattered on everything. It looked like a chain saw massacre had taken place. I sat there on the couch. MTV was still on but the screen was covered in blood. I wiped it off with my shirt and sat back down. Sirens were coming my way.

Within a couple minutes the police ran in, guns drawn. Surprisingly I didn't go to jail.

After the story was told by all involved, the cops thought I should just find a different place to stay that night. I put my stuff in my car, drove around awhile, and ended up at my new temporary home, a strip Motel on Columbus Avenue, not too far from my job at the Carriage House.

The strip Motel was $85 a week and in a seedier part of town. I would see hookers walking up and down the street and got propositioned quite often but never took the bait. They were fun to talk with and occasionally would leave notes on my car. The room next to mine was an hourly room.

From there, I could walk to work within 30 minutes and often did. My car was a gas hog and I wasn't getting paid a lot. Sometimes I'd catch the bus, get a ride or even hitch.

I was picked up hitching home one evening by a guy in a new Monte Carlo. He had a bushy mustache and was wearing what was back then called a tank top (*today, a wife beater*) and silk running shorts. Back in those days, a colorful tank top was a standard type of shirt to wear in Florida for guys. I might have been wearing one also, but the silk running shorts were a tell. He had to make a stop at the 7-11, *"did I want anything? what kind of beer do I like?"*

I was still quite naive' but catching up quick. When we got back on the street, he handed me a beer and started in with personal questions. The door locks clacked and he reached out for my knee. I already saw what was coming but hoped for the ride back and a short brush-off. When we stopped at a light, he said we should go back to his place. I was pretty quick and hit the door lock pulling the latch at the same time, stepped out of the car and onto the curb.

One time when going home from work, sitting on the bus bench waiting, I picked up a small news circular I thought was a grocery store tabloid. I was going to toss it in the trash can next to the bench when a couple words caught my eye. It was published by *"The Swinging Door."* That was also on a sign across the street a few buildings down. I'd seen that sign before and wondered what that was. The paper was a sex want ads. I tucked it away and looked at it when I got home.

It was quite extensive, several pages front and back, offers for services and want ads for services, all kinky stuff... intriguing. There was a help wanted ad there for the company, it wasn't for sex but for janitorial part time. As I remember it offered 15-20 hours a week at $10 an hour, I was even more intrigued, that was good part-time money.

It took a few days to get up the nerve but I answered that ad. I took off from work and showed up at the time agreed during the day. I thought the job would be at night but that was my naivete'. It was for during the day so I had to turn it down. But then the guy offered me another job... as a "valet."

At 19, I was thin, buff and pretty good looking. I spent a little time getting a tan, and when tan, my skin evened out, head hair got lighter and body hair took on a strawberry twinge. The guy called a middle-aged woman wearing leopard skin print into the room and they discussed me like I wasn't there. She came over and rubbed my leg, *"What do you think, are you available at night? The tips are REAL good, here, let me show you...."*
She then proceeded to convince me while the guy sat in the chair greedily watching.

I worked there three nights a week for $150 per night plus tips. I made a lot in tips also. That only lasted about two months. I was always tired at my day job and there were too many gay and Bi guys who wouldn't leave me alone. I hadn't yet come to terms with gay guys. It's hard to imagine for many people, but after a while I was repulsed by all the ravenous sexual attitudes. For the clientele it was occasional, for me it was 7-8 hours constant, three nights a week.

There were other young guys (*and girls*) that worked there also and I met a few friends I kept for a while but continued my job at the Carriage House and stopped working there. I didn't really need to be surrounded by depraved middle-aged sex freaks, I had my own prospects at every turn. I saw what it did to one of the other valets at the club and didn't want that to be me. Him and I had gone out to a sports bar a couple times and girls would not leave him alone.

I was not in his league at all.

He had a deep cut body with dark skin and electric blue eyes that sparkled from across the room, he was a beacon, a completely wore out beacon. He started to loathe women and had a pretty hostile attitude toward gay guys. I felt lucky not to be him.

I was sitting out front of my room at the Motel one weekend when a couple girls walked by. They were young like me, maybe a little younger, not hookers though, maybe hookers in training. I chatted them up and they would stop by occasionally to get high. The Motel manager, Vinod Patel, a greasy haired Indian dude wearing polyester slacks and flip-flops, did not like that. If I shut my door with the girls inside, he would come across the lot and pound on the door.
"We'll have none of that I tell you!!"
This from a guy who rented the room next to me to hookers by the hour. Many nights the headboard pounding the wall next door would keep me awake.

My room was originally a bedroom suite to the one next door. It was twice the size of mine with a locked door between the two. He tried to get me to switch rooms a couple times so he could rent my smaller one to the hookers. I found it was because he had a peep hole in the painting bolted to the wall. There was the same on the other side of the room.
I covered them with tape when I found them. He had his whole family living behind the office, wife and two kids. *Hmmpff.*

One day I took the girls for a ride home in my car. I got stopped by the cops for a tail light out and was taken to jail. It turned out Chuck had gone to the police station when he got out of the hospital and swore a warrant out on me. I was in jail for three days before my Mom talked him into dropping the charges. It cost me $200 to get my car out of impound and almost cost me my job. The girls were spooked, I never saw them again.

I met a friend at the Carriage house, he worked in the warehouse in back. I was a showroom and Interior Designer do-boy. Ray and I were fast friends, he would be the best friend I had in Tampa the entire time I lived there.

Eventually I got fired from the Carriage House, I worked there about eight months. The reasoning was a mix of it being time for a raise, and myself and one of the Designers having a go. She was another divorced Mom and could not be subtle. I was told not to fraternize when it was first noticed, but we never really stopped. Also, my job was easy to fill cheaply, why give me a raise?

By that time, I was out of the Motel. Ray and I were rooming in the back portion of his parent's house. I was paying his dad $175 per month. It was a very big house and he had a very big family, most of which no longer lived there.

They were Puerto Rican by way of Chicago. His Dad used to be in a gang there and decided to move to Tampa when things got too real for him in the 70's. Here, he helped move cocaine around town as a side hustle and lived the life of a retired gentleman. Ray's Mom Paquita loved me and was always stuffing both of us with food. She was hoping I would take a liking to the youngest daughter still living at home but I wasn't interested in her. I *was* interested in his older brother's girlfriend and we eventually ended up together... kinda.

When it was noticed I had no interest in Letti and had eyes for Glathia, Ray's Dad started in on the "Mike has to go" campaign. I was good at saving and had a little reserve.
I sold my car for $800 and when my tax refund came in, found my own apartment. I had enough to furnish it well with a good stereo and TV, it was a great Bachelor pad. The upstairs of a house on the Hillsborough River. Strangely, about a mile from the Motel I'd stayed at and just off Columbus Ave.

It was insanely cheap too, $195 a month. Like all good things, there was an uncomfortable catch. The Landlord knew me from The Swinging Door. Not that there was anything expected, there wasn't, but I was on the edge of this crowd again. His girlfriend lived in the boat house and there was a constant stream of renters in the bottom two apartments of which many were in that circle. I stayed in that apartment the entire time I lived in Tampa with no rent increase. The cost was easy to maintain and a welcome benefit since I went through several jobs.

When I sold my car at Ray's, I asked his Dad if I could use the old Station wagon sitting in the back yard under a tree rotting. It didn't run but he said I if I could fix it, I could have it for free. It was a 10-year old Oldsmobile Vista Cruiser station wagon. Kinda cool, it had wood paneling on the sides and a glass roof.

I fixed it, then Ray and I went out one night and "scavenged" a new set of tires for it. After cleanup it looked nearly new. His Dad was visibly perturbed, he had underestimated me. The first night I was in my new apartment, I came home dead tired and left half my stuff in the back of the wagon. The next morning, I came out to a broken window and everything gone. I eventually learned to leave the doors unlocked and a half pack of cigarettes and some change in the console of my cars. Protection money from being vandalized.

In a few short weeks, Ray's Dad got jealous of the car and had second thoughts about giving it to me. It was clean, ran great and had new tires. I'd replaced the window but it happened again to a different window. The second broken window gave him reason to rant and he took it back. He was a shyster at heart and didn't care nothin' about no white boy.

I was walking for a while and shortly ended up passing a "Buy-Here-Pay-Here" car lot. I came out of there with a yellow 71' Mazda Cosmopolitan.

It was a strange car for me but it was cheap, $385 with $35 down and $50 per week. I had a hard time getting a job for a while and Ray and I would go siphon gas from trucks at the ship yards for both of us.

The Mazda would have been good on gas if I could keep my foot out of it. It would spin and smoke the right rear tire damn near off. Shortly after it was paid off, the motor started smoking and I had to constantly put oil in it. One of these times, I didn't put the oil cap back on the motor, and while I was going down the highway, all the oil spit out and it slowly ground to a halt. I left it right there and never came back for it. I never heard about it from the county, I always wondered what happened to it. I then bought my downstairs lady friends Toyota for $300. It was pretty good shape and lasted a while.

Some of the people who went through the apartment downstairs were a study. Some became lovers, some friends. Carol, the lady I bought the Toyota from wanted to be more than friends but I didn't, we were still good friends though. Her and her Brother lived off a trust from land their family sold long ago.

Once a year their attorney showed up and gave them each a pretty big check, it was quite a sum. Since they lived in a regular fashion they really didn't need to work. Her brother was an extreme pot head, I would buy him pot a quarter pound at a time. He played the guitar real well and was a very nice guy.

One day I saw a cool old car I liked in the Auto Trader. I was talking to them about it and they insisted I buy it. They would front me the money, I would sell the Toyota and pay them the rest as I could. To this day I still owe them a bit.... I had that car for thirty years. It was a 1968 Dodge GTS program car. It started its life with every option available, spinning on a turntable inside the Dealership as a display model.

Carol eventually moved out to a bigger place. She got pregnant after a night of spontaneous hoochy-coo with the guy living up front, I'd dodged that bullet. She moved out and her previous ex-boyfriend moved in.

Colin was from England and spent time in Africa during his military service. He was a pretty cool guy, a lush, and always with a story that ended in a bar fight.
One Friday night he knocked on my door and pointed across the river. He was snockered, pretending to be quiet and sly.

Across the river there was a more affluent part of town with some very lavish houses. I looked over and one of the houses had the complete back yard and large party dock lit up. There were people milling about and you could easily hear the music. He recommended, in his words, that we "crash the brigade."

"We'll take the dingy, sneak in from the sea, and catch em' with their pants down!"

The dingy he was referring to was the landlords two-man, twelve-foot sail boat, bobbing, tied to the dock.

The river there was brackish water and affected by the tides. At that time it wasn't running fast, I now know it must have been at slack tide, back then it was dumb luck. We took two oars off the rack at the boathouse and took off. When we got over there, he set into a Pirate character and the people there were so amused at the crash, one guy friended us and gave us a whole roll of drink tickets.

This was a charity Gala for some pet project and the bar was giving out drinks by tickets bought at the door. Colin went to get us drinks, the bar was closer to the house. After a couple drinks and Colin getting much louder being encouraged by a few of the more bored guests, a couple big guys came to escort us back to our boat.

Colin threw down his drink glass, breaking it on the patio and went running to the dock. He then jumped in the River yelling for me to follow. I was led there nicely and got into the sailboat, finally picking him up in the middle of the river. He never got back inside the boat but grabbed a lead with his teeth and swam all the way back. I left him on our dock breathing heavily, nearly passed out.

Ray had been fired from the Carriage House warehouse; at that time I was between jobs also. I just quit a job after a few weeks in the blazing sun at a metals recycling plant. Halfway through my third week, one of the guys set a hopper full of titanium on fire and the business was out tens of thousands of dollars. Attitudes were as hot as the sun and that hopper full of ash. I thought that was a good time to look for another job.

Ray came over with an idea. Through his father, he knew some guys which in the old days would have been called "second story men." They were burglars who only hit known set-up targets and already had a buyer for whatever it was they stole. I had no prospects at the time so it wasn't hard to ease me into the idea.

We met with a couple of them and within a few days they gave us a couple jobs, told us how to do them and came to pick up the goods with cash the same night we finished. Ray and I were excited. We had a promise of at least a couple jobs per month but it wound up being a couple per week.

It was real fun stuff and I was getting fairly cocky feeling like a character in the movies. We would be working at night doing stake-outs and skulking in the shadows. We were doing this all over the Bay area. Tampa, Clearwater, St. Pete, only in the more affluent areas. We stole cash and Jewelry, guns and drugs, one time even a truck and trailer.

Ray and I had been at it for several months with quite a few jobs under our belt. We'd been given a key to a house on the channels and a time window. We came back with a bag of jewelry and several automatic guns from a very nice house. After the job, we were to meet and switch cars. We'd leave the stuff in the trunk. Two guys we didn't know from the crew picked it up from us and we took their car back to a parking lot where we'd left ours. We got eight hundred each for two hours on a Thursday night, real good money.

Long story short, that car we used was found the next day at the docks gutted from fire, covered in bullet holes. Nobody ever heard from those two guys that picked it up again. There were a lot of phone calls, a couple meetings and a lay-low dictum. I didn't need to be told, that was the last time for me and Ray. I was looking over my shoulder for months after.

Ray and I hung out together a lot. We would go to the Night Clubs and scheme ways to make extra cash. We sold pot for a while but Cuban and Jamaican gangs controlled that and you didn't want to be on the wrong side of them.

We had "friends" who sold pot for one of the gangs. They knew some people who worked at a Club on the Causeway and one night we all went there to see if we could work out a way to work together. These were people Ray knew from his Brother, I didn't like them very much. They were loud and too cocky for my taste.

There was a pretty long line to get in. We were standing in line talking and smoking when a guy a few couples ahead of us started getting loud with his girlfriend. Ray was intently watching. This guy was with a group of couples and was calling his girl names and lightly smacking her. Ray was a real Macho guy and a protector of ladies, he did not like this. He made us all pay attention and said if that guy smacked her one more time, he was going over there.

He was of-course over there in about 30 seconds and semi-nicely asked the guy to stop. The guy copped an attitude right off and asked if Ray wanted to do something about it. Wrong thing to say to Ray.

After being hit four or five times real quick, the guy pulls out a knife and his friends jump in. Then I and the two guys we're with had to jump in. The next thing you know there is a huge brawl with more people involved than you can figure. Knives were out, people were getting stabbed. Ray caught a blade in the shoulder. I hit and got hit. I ducked a knife and started side kicking knees as I headed for the parking lot.

The girls we were with, were previously schooled. They saw what was happening and left to get the car, they were honking the horn at the entrance. Ray was the only one hurt bad. He ended up with a good scar. I had a popped lip and a broken nose. The other guys had torn clothes but that was it. You gotta be careful in Tampa with the Cubans and Puerto Ricans. Knives and guns come out when tempers flare.

I got a job at National Sea, a seafood company on the docks. It paid well and was an easy cold storage warehouse job. By this time, I was together with Ray's Brother's old girlfriend Glathia, she was selling coke for a living. In Puerto Rican terms, she was a "Pericara," a female coke dealer, legit. We were together for quite a while.

On Friday and Saturday nights we would go to the hot clubs. There was one downtown called the London Victory Club, she unloaded a lot of coke there every weekend. I'd drive her around town and she'd sit next to me giving me little bumps with her pinky nail. We'd hit the clubs, sell coke and dance, sell coke and dance. Tampa, St. Pete, Clearwater, it was crazy fun. Mainly because we never got caught or got in any trouble.

We could bypass the lines at the clubs because all the door guys knew us. I'd slip them a few lines in a dollar bill. We weren't the only ones selling though, there was some rivalry. Glathia would take care of that. I'm not sure what she would tell them, I would be off on the side watching. She wasn't talking about me, nobody ever looked at me. I think she was telling them who she was slinging for. I met a few of those guys, they were dangerous heavies.

There was a guy I worked with at National Sea who was in a local band, I would sometimes "roadie" for him and go to his shows humping amps and equipment. After the shows there was always a party at a place on Dale Mabry Blvd. called "Shad Row," it was a bottle club.

I don't know if it's still a thing in Tampa but there used to be places called "bottle clubs." They were essentially bars that opened up after last call at regular bars. At a bottle club, you paid a cover charge to get in the door. You brought your own bottle and they put your name on it. When you ordered drinks, they made you drinks from your own bottle. Drink prices were the same and tips were expected same as any other bar. A unique and legal way to get around the laws.

There were also other things going on at Shad Row. There was a big, Big, BIG guy they called Pineapple at the end of the bar. He was the bouncer and the filter for two rooms behind him. One room was a large sectioned off sex chamber and the other, a place where one could go in and do whatever drugs you preferred. I told Glathia about this place and it upped her weekly quite a bit. Her and I would go there a lot after the clubs closed and supply coke for the drug room.

One early morning we were there hanging out, she made many friends and was making the rounds. I was with some people and a very hot chick came up to me and got friendly pretty fast.

Someone in the bar told her, "*I was the guy to see,*" she wanted some coke. I always had my own stash so after a few minutes I snapped her off a bit in a dollar bill. A short time later she came back with a story that her and her girlfriend accidentally dropped it in the toilet, she wanted more.

We headed out to the car, if I hadn't seen the badge in her purse twinkle in the light, I might have gone to jail that night. As it was, I told her to wait a sec, I had to pee. I went back in, dumped all I had on me, told Glathia real quick to find a way home then went back outside to the car.

We sat there and she acted like she was going to give up something for a few lines of coke. She was all up on me and feeling me up. That was too bad because my balls were in my throat, I could barely talk when I told her I knew she was a cop, I had no-more, there wasn't anything in the car, and she might as well leave since I just told everyone inside she was a cop.

Her act stopped immediately, she got out of the car and went to stand next to another car across the lot. She was talking with a guy in that car when I left the parking lot. I never went back to Shad Row.

I wound up losing my job at National Sea for being constantly late, there were many late nights with Glathia. I got a job not far away at another Seafood Company where the Dock Manager wasn't so strict. In-fact, he had a coke habit, I was a favorite guy of his. On his lead, he gave me overtime for weekend work. On Saturdays I would take his list of product from the warehouse and toss it over the fence to him. He would sell it, and in turn, buy coke. I did the same with Ray a few times, we had big parties at his Sisters house. Ray and I supplied the seafood, Glathia the coke.

A few of the girls who worked up front would come back to the warehouse on their breaks.

There was an upstairs breakroom for the warehouse above the offices and a lot stuff went on up there during working hours. Yeah, coke and sex. Some of the guys would buy a few lines from me, and next thing you knew, one of the girls from up front would be in the break room. I was guilty a few times.

I remember very well the last time I had a big deal with Glathia. I also remember the exact time it clicked in my head I had to get out of this life, both times were within weeks of each other.

My manager at the seafood company was having a big get-together party and needed a lot of coke. Supposedly these were heavy hitter friends of his and it needed to be *"real pure."* No problem with that, Glathia controlled how pure it was, I set it up.

Glathia and I weren't exclusive. She was a very good-looking Puerto Rican woman, but this was Tampa Florida. In her Puerto Rican and Cuban circles, it would not do for her to have an actual white boyfriend who wasn't a heavy hitter. We both enjoyed our freedom, and the taboo feeling of being on the hush. Our relationship wasn't exactly plutonic, but to people in her circle, I was her enforcer and bodyguard. It was true, I got mean a few times and carried a gun in a holster under my arm when things were iffy, but I never needed to use it or even threaten with it.... except one time.

I told Glathia this manager guy I knew from the Seafood Company wanted three ounces, there was going to be a big party. He needed enough pure coke to lay a thick line down the middle of a twelve-foot table and have some as party favors for the road. The party was to be at an exclusive club on Davis Island, a very posh place.

The deal was half and half, half now, half on delivery.

She reminded me, with this and her regular weekly amounts, the dollar value was high and there couldn't be any hiccups. Through me, this guy already bought quite a lot from her over time, usually an eight-ball or two per week. He held down a good job and I'd been to his house, he was good for it. She added it to her weekly call.

Glathia was well connected through Rays Dad, but over-time, she no longer got her stuff from him. When her and Rays Brother split, things were a little cold so she went to the source. She would make a call before noon on Thursday. A guy with a briefcase would get on a Miami/Tampa shuttle and then once in Tampa, take a cab to her place. She was just one on this guy's delivery route. He would leave her with hard, pure chunks of cocaine the size of a Brownie. Pulled from a baking pan where it solidified by process after being laid there as coca paste, straight from the source.

She would buy inositol by the pound from a pharmacist "friend," to use as cut. Together we would crush and mix the coke. She would give me little bumps from a long, 18k gold, false pinky fingernail I'd given her for Christmas. She *loved* that pinky nail, it had a small diamond burst on the outside in the middle. It was the little things that endeared us to each other.

On one occasion, her and I met several of these guys in Miami. We took a weekend party jaunt on a forty-foot yacht. She asked me to go as her body guard / partner friend, she needed to represent as both a player and as someone who got around to all types of high-end people in Tampa *(rich white folks)*. These were the kind of guys "Tony Montana" was familiar with. Truly, I was playing *waaaay* out of my league, but I could still lightly play and enjoy the game.

The guy from Miami showed up Thursday afternoon as always, we then spent Friday afternoon crushing and mixing it up.

You can't actually snort pure cocaine until you are such an addict you are close to death; ALL cocaine is stepped on. If you are snorting it pure, it's in very small bumps well spread out.... like Glathia and I. She lightly stepped on even our own supply.

A line down a twelve-foot table snorted up pure would surely kill someone, if not everyone. You never know how many lightweights are playing a game at the party.

We showed up dressed well an hour before the thirty guests were supposed to start arriving. This Seafood Manager guy led us to a conference room with a huge inlaid wood table. He wanted to test it before paying, Glathia gave him a little gram pouch and he tried it. The stuff we brought was far and above anything I'd ever given him before, it was the same ratio we saved for ourselves, about 8:1, where the norm was usually cut by a quarter or more. Pure cocaine isn't pure white, it is crystalline and has a light glassine yellow hue when in a big pile. It's the inositol or other inert media it's cut with that evens out the color to a more-pure white.

Spread thinly, this stuff was showing a hue and he was telling us that meant a heavy cut. He was a lightweight already half fiend. I tried to explain but he got mad and wouldn't pay the rest. Talk got heated, I had to get heavy with him and show him a gun. It was mentioned that Seafood people and Cocaine people were different kinds of people. It was mentioned that all his friends at the party could possibly be in danger.... etc.

He paid Glathia the rest after realizing he brought whatever came next on himself. She gave him a few bumps from her pinky nail and soothed him with her feminine whiles while laying out the line down the table for him. I stood against the wall quietly. As we left, he mumbled to me not to show up for work anymore.

Yeah, I'd already figured that one.

Now, I didn't have a job, it was job hunt time. I didn't really make a lot of money with Glathia, that was her gig. For me, it was just for fun. Any money I made with her was reinvested in the party life. Clothes, Jewelry gifts, trips, restaurants, all the fun stuff.

I put out a lot of applications and was at home a few days later when Ray came over. Ray hadn't been around lately, he got a good job with the city bus company and was now a bus driver. I'd talked with him a few times since he started his route. His take on the job was that he made good money and other than that, at least he met a lot of girls. He recommended it to me but I never even considered it.

He mentioned he met a sweet girl on the bus that day and he needed a date for her cousin, she wouldn't go out alone on a first date, she wanted her cousin there. He convinced me, he would pick me up at seven on Friday, I should bring coke.

Ray showed up in his Sisters convertible, she was gone on a business trip and he was hanging out at her new house in Carrollwood. At the time, Carrollwood was a new upscale area of Tampa. I never really knew for sure, but I think his Sister started her own business with backing from her Father's coke money. However it happened, she was doing real well in a legit Title Company and it was taking off.

We picked the girls up and I could hardly believe they ever rode the bus. They were fresh from Haiti. Beautiful glowing skin black girls. By now you know I have a little history there.

We went out to dinner, dancing and drinks then ended up at Ray's Sisters house. We were drunk and coked up, the night turned out well but I did too much coke. I laid there in bed next to this fine Nubian chick with my heart about to explode, I was real paranoid, *what the hell was I doing with myself?*

The next Monday, when out looking for a job, I drove by a place I often mused at. Every time I drove by, it took me back a few years to that time I was thrown out the front door of the Police Station in Thomasville.

I turned the car around and went in, about an hour later I was enlisted in the Navy. My juvenile record was behind me and sealed, this time they took me with no questions.

I was a little worried about the required drug testing but the intake schedule would put me out far enough if I just stopped smoking pot right then, that's what I did. Cocaine leaves the body untraceable in a couple days.

The next day I got a call, I'd been hired at a plumbing supply company. I still needed money and wouldn't be leaving for boot camp for over three months so I went to work. It was a bitter sweet job. Good starting pay, I learned a lot and it was pretty easy. The owner's daughter was a knockout and I caught her looking several times.

Three weeks before I was scheduled to leave for boot camp there came a company meeting. The owner told everyone all the loans were soon to be paid off, everyone was getting a big raise and I was officially welcomed into the family business as a permanent and valued employee.

Those were great folks, it was real hard to tell them I was going in the Navy, I almost wanted to stop my enlistment right there. I told the owner the next day, it was three weeks before I was to leave. He got upset and fired me on the spot.
I spent those next weeks getting ready to go.

That feeling of; "time-to-go" had come back to me, but this time it wasn't like I was escaping the ludd soon to be trapped if I didn't act, no. This time it felt open, inviting and exciting.

As I now think back to that time, two things come to mind. First, those two weeks were the best I could remember ever having in Tampa. Two girls I'd struck out with came forward so I had plenty of playtime. I was able to sell a lot of personal stuff easy and left for Boot Camp with a big wad of cash. I partied for free, everyone I knew was treating me like a King.

I could have been caught in so many ways doing so many things; but I wasn't. Was it luck? subconscious skill?
I skirted death and the law several times in Tampa but considering how I think of my previous life, I'm sure my best luck was not catching any diseases. These were the days of HIV/AIDS and as we now know, it wasn't just for gay guys.

Lucky S.O.B.

Chapter Seven

See there, how could I tell my Grandfather much of that? More to the point, at this time in our lives, *WHY* would I tell him *any* of that? I doubt he would find any of it more interesting than disturbing. I have mentioned sanitized snippets on occasion, but nothing close to inferring the realities.

I have thought a lot about this. The reasonings for not going through my younger years with him in more detail are several. One, as I've mentioned, is to save him from grief. I wouldn't want him to think he failed me in any way. He also would not see much of it as having any redeeming value, so that angle is no-good. I'm past bragging about any of it, always have been actually. I'd rather keep it all hush anyway. Much of it is a bit embarrassing after-all. Learning my lessons out in the open one-time is enough for me. Besides, I was still in second gear.

One morning I woke at 5am hearing him lightly moan from his bed. He was having prostate and intestinal issues again. He couldn't relieve himself. I called the hospice doctor, they showed up right away. They were able to help him right there in the apartment that time, but within another week, the doctor was by his side giving him the talk.

You could tell the team was practiced at this, they were very good at their jobs all the way around, yet Gramps flipped the script on them.

Ok Doc, I really appreciate you-all, you have done an excellent job. Don't worry about me, I am set with the Lord.

How about you, do you-all know the Lord? Have you given yourselves to Jesus?

He was looking around the room at everyone there. Suddenly, it went from the doctor's hand's holding his, to him holding the doctor's hands giving him back an imploring look.

Gramps had done what he could always do best, turning any conversation into a testimony. All the members of the hospice team spent several more minutes with him, each professing their beliefs. Next came more instructions for me from the team, we all expected the worst at any time.

Things calmed down till the next evening. Gramps called me in his bedroom and came out with it. He couldn't go and really needed to. I called the team, it was too late for the regulars. Night shift came over within minutes. A fresh young RN, she couldn't have been more than early 20's.

She was going to run a catheter. I'm not sure what was done previous to help him with these issues, I wasn't in the room for that, but it wasn't a catheter. After several tries and Gramps screaming to the moon, she called in reinforcements. More fast response brought another very young attendant. I was in the other room not 15 feet away, they were in there yanking and pulling on poor ole' Gramps.

He was howling, blood curdling stuff, hair raising stuff. I was inclined to go in there and put an end to it. I was really starting to freak out. Then he screamed like he'd just given up and started sobbing. Both nurses were out of his room throwing things away, slightly straightening up, moving pretty fast, talking pretty fast. They both left pretty fast, like they'd just robbed a bank.

I checked on Gramps after they left and he was lucid but thrashing around. He was mad, actually quite mad. I'd never experienced him this way before.

There was still a bit of a mess so I was going at it when he just threw me out. He yelled and flailed his arms, he was pissed. I was to leave right now. He seemed quite aware and serious.

I went back to my apartment and fell asleep on the couch. Not knowing what waited, at 6am I opened the door to his apartment. The lights were on throughout, everything to be seen was neat as a pin and in its place. Gramps was fresh looking, fully dressed sitting on the couch in his normal spot. Hands in lap, looking down with eyes closed. He probably started out praying and ended up asleep. He was snoring, walker and cane within reach.

His bedroom was straight, bed made, no signs of last evenings struggle. Bathroom across the hall, the same. I was ready for clean-up, but now, nothing. He must have been up all night. I went in the kitchen and started making breakfast. Just as I thought, he woke when the sausage aroma started to waft. Morning niceties and small talk. I had to ask him all about how he was feeling, but figured I would wait till after breakfast was cleared.

Catching up with the morning news show on TV, he was half way through his morning food shuffling ritual when he reached over to the remote control, miraculously hit the mute button on first try, looked back at his plate then shook his head.
"I don't want to see those two girls again. I'm feeling ok this morning, I think I'll get better."

And he did.
I talked with the hospice team a few days later, they looked him over and re-evaluated him. All I could tell them is that all indications were he had jumped back about a year. Something had rewound his spring.

Directed by him, he was back to visits from church friends, two eggs in the morning and a full glass of milk for dinner.

He tried not to use his walker but called me into the kitchen a few times to bring it to him.

My Mother visited from Florida a month earlier. In October she moved back to Des Moines for good. You can never be certain of other peoples' reasonings, sometimes they don't even know themselves. But I'm pretty sure a good piece of my Mothers reasoning was guilt. I knew she felt guilty it wasn't her up here taking care of her Father. There had been a sharp upswing in her interest since I'd moved back to Des Moines.

Gramps noticed this also and asked me about it a few times. He was as dumbfounded to her reasonings now as I think he was of me when I first showed up. There may have been other unspoken truths there also. My Mother was no Spring Chick, and not of her Fathers physical or mental constitution. In Florida, she lived down the street from my Sister, here, she would be down the street from me.

She helped with Gramps when I asked and was worried she should be doing more. But there really wasn't much more for her to do that I wasn't already doing. She was indeed on the ramp-up program. There were certain days and times it was ok for her to visit. I was the only one now with free reign. She had keys to his apartment but they were emergency use only.

Gramps didn't think twice about doing or saying anything around me. He would ask me all kinds of questions about things he saw around him. This was a distinct difference from before his episode. He was basically chipper but occasionally would be testy. He was increasingly frustrated with his state of mind, his declining physical ability, being stuck in his apartment and sometimes, even me. This is a condition I would not wish on anyone. Either to experience it, or to stand by and watch it play out.

When I first arrived, he thought I was here as a spy to evaluate his geriatric state and report back to.... whomever. So I left him alone and did my own thing. He now likes me being around, and I enjoy being here for him. I do still sense as we talk, he still considers me a heathen, but a heathen keeping him out of an old-folks home to waste away, so... ok then. I imagine, he imagines, I'm the heathen slave sent by God to ease his situation. His own bible story in the making.

I had been spending all this time with him for close to a year and we talked quite a bit. I was surprised many times at the things and ideas he actually had no idea of. As we converse, he often asks me; "*How do you know that?*"
I'll expound a bit and he will look befuddled. I like to watch the game show Jeopardy and he'll sit on the other end of the couch and shake his head.
"How do these people know all this stuff?"
My simple and non-controversial answer to him is;
By watching Jeopardy.
The Jeopardy game show usually has a few biblical categories and questions which keeps his interest.

As it turns out, My Grandfather has a grand all-encompassing knowledge of one thing and one thing only, everything else has been shut-out. This occasionally presents a spot where he might get uncomfortable so I give validating answers to him instead of expounding on things he cares nothing about or having to repeat myself over and over.

For instance; I rarely eat with him. He's been a rail his entire life and has always eaten whatever was put in front of him and even more. To this day, although he can't eat much of it, he wants some of the worst food ever put in front of him for dinner. I'm not that way, he gets to eat whatever he wants, and I make it for him, but I just can't eat that stuff.
So several times he asks; *"Don't you ever eat?"*

We played this scenario again the other day and this time I gave him a different answer, playfully sarcastic.
"No, I take my sustenance from the Lord."
He liked that.

"Oh yes, I know what you mean."
He then went back to eating. I thought I would keep it going; "Kinda like the Buddha, I just sit here under your tree and eat leaves."
I thought I was being humorous using a very lame paraphrase.
He looked at me like I was nuts... *"Huh?"*
"Yeah, you know, like the story of the Buddha."

"Well I've heard of the fairy tale, but don't know anything about it."

"You don't know about Buddha?"

"Nah.... why do I need to know anything like that? Fairy tales aren't anything to know."

"Uh, Jeopardy, *helloooo*."
I try to be funny but it's only to myself. He doesn't have time for this kind of nonsense. He's busy waiting for his reward, now truly disappointed each morning his eyes open.

Grandpa knows one thing, and he knows it inside and out. He knows it upside down and backwards. He knows it from his experience of going to church his whole life and reading every form of Christian Bible ever written or annotated. He knows his brand of the Evangelical Christian Religion, *that's it.*

He Doesn't know of Jehovah Witnesses, or Mormons, or Catholics, or Greek Orthodoxy or the Crusades or the Templars. He knows nothing of Judaism past his own memorization of the Old Testament. He has absolutely no idea of any faction of Islam, Sikh, or Hinduism.

Forget about Buddhism or even, crazily enough, even all the ins-and-outs for the Lutheran Reformation.
All those people are going to Hell.
Quite a study indeed.

We aren't alike in any overtly discernable way, so why do I have such an affinity for him? Within the family I seem to be the only one. Yet, as they have aged, they have softened also. Until I injected myself into this situation, my Mom and Uncle would just as soon heard of him passing from a dark room in an elderly care center. They were alienated long ago, and even though Gramps knows why, and is lightly repentant of his previous actions, he would never say he was sorry. Sorry for being a champion of God, no matter how you oppressed others is not within the convention of the greatest generation... or their children. I mean, no-one has ever apologized for the inquisition have they?

I guess somewhat luckily, I was only very lightly touched by his attitude. The parts I experienced were merely the lighter side of humanity, caring, and what I took for Love. I didn't get a lot of that from my parents growing up, and the few times we interacted as I grew, he never said a mean thing and was always very thoughtful. If you can work hard to avoid all things religious, he is a pretty thoughtful and nice guy.

As a child, one time when at my Grandparents house spending the night, I wet the bed four times in a row. I was six or seven years old, embarrassing stuff, but he changed me and the bed without a word. In my house it was a problem you were threatened with, also within my childhood home were the reasons I wet the bed until such an age, even later.

Back then I was being indoctrinated into the Christian Religion and my Grandfather was the one trying to impress upon me the virtues of scripture.

He paid to send me to a church camp for two summers. He seemed to care about me and how he did it made no difference to a kid as young as I was. It was the positive attention I was not getting at home.

Later, after my Grandmother passed, he remarried to a lady who was probably the nicest person I have ever known. Always genuinely smiling and happy. She would pull you aside and tell you how good she thought you were. She was always doting on my Grandfather and saying the same about him to everyone. Out of character, he would respond to her the same way. He now refers to Betty as, "a very good wife." She left in 2016, truly, Betty was light.

That was something my Mom and Uncle took a smidge of offense to. I saw it as her smoothing out his sharp religious edges. Even though she was just as bible thumping as he was, he softened with her. I have great memories of my actual Grandmother; no-one can take that away. She just wasn't as happy in her marriage as we all hope to be.

One thing that resonates with me about my Grandfather, despite the disparity of generation and thought, is the small similarities in our lives. It's hard to pick out because it's not similar in action, it's in the complete disdain we feel for our environments. We both shun the conventions we are trapped within, his secular, mine societal.

His life is in the realm of what has come to be known as the "Greatest Generation." When he became aware as a youth, the technologies we all take for granted today were in their infancy, barely recognizable as a beginning for what we have now. When he was born, a telephone was a wooden box on the wall an operator had to connect you through. Perhaps a candlestick looking device with a very limited range. There was no TV. Flight was a novelty, radio was also sketchy and new.

Cars were also a recent invention, science and medicine were still in their infancy. They thwarted evil and "saved the world."

Conversely;
When I was born, it was in the years of human enlightenment. Although one could argue the technologies of the 1960's had, and realized, the most grandiose of intention, His was of the material, mine was within thought.

Here we are today with a screen frozen to our hands which offhandedly can be used as a telephone if anyone actually wanted to use one. Flight has taken us into outer space. Television is passé.

Yet once again we are being brought full circle by superstition and the greed of humanity. The attitudes and practices of the American-German Bund have come full circle, without any of the lessons. According to every generation since the first; another fall of an empire on the horizon.
My Grandfather and I come together with a final thought. Why are we still here? We both helplessly wait.

Yet the longer we spend time together the deeper the reveal. I'm not sure if it is his brain solidifying or not, but what has become palpable is his lack of compassion and empathy for friends, family and the world around him.

I tend to think it is because he has very little life experience and lives within the convention his chosen editorial "News" allows him. My Mother attributes it to him being of German descent, like that is somehow strong enough to overpower the rest of a person's existence, "*He's just German stoic.*" It may be that he has simply become desensitized to the world around him after everything and everyone he has ever known leaving him behind.

There are times when I almost take his glib replies as offense.

He'll say, *"Oh, that's too bad,"* in a compassionless deadpan manner while completely absorbed in seeing what's at the bottom of his dinner salad. He'll shake his head with a confident wry smile while relaying the latest plot he's absorbed off television. When you ask him the reasonings, he has no idea, can't give any examples. He gets miffed when you don't accept the point he picked up from TV editorial.

One Particularly good Sunday we went to Cracker Barrel to have lunch. He was feeling spry, cane only, still quite slow.

A couple passed the table and one tripped over his cane which had slipped, and tipped over unnoticed. Gramps apologized and had a lite cheerful few words with them for a minute. Later while eating he asked me about them. They were obviously different. What did I think about them?

"What do you mean, the hair, the mannerisms? That they were a gay couple in the Cracker Barrel? That *is* a bit unusual."

While saying that to my Grandfather, I was thinking this was uncharted territory. Little did he know, there was a lot of it close to home if he chose to go there.

"Is that it, do you think they are gay?"

"Yes, definitely so, I think you disappointed them by being so nice. I think the blue haired one expected more of a shock."

Why shock? why do you say that? I've seen these people before."

"Well, they probably have a different idea of you... and most likely this place, just a feeling I get. Are you used to openly gay people being around? are there any gay folks in your church you know of?"

"I haven't known any myself. But I have been in company with a few I was told later were gay. They seemed normal.

But make no mistake, the Lord won't stand for it, it's an abomination."

Gramps went into a few Bible verses, I pulled one out of my own hat. A deep cut, a different angle of the story of the coat of many colors. Giving away the symbol of power and leadership to his best friend, with a kiss....

I was surprised to see a look of contemplation on his face, he was actually thinking about it. I hope I didn't ruin the Old Testament for him. None of my interpretations are worthy of their own argument, just pointing out different angles.

In a spur of the moment I decided to lightly address the subject and break previously unbroken ice.
"You know we have a few gay people in our family don't you?"

He looked up from his food and sat straight up.
"*Who is that?"*

"Beth and Ian of-course, two of your great Grandchildren; Kelly's kids."

"When did they turn... how did that happen?"

"I thought you might know about Beth. She's married with a little girl in Indiana.

"Married!?"

We've all known since she was young and Ian says the same of himself. It's not a choice Grandpa, they are born that way, that's just who they are."

"So it was from their Father then?"

"No, I don't think so, that's the funny part to me, those two have different Father's. If it worked like that, it would be Kelly's side, my side... *my Father's side.* I'm sure that bugs my Dad."

"What do you think Mike, how does that happen?"

I don't know, I would have to say; God's will. I just know it doesn't bother me. I've known quite a few gay people over time. None of them were recruiting. Beth and Ian are nice and successful people. I'm proud as I can be of them on that point alone. I know people hover on it, but if a person can't get past something, they need to figure out a way to put it out of their head and leave others be."

Gramps honestly mulled it over, I didn't see anything negative in his face. These were people he knew, hugged and visited with in the not too distant past. After a few seconds he went back to his plate. He picked around in his salad shaking his head*; "That's too bad,"* was the last thing he had to say on the subject. His tone said a little more.

I can imagine a time in his previous life when this would have been the prelude to a rant. A Biblically based fire and brimstone condemnation with a demand for penance. I think it was just the needed energy for all that he was lacking, it was still there. Yet I could see there were changes going on behind his eyes, as I, someone from outside his crowd, introduced subjects and viewpoints he was not used to hearing. Over time, I learned he was more open mindedly accepting than we all previously gave him credit for. Much of his acceptance has come with his age. I think at some point we all soften a bit when we finally come to the realization we can no longer change anything.

We got out for lunch a few times before it got too cold outside. Sometimes at his favorite Cafe' we'd run into a few of his Church buddies. On Thanksgiving we had what remained of close Family coming over for dinner and conversation. My Mom was there, and with the other older cousin family members around, there was a hundred years of memories to pick through. I'd heard much of this before but there were others in company who had not...

After getting his draft notice, Gramps went to Basic Training in Idaho. The last week of basic, he got appendicitis and spent three weeks off-duty healing. In that time, he applied for a position at Radio School in Washington State.

"It was fortunate I went to Seattle, Bainbridge Island actually, but better than half the time I stayed in Seattle at Otto Carnie's place. They lived a block or so from a nice lake. Otto was a man from my childhood who grew up with my Uncles. Story was; our family took him in when he was young. He was an orphan that came from the East on a train with a note pinned to his jacket. He was treated just like a member of our family. I never knew his story until I was much older, I thought he was another Uncle. I was only there in Seattle for six months though."

"I'll bet that was the Green Lake neighborhood in North Seattle. I used to go there occasionally, there was a good Fish & Chips place there and the atmosphere was pastoral.

You know, that's two off the Orphan Trains in our family. The other side, Grandma Gill, had an adopted sister who came off a train in Chicago before they moved to Iowa. Auntie Pete was what we called her but I think her name was Petunia. Her life turned out great. She married Mr. Grubb of Iowa Real Estate fame. I only remember seeing her when I was young."

The others in attendance were surprised and wanted to hear more. Mom already knew all of this of-course, but Grandpa's niece and nephews hadn't heard any of it. They were in their late 70's, children of his Sister, and also had rarely seen Gramps throughout their lives. They showed up for the occasional holiday but still lived not far from where they were born and raised in Waterloo. I remembered them from my childhood when we would go there to visit.

...Gramps was 23 and learning Japanese radio code on Bainbridge Island, Washington, a ferry ride from Seattle.

When finished, he was sent to Guam on a Navy LST ship where he spent the entire war intercepting and decoding Japanese communications. Perhaps one of the more charmed of all World War Two Navy stories I've heard. He attributes his entire time in the Navy to being guided by Gods hand. Without that bout of appendicitis, it was quite possible he would have been sent to a combat position of some sort. He considered that hospital stay, God's doing.

When he got out at the wars end, he came back to the states on another LST ship to San Francisco, then a long train ride back to Iowa. He didn't want to go back to the packing company, so he used his G.I. benefits and went to Chiropractic School in Chicago, Illinois.

"One evening when coming home from school on the train, my homework fell out of my satchel onto the floor. All the folks were scared to death. I had an embalmed hand in a bag I was supposed to study. That was quite a stir, the police were called and I was held up for a while."

He, Hazel and young Jacky lived in Chicago for two years until he graduated there in 1947. Then he started a practice a few burgs away from his home town, in La Port City, Iowa. Chiropractic was a new thing back then, but once people took a chance on him, he stayed busy. He was charging a dollar per visit and sometimes people would pay with animals, food or other goods. My Mom got one of her first pets that way.

La Port City was fine, but was a small town with no way to advance his business or make more money, so in 1952 he moved his family to Des Moines. He bought a two-story home, they lived upstairs and his offices were downstairs.

Living in the "Big City," life was a bit faster all the way around. He found many temptations and vices in Des Moines.

Before long he and Hazel were going out to the Val-Air Ballroom dance club every weekend, smoking and drinking. He said it was the lowest point in his life. Not only had secular life crept up on him, he and Hazel were having marital issues. Gramps says he was being the biggest hypocrite he knew. Drunk and carousing Saturday night, up and in the pews Sunday morning. Deep inside it was preying on him and after a year or so of this, Hazel was just about fed up. She threatened to leave him if he didn't stop.

This was a wake-up call for him he paid attention to. He doubled down on Church, took on responsibility as a deacon and became part of his Lutheran Church hierarchy. This was Evangelical Lutheranism and through his exploration of doctrines, by 1956 he put the Lutheran part behind him. He changed his religion to Evangelical Baptist. This felt like a good fit for him and was closer to how Hazel was raised. It smoothed out their relationship for a while.

From this point on, he would remain steeped in religion. He even took a few Bible courses and set a goal of becoming a Preacher. This exact opposite swing to hardline Christianity was again opposed by Hazel. She told him she did not want to be a preacher's wife and have a church be her second home. By 1959 they had come to an agreement on this. Gramps would spend as much time as he wanted there but she would be at half his pace. Grandma Hazel had a very active mind and several hobbies she was very good at, she needed creative time for herself.

In late 1959 their second child was born. Seventeen years after their first, Chris arrived.

"Jacky was close to high school graduation and soon left the house. It was all that making up hazel and I were doing."
... is how Gramps put it.

By this time, his Chiropractic business was doing well, his family was living in a brand-new home and life was good. He attributed all this to God and his reaffirmation in faith. Perceiving he was experiencing God's blessing, again he dug in and went deeper into his religion.

"From the early 60's through the 80's, pretty much all I did was work and praise the Lord. Mike was born, then Bill and Jacky moved to the apartment above the office in '64.

Let me see... what else... Well yes, we-all, other Chiropractor friends of mine and myself, started the Iowa Chiropractic Society in "65. I was voted the first President. That was pretty involving for awhile.
I also bought a couple rental properties....
Oh-Boy was that a Job. It got to be too much by the late 60's so I sold them. After that we moved into that big house in Beaverdale."

"Hey, I remember a movie you had us all go to back in the 70's. I think someone said you had something to do with that?"

"Oh yes, I'd forgotten that. "A Thief in the Night." It was a rapture movie made right here in Des Moines. There were a group of people, I guess you could call them movie people, who solicited all the Churches in the area for help, paying for everything I mean. I and a few friends passed the plate all over town and put up several thousand dollars ourselves. It was a lot of money back then."

The nephews and niece chimed in, they remembered that also and were invited. It was kind of nice with a group of family members reminiscing on like experiences from the past.

After another month or so, it wasn't unusual for Gramps to need help getting to his feet. It was chilly outside and being a rail, he couldn't take much cold, he liked it warm to the hottish side. He was eating a little of everything.

His main movement and exercises were making his bed in the morning, getting fully dressed, getting down the hallway and back for mail, then the up and down, back and forth to the bathroom during the day. It was a meager existence I tried to liven up if at all possible.

The most exciting part of each day was preparing to go through the mail. For a guy with very little going on, he would get a literal handful of mail every day. Most every piece was a come-on for donations from some religious entity. He would slowly inspect the entire outside of each envelope to register where it was from. Then each was opened a certain way with an old-fashioned brass letter opener. After reading each line of each letter with a magnifying glass, he would decide which pile it would go to, in the trash or donation worthy.

When I first came, he would send out a couple hundred dollars per month, $50 each to charities he deemed worthy. Many he had been sending money to for decades. This is why he got so much mail, he was on the list. If you donate to one, you will start getting come-ons from all of them. They sell your name similar to how things are done today electronically on our phones and computers. After a while, he was tired of the effort it took him to write the checks so he had me get him fifty-dollar bills. He would wrap them in a separate sheet of paper and mail them in for donation. On a personal level, it was hard to watch considering at one time or another he had donated thousands to the Falwell's, Baker's and many other failed TV ministries proven as fake, grifting, shysters. But it was his money... *Whatever.*

Towards the end I would just put those outgoing letters back in his desk and they would never get money inserted into them. He would forget about them and be ready for the busy feeling of tomorrows mail.

I was back to the 6 hour per day, gone at night routine of previous. It didn't sit right with me but he insisted. Every morning when I showed up, I was apprehensive about what I might find when opening the door. It was a little hard to watch but I could empathize with him. He spent most of the time sitting in his spot on the couch, eyes closed, sleeping and praying.

One particularly cold day in January we were sitting on the couch talking about my kids.

"You never say anything about yourself, what have you been doing all this time? I'm tired of dragging it out of you. You've asked me all about my life, I'm dry, it's your turn. I'm gonna rest my eyes, you go ahead, tell me about when you were in the Navy. What did you do in the Navy, You were on a Submarine weren't you?" Whew!... that had to be something else."

"That's right, where did we end up?
I enlisted in Tampa when I was 21... "

Lucky S.O.B.

Chapter Eight

Gramps wanted to know about my service, what it was like on a submarine, where did I go, things like that. Again, I would skip over the bad stuff and stick to the basics. There was plenty of basic stuff and lesser evils he heard, but aren't worth space here. That's the trade unless there are a few pages left over.

...March of '85.
I'd already taken my pre-enlistment test and physical. The recruiter was very happy with my test scores but the urine test for drugs *(marijuana)* was *"inconclusive."* I was required to sign a drug waiver swearing I would never be a bad boy again.

Boot Camp was in Orlando, Florida.
One thing for sure, my timing could have been better, it was June. Luckily Navy Boot Camp is more classroom and teaching than a true physical experience. We were only required to exercise an hour in the morning before breakfast, I could easily handle it, no mid-day heat and humidity outdoors.

I got in trouble three times in my six-week boot-camp stint. Once was for publicly pointing out a bright red stain on the crotch of a female company Commanders uniform during grinder calisthenics. She was a real ball-buster, though I'll bet she wasn't familiar with testicles at all. Then once for a debacle at the Dentist when they were pulling my wisdom teeth. And once for disobeying orders.

Punishment: One half day "I-T," for each of my indiscretions except the disobeying orders, that was a bit more involved.

I-T is short for, "Intensive Training."

It is a place where all those given I-T, line up and required to exercise for two hours straight without stopping. Done with a dummy M-14 rifle weighing 20lbs. while listening to "God Bless the U.S.A." in a never-ending loop. *Over-and-over-and-over...* continually. Two hours in the morning constitutes a half day. Another two in the afternoon was a full day.

I was called into the Commanders office at the end of week four. My scores provided choices for service path, I chose Submarines. That required, a more thorough look by Naval Investigative Service. They found I had a juvenile record but not what was in it, they wanted to know. I told them it was marijuana related and about my debacle with the car chase when I was 15. I didn't mention anything else. They noticed my drug waiver and accepted the other. Again, I had to sign more paperwork promising not to use any kind of drugs and that all my previous statements about my juvenile record were true. .... yeah, what I told them was true, omission notwithstanding.

I was barely healed from the dental debacle by the week before graduation. One of the last things was a taste of Liberty (*approved, timed, off-time)*. The company was split in two, half were given liberty the first Saturday, the other half, the last Saturday before graduation. I got the first weekend. Glathia came and picked me up and we went back to Tampa, I had a great time but was a freak show for everyone I knew, including her. I was still mostly bald and had only the Navy, white ice cream man uniform to wear.

Glathia was acting particularly sweet to me, it seemed strange but I liked it. I even made it back to the base in time with no problems. The next week was a breeze and then the other half of the company was to go on their Liberty weekend. My half was on "watch," confined to the building.

We had our ID cards by then and I was bored. I was also the only guy there who was of age to drink.

I heard of something called the EM club and knew where it was. I'd passed it when I went to the Dental building, it was on the other side of the gate on the training side of the base.

That night I snuck out and got to the gate, presented my ID to the sentry and went through. I went to the Club, had a few drinks and went back. When I snuck back in, I quietly took off my uniform and crept into my rack. All the lights in the dorm suddenly came on. I was busted. Someone squealed on me sparking a surprise inspection, I wasn't there. Strike Three.

On the walkway leading into the Command building there were colored footprints painted on either side. This is where recruits in trouble stood until they were dealt with. I stood there till Monday morning. One meal a day, two 15-minute bathroom breaks every six hours, continue standing. I was set-back one week to graduate a week later and had to attend I-T twice a day for the remaining week. When I wasn't doing that, I was picking up trash.

The physical exercising aspects of "IT" weren't actually as bad as that song playing in a loop. "God Bless the USA" playing constantly nearly drove me insane. *I loath that song,* a true torture device.

Luckily, on the last day before graduation I was called to the command building and got a lighter talking to. *"I was scheduled for Submarine school, I had high scores, I was older and should set an example. I had promise and if I agreed to swear to fly straight from now on, in my file, they would attribute my set-back to dental issues."*

I Promised.

Submarine School was a breeze. I had one brush up with a kid for some reason I can't remember but nothing came of it. There in Sub School I was given more choices, I chose to be a Navigational Quartermaster, they were really pushing it.

I had the scores and there weren't many equivalent jobs on the outside so not many guys chose that rate or were even able to choose it.

Because I chose Quartermaster, I got another visit from the NIS. Quartermasters are privy to secret stuff, so I needed to be vetted for further clearances up to Top Secret. They wanted a background statement from me including all my parent's personal info and my employment history.

A week later I was called back in to answer discrepancy questions. It turned out they found more jobs than I remembered. I had to answer why I tried to enlist when I was eighteen but didn't go in. Why I lost my driver's license when I was 16, why this...why that...*why, why, why*?

I sidestepped and left things out, I thought the jig was up, but after a week or two of hearing nothing else, I calmed. The day before graduation, I was called into the section leaders office. He gave me a quartermaster insignia for my uniform, I was in.

I called Glathia once to say hi and found out why she was so sweet to me after bootcamp. She asked if she could come up to Connecticut and stay with me. I told her there was no-way since I lived in a Navy Barracks and wouldn't have a real place till I got to my permanent duty station. She then asked me to call her when I got there, she would come then. I really hadn't expected to see her again but told her I would call. I then called my good friend Ray, he told me the whole deal.

After I left, she got a real job to look more legit, working as a parts runner for a NAPA auto parts store. She was also selling and delivering coke with the company truck while delivering car parts. She got caught red-handed and had a court date. Her Miami people bailed her out but told her that was it, no more for her. I later heard she went back to Puerto Rico.

I graduated Submarine School bumped a pay grade to E2. Nobody gets their choice of duty once you're in the pipeline. There are openings to be filled throughout the Navy. If your training fits the hole, you are the peg.

Of-course everyone wanted to be stationed in exotic places and on fast attack subs. The Los Angeles class fast boats were the hot ticket back then. I don't remember having a preference but I pulled what turned out to be a great job. I was sent to Bangor Washington to be a Quartermaster on the Gold crew of the USS Alaska SSBN 732.

The USS Alaska was a brand-new ballistic missile boat. When I got to Bangor, the boat had only been there a few weeks. Fresh from the shipyard in Connecticut, it had just arrived to its permanent port there at the Sub Base after making the long trip around and through the Panama Canal. The boat was getting ready for its first patrol deployment and the other crew was going to take it out first. They would be gone for three months then come back for a two-week re-fit. Then my crew would take over, until then it was training and off-time.

In these months, I got to know the base and the whole area. This corner of Washington was pretty much dedicated to the Navy. I took advantage of all the programs and facilities on base for the sailors to enjoy.

When I left Tampa and joined the Navy, I'd sold and gave away a lot of my stuff. What was left was taken to my Sisters house. That's where I left my old 68' Dodge. After my first patrol I used my three week off-time to fly home to Tampa. I was going to drive my old Dodge back.

There was a new recruit on the boat named Steve, we got along pretty good. He didn't have plans for the off-time so I asked if he wanted to come with me to Florida and drive back.

We flew down there and it turned out my Brother had been driving my car at night behind my Sisters back. I guess he learned that from me. I had to do quite a bit of repair and we took the seats out to have them reupholstered.

While we were there, Steve and my Sister took a liking to one another, they were on the phone constantly. Later, it turned into marriage and kids. Half the turmoil that happened to her in her whole life started with me bringing this guy to Florida. Steve drank like a fish and would later be my good-for-nothing alcoholic Brother in-law. Who knew? *Sorry Sis, really.*

Steve and I drove back, along the way stopping somewhere in Tennessee for fireworks. Part of the plan was to stop in Aurora, Colorado and see his family. We headed there and kept the party going. We pretty much stayed half drunk, did burnouts and tossed jumping jacks out the window all across the USA.

In the early Summer of 1987, our crew brought the Boat back to Bangor and got a little surprise. There would be a standard two-week re-fit to get the boat ready for the other crew's three-month deployment, but when they left, they would be going to Seward Alaska to dock there for eight days and give tours for the 4th of July Holiday celebration.

There wouldn't be enough crew to do all that needed to be done, so our crew would be flown to Anchorage on a MAC flight (*Military Air Command*) and driven to Seward to help with daily cleaning, standing watch, Sentry duty and giving tours.

When we got to Seward, the boat was already there, our crew was first split into two groups. One would work the first four days, the other the next four. As I learned always seemed to work best, I volunteered right away for the first four days.

One of the first to volunteer, I also got first choice of what kind of duty would be required of me.

I chose giving tours and sentry, these chores were for ten hours during the day. We got off at 6pm and had to be back each morning at eight.

Seward was/is a very small fishing town. There were only two small motels there and they were booked solid. All the sailors had to sleep on the Sub or on the tender. Luckily, I never slept in either place. It seemed the entire State of Alaska showed up for the 4th of July and tours of the USS Alaska. There were no rooms for rent even in sheds. The beach areas were literally full of tents two feet apart for a mile up and down the shore. There were probably close to ten thousand visitors there.

Something strange was that women were everywhere, absolutely everywhere. There was a specific reason I found out much later. Also, no matter where we went, sailors never paid for a meal or drinks the entire time. There was always someone treating you or paying for entire groups of sailors. There were a lot of sailors besides the Alaska crew there. The Sub was tied up alongside a Ship called a submarine tender, the USS McKee. These are big ships with several hundred crew, they were enjoying the spoils also.

The days were standard. Our crew arrived, was sectioned off, and I immediately started in on my first day. Off at six I put on the required "Cracker Jack" uniform and hit the town with a couple other guys. Long story short, if you were off the Submarine, you ate free, you drank free, each of us had our choice of several women vying to take us home that night, it was fantastic. I spent the first night in a hotel room and the next three in three different tents on the beach, all courtesy of four different ladies.

The fourth evening was the most memorable. A few other guys and myself were invited to a barbeque and then later to a small bar. I was hit on very hard by a beautiful native Alaskan woman, she was Inuit (*and definitely in-to-it*).

Elaine had long black hair down to her knees. Her and her girlfriend came from Anchorage to meet Sailors.

While my sailor buddies and myself were sitting at the bar I was having my evening standard so I didn't get too drunk, a flaming shot of 151 Bacardi and a beer chaser. This was always fun as a display but I would only have two of these a night, spread apart by an hour or so.

This was my second of the evening, the sailor next to me at the end of the bar was already shitfaced drunk. He was a guy off the tender and without a lady companion, mainly because he was a bit messy and loud. My new Alaskan girlfriend was next to me and a few people gathered to watch me toss down the flaming shot. I did it, and this Tender guy got loud saying it was nothing, I was just a show-off and wasn't drinking all night *(till I passed out like a man, lady-less I guess)*.

He demanded a shot and a beer for himself, it was delivered and he proceeded to pontificate on several subjects of no particular interest. He was sitting at the end of the bar, next to the caddy of drink garnishes and napkins piled up. No-one noticed right then, but he had knocked over his shot and it ran shortly into the napkins, setting them on fire.

People were trying to help him, he was loud and incredulous, pushing people away. Things happened faster than anyone expected and when the flames crawled up the stack of napkins, someone yelled *"FIRE!"* Then a few other drunks yelled *"FIRE!"* then there was a stampede.... The fire got larger as people were pushed back and forth. That bar nearly burnt to the ground. There was a lot of damage but I heard they were open again the next evening.

My Alaskan girlfriend and I retreated to her tent on the beach. After an hour or so, her girlfriend showed up with a sailor from the Tender, him and I were high fiving each other.

Those girls howled like wolves, it was nuts.... and a little embarrassing since there were tents literally next to us in every direction. People were laughing and urging us on... The next morning as we exited the tent, we got an ovation, hoots and howls from a dozen people all around.
It was in order; I took a bow.

This was the beginning of my four days off. She wanted me to go back to Anchorage with her but I previously made plans with some folks we met the evening before. She gave me her number and told me to call her if I wanted to go later. She would come back and pick me up, right then, her and her girlfriend were heading home.

I'd made friends with several guys off the tender over the past few days and the day before, one of them pointed me towards the community bulletin board. One of the guys off my crew and I went there to look and we found plenty to do. On there were hand written notes from people visiting town who were offering sailors everything from dinner, to Barbeques, to drunkfests to sex *(and not just from women)*.

All of it was very interesting and I spent several minutes with my crewmate there pouring over offerings and making fun out of it. One hit both of us as too good to pass up, we took the number and found a phone.

I went in and told my section leader what I was doing and was told I just needed to be at the airfield in Anchorage to muster together at a certain time with the rest of the crew to catch the flight back, otherwise, have a good time. *So I did.*

Myself and another guy off my crew met a guy in front of the Seward Community building. We took a two-hour drive to his cabin in the wilds of Alaska. There, his wife and another couple had dinner and drinks ready and we had a great time.

We talked about the Navy and Alaska and just about everything else related before passing out.

The next morning, we were roused early and helped load gear into a pickup truck. This was July, the sun never set, it just dipped around 2am. At 7am we met the other guy from the previous night at a huge boat shed on a nearby Lake. In that shed was a big "small' airplane on pontoons. We stowed everything in the plane and soon we were on the lake and in the air.

Fishing in the lake where we started would have been fine by me, but that wasn't good enough for these two. We flew for about 45 minutes, then circled another lake with no cabins or dock on it. This lake was deep in the woods and they said; only accessible by plane.

When we landed, he moved the plane to a spot within 50 yards of the shore. He and the other guy got out on the pontoons and each tossed an anchor in the water. Then they untied and unrolled a floating dock from each side of the plane.

It was shaky, but we quickly got used to it and no-one fell in. We fished off one side and cooked on the other. There was a cooler of beer in the plane and they each had pot but we of-course as two sailors couldn't partake in that.

Over-all, it was a glorious day. Fish bit immediately, and they were biggies. It was more like dipping in a fish barrel, it took no actual fishing prowess or effort. We had a boom-box Booming, a small grill grilling and several strings of fish dangling.

We got back that night and sat around a few hours before falling asleep. The next day Bill drove us back to Seward. I called my new Alaskan girlfriend Elaine and she came to pick me up at a store on the road outside Seward. I spent the last day and a half there with her at her place in Anchorage. She showed me the town and we indulged.

Elaine worked for Alaskan Airlines in their ERA Helicopter division offices with access to free stand-by flights anywhere Alaska Airlines flew. She came down to Seattle twice after that for visits. Like many of those women who went to Seward on the fourth looking to meet Sailors, Elaine was really looking for a way to permanently get out of Alaska.

The Sun never set the whole time we were there. In the Winters the Sun hardly came up. Elain told horrific tales of how women were treated up there by the gruff Alaskan men. All that darkness and then blazing light with oppressive misogyny thrown in, I couldn't have stood that for very long myself. Elaine was very nice but we weren't well matched. When it came down to it, I could not oblige. She was kinda ticked off.

There was a convenience store on base. It was like any other off base but prices were lower because it was part of the Navy Exchange store system. One day while in there, I saw a slight, coquettish girl carrying a case of beer to the register. She couldn't have been even five-foot tall, certainly not even a hundred pounds. I looked at her and didn't think she would get away with it, she looked way too young to be buying beer. The service let the underage members drink in the enlisted clubs but not take any out or buy it in the base stores.

To my surprise, the cashier took her ID and she started out the store with the case. Struggling a little, I took it from her and helped her out the door with it. Her name was Lisa, she wasn't in the military, she was a dependent. A family member of a retired Navy Sailor. They lived not far away in a little town next to the base called Keyport. She was getting the beer for a party she was going to.

I ended up seeing her a couple more times in the next month and we started up a relationship of sorts. She was a bit loose, but so was I. I figured she would be nice enough to spend time with here and there.

Here is where my learning curve with deranged and broken women started. But hey, what do you know when you're a kid? The only way people know how to make proper decisions is by practice and example and at that time, I had neither.

It was the Winter of 1987/88. As Trident Missile Submarines do, we were slowly "punching holes" in our assigned patrol area, tracing large circles in the depths of the Pacific. I was in my off-watch section of the normal 18-hour day and was awake doing .... something, when a call came over the 1MC (*ship-wide announcing system*) so everyone in the ship could hear. It was the beginning of a drill. By the nomenclature of the announcement I could tell it was a drill involving the engine room and more specifically, the reactor compartment.

After a while, in the Navy at sea, you go through so many of these readiness drills of so many types, you know what you will hear next and what the responses should be. Even if the drill doesn't involve you, you kind of follow along in your head. Many times, they involve people running past you in a hurry, or taking over a space you are in, or loud alarms and exclamations. Because of this repetitiveness you are ready for what comes next. They are designed this way and is one of the reasons there are very few incidents on U.S. Navy ships that can't be taken care of.

Battle Stations, Periscope depth issues, Submerging/Surfacing problems, Fire, Collision and any other imaginable catastrophe has a finely managed process to be gone through and every space in the ship and sailor in them, knows or has the means to know, what's going on in each case.

This drill was a Reactor SCRAM.
SCRAM is short for "Safety Control Rod Axe Man," a term from the early days of nuclear power when to shut off the reactor quickly, a man would cut a rope with an axe.

This drill imitates a situation where the ships nuclear reactor suddenly goes out of control in some way and must be shut off quickly. The drill is for both safe emergency shut-off and safe start-up.

This was a routine shorter version and the course was to hover the ship and maintain propulsion under battery power while the "nukes" (*a moniker for nuclear trained engine room personnel*) scrambled to get the reactor back on-line.

Over the ships announcement systems, I was hearing all the normal back and forth from the control room to the engine room and from the chief of the watch to the forward spaces to maintain ballast trim to hover the ship. The chief of the watch (COW) kept insisting to the machinist mates and torpedomen in the torpedo room to re-check their assigned valving and switching configurations. He was being answered in the affirmative, yet the COW kept insisting something was wrong and was counting off timing and trim status. He started naming off specific valves which is something he would never have to do from the control room.

Soon, the boat started to take an upward pitch. The COW became more insistent and next called for available personnel to the torpedo room to verify the status. In normal daily drill operations, this was immediately noticed by the entire crew as not usual, heads started popping out of doorways.

The next call was for specific people to move forward and all other off-watch personnel to stand still. This was to avoid confusion and make room for free movement of needed personnel around the ship without groups of sailors being in the way.

Next, bunks were called. Everyone not on duty or called for service was to get to their sleeping bunks.

I was in the library/movie room in the forward missile compartment, it was only a few steps down the corridor to my berth. Outside my berth was the midships depth finder. The pitch of the boat was now pretty extreme, I could tell there was a problem with ballast water movement. Looking at the readout on the depth finder, we were a little below normal patrol depth and the number was ticking up slowly.
Ticking up, means the boat was going down...

Next, the call was for all spaces dark. This was to use all battery power for the screw to maintain propulsion. The only lights are emergency DC lighting in the corridors. I sat at the curtain to my berth and watched the depth finder as it kept ticking up, the calls over the announcing system became more frantic. The boat was pitched up pretty steep, battery power only gives so many turns of the screw to maintain a couple knots. At the angle of the boat, the slow turn of the screw served only to slice the water at a useless angle. The rear of the boat was getting heavier, battery power could not move us forward and we were sinking.

The reactor cannot just be "turned on" once it is SCRAM'd. It is an entire process to keep the nuclear reactor and coolant systems in balance, it usually takes at least 30 minutes in the fastest methods. We were sinking, and by the depth finder, picking up negative speed, slipping backwards into the depths of the Pacific. We were at a 30-degree pitch and descending about 20 feet per minute, I was scared.

I just sat, staring at that readout...600... then 700... 800...

The 1MC screamed... THIS IS THE CAPTAIN, I HAVE THE CON.

The Captain started talking in plain language and calling people by rank and name, directing people all over the ship.
900...1000...

"RIG SHIP FOR COLLISION THIS IS NOT A DRILL !!"

On a submarine, collision means hull breach.
The Collision bell rang. Sailors were running to their stations. My station was at the plot in the control room. Just before turning to head that direction I took one last look... *1250.*

I was an SS qualified Submariner, I knew the math and dynamics of what was taking place. There were only two things that could happen at this point. We were nearly out of the envelope for one and consequently, would then be doomed to the other.

The boat was creaking and snapping, normal for a deep depth ride but it seemed a bit urgent right now. It was real hard climbing forward and up the ladders to the control room.
As I struggled up the ladder and lifted myself into the Control room, I heard our last chance being called out...

"CHIEF OF THE WATCH FULL BLOW ALL BALLAST TANKS !!"

I'd heard this din of clacking valves and rushing air before, during a dependents cruise. We took family out to cruise around as a fun day on a submarine and the finale was to pop up nose first from a few hundred feet and give everyone a thrill like they were all in a Clancy Novel. In that instance, the call was for all ahead full and a 10 second blow on the forward ballast tanks so the nose would lift.

Here and now, there were no other options. This order wasn't broadcast to the entire boat. Those in the control room were the only ones who heard the Captain's order, but by the noise, the entire boat knew in a second what was happening. If the boat is too deep, blowing the ballast tanks with compressed air to expel the water in them won't help. Sea pressure becomes more than the pressure in the air tanks.

It didn't seem to help. I could read the depth gauge on the helmsman's control panel... 1320 and it was still ticking up... yet more slowly.

Then after a few excruciating minutes, it stopped at 1335...1334....1332....

It was roughly ten minutes before we bobbed to the surface. Slowly at first, then we picked up speed and finally broke free of our fear. I could feel the air in the boat change and hear the collective sighs of the entire crew. We were still at an uncontrolled angle and pitch, bobbing like a cork.
...But we would all live to punch holes another day.

The cause? One man, one out of place valve. A mental mishap, in the Navy, commonly called a brain-fart. He was too senior and experienced and sea hardened for people to question him or check his work.

When we got back from that patrol, I got a call at the office. Lisa, the girl I had been going out with on and off with for the past year, had a surprise for me, I had a daughter. I hadn't seen Lisa during our last off cycle and wondered what happened to her, now I found out.

The baby had been born while we were out to sea this past time and was already a month old. We met so I could see her for the first time. There would be no need for a blood test or anything like that. She was definitely mine. I was not in Love with her Mother but I was struck immediately by her. I was instantly in Love, and have been ever since.

In the fall of 88' we got lucky, the boat was to split the patrol with a trip to Hawaii. After spinning around in our patrol area for a month we took a detour and spent two weeks in Honolulu before getting back to business. Two things of note happened there, one would follow us back to Bangor.

A submarine has a very dry and cold, controlled atmosphere. We are all dressed for it and you get used to it. When we opened the hatches in Hawaii, the air hit like a sledge, it was thick and warm, it felt like I was back in Tampa, yet worse.

Several of us got together to see the sights. I rented a convertible Mustang and we made a ring of the Island. We stopped in all the typical places, then decided to hang out on Sunset Beach on the Northwest corner. It was a great place but the water and its action were MUCH different than anything I'd experienced during my time in Florida. Sunset Beach has some of the best surfing on the Island and the undertow is so great it is recommended to get instruction before swimming there. There were "No Swimming - Severe Undertow," warning signs all along the beach.

I was playing in the surf and the further you stepped out the harder the waves hit and you could feel the water rush back real hard. A larger wave came in and I dove into it. It lifted me off my feet and churned me around, kinda fun. I did this a couple times and confident in my swimming ability, I ducked under a couple more times as waves came in.

I popped up and saw I was 30 feet off the beach so started swimming back. Another wave hit on top of me... and another until when I next popped up I was 50 yards off the beach. I started to swim in and looked behind to see a real big wave swelling and was pulled under. When I popped up, I was even further out. I swam hard, but each time a wave would kick me under then pull me back. I tried to get back in for twenty-minutes; I was dead tired. I resorted to treading water and floating on my back to rest but this did nothing but drift me away from the beach further.

I was laying there on my back thinking this was it, when I heard someone close calling out...

"Fuckin' whiteboy, can't read the signs huh? How they let you into the Navy and you don't know how to read?

I looked around to see a lifeguard with a floatation buoy swimming circles around me.

"You good? You want me to leave you alone?"

I was dumbfounded and could barely get it out.
"No, I'm dead tired."

"Ok, here's what we're gonna do." He slid the buoy's lanyard around my arm.

"You hold that under your arm, I'm gonna lock my arm under your other one here. If you thrash or fight me, I'm gonna have to knock you out and drag you in, Got it?"
I sputtered "yeah," and nodded.

"Ok, here's what we do, see the wave starting to swell? we're gonna ride it. Stay on top of the water, swim up, don't let it put you under."

Before I could answer, he was pulling on my arm.
"Up, Up, stay on top."
The wave was swelling, I dog paddled up as it started to go over the top of me and he kept pulling me up. When that one passed, I wanted to look towards the beach to see progress but he yanked me around to look towards the next wave.
"Here it is, up, up...."
It took three waves and I could feel sand under my feet, less than five minutes. I drug myself out of the water as he walked away.
"I'm not going after you again, stay out of the water."

The small crowd there watching dispersed. I wouldn't need to be told again. I was so tired, I laid on the beach 30 minutes before I could even stand up.

Later, when back in Bangor on our three-month off time, I would see a two-week open ocean swimming and rescue course available. When I saw that, the Hawaii incident rushed back. What the hell, it was free to me, I took it.

Starting after my second patrol, I took a lot of extra-curricular courses in my off time while at Bangor. It helped keep me out of trouble and was a plus for my advancement in the Navy. I found out later there were directions and places I wanted to go that needed precursor training I already had. Later, I would be chosen to do certain things because I was the guy who already had the certifications. I took advanced Firearms and munitions courses, Hand-to hand and self-defense courses, Advanced navigation, scuba and survival courses. All available free through the Navy, and a real plus was that if they weren't in the area, I could take a Military Air Command (MAC) flight for free to get there. I went to San Diego, Jacksonville and Pensacola on short, all-expense paid vacations to take a couple courses.

Everything was pretty expensive in Hawaii for junior sailors but submariners made a little more money than most of the same rank so we got out a little more. One of the places we weren't supposed to go was Hotel Street. There were a lot of hookers and drugs there at that time so the Navy made it off limits.

Three days in, that's where I got my tattoo. I had a pretty good drawing of a Griffin I made from a dream on the way to the island and chose to have it put directly in the middle of my back so it couldn't be seen. Sailors are Navy property and you couldn't do anything which might hinder your service. Being laid-up healing or getting an infection would get me in trouble. I got it early-on so it would be healed by the time we left.

After the first week, we'd seen most everything, a lot of us spent our off-time on base at the EM Club (*Enlisted Men's Club*). Nothing more than a bar with a dance floor, TV and games. Many guys were out of money but I and another junior friend on the boat hadn't spent our wad, we were like minded guys, in more ways than one.

About three days from shove-off, a friend Tim and I were at the Moose, a restaurant and bar in Honolulu we both went to a couple times. I was chatting up two girls at the bar, he was off somewhere then came back to get me. He said he ran into two guys playing pool I needed to meet. These guys worked for Texaco and were taking a break from a big party going on at the Hotel they were staying at just down the street. After 30 minutes or so, Tim, the two girls and myself went back to these guys Hotel.

This wasn't just a Hotel room, and this wasn't just a party. It was two adjoining 4-room suites with outdoor patios and hot tubs. There were two kegs, booze of all sorts and the continual waft of Pot being smoked outside on the patios.
Everything was a dream come true... except the pot. Neither one of us could take a chance of even catching a contact high.

There are many jobs and duties on a ship in the Navy, so many in-fact, there aren't enough people to do them all. Because of this, many guys on the ship have ancillary duties as well as their regular jobs on-board. One of these secondary ancillary duties is called being the DAPA. This acronym stands for "Drug & Alcohol Program Advisor." I was in training for this under the ships current DAPA.

The DAPA keeps his eyes open for sailors turning into alcoholics, alcohol abuse and drug use. The DAPA conducts screenings of personnel as needed and conducts random drug tests. The randomness of drug tests is whenever the XO of the ship says it will happen and dice are rolled to choose the sailors who will be tested. The sailors whose last number of their social security number matches the roll of the dice, show up and take a pee test, actually pretty random.

I knew the schedule of *when* the dice would be rolled, but of-course not the number it would be. There would be three tests, we already had two, the next was tomorrow morning.

I had a few drinks and mingled inside, away from the outside doors, Tim was all over the place. I found my way back to the ship around 10pm but he said he would stay.

The next morning, I was in the control room for the roll of the dice. The number was called out to the ship. All those with that number, report to the forward head for urinalysis. Being in training, I was on "weeny watch," I had to watch while people pee'd. I didn't know Tim's last number but kept my fingers crossed he didn't show up in line. He got lucky and didn't get called. I talked to him earlier in the morning and he told me he'd gotten drunk and took a few hits. I was worried for him but it turned out ok.

Later that day when I got off duty, I went to the EM club. Tim was there and he called me outside. He showed me a bud in a cigarette cellophane, some heavy stuff. After so much extensive "research" throughout time, you can tell the good from the bad by smell, this stuff was top-shelf killer. He said I could have it, *he bought a quarter pound.* It was wrapped up tight and double bagged inside a coffee can.

He thought he would mail it home but tried earlier in the day and something (*can't remember what*) spooked him about it. *"Did I have any ideas?"*

Something else I knew, was that tomorrow, two hours before launch, after all hands were aboard, the base MP/K9 unit would be brought on the boat for a sniff around. Also, there would be a surprise pee test in the morning that would be popped even on me. I wasn't told, I didn't know about it until I was called to the Control room the next morning. Both myself and the DAPA had to pee, as well as *this time*, TWO random numbers were called. It seemed as if the command knew or heard something and was trying to catch somebody. I half thought it was me and took light offense.

Later, when back to Bangor, I heard the whole story. The last two numbers weren't random and they did catch two guys. There was reefer madness going on in the Navy at Pearl Harbor back then. *Maui WoWie.*

Tim asked me to help him think of a place to hide the pot on board to get it back to Bangor. Crazily, I told him the only place the dogs can't go is in the sail. There were lockers in there not being used, and the sail is shut tight underway, it wouldn't open again till we surfaced in Washington. So Tim used one of his own division locks and put his pot in a locker in the sail. The plan worked...-ish.

I was also a bit stupid with that bud he gave me. There was one more place the dogs couldn't smell anything on the boat but people were in there regularly and Tim's coffee can would have been noticed. The Fan Room has huge charcoal filters, all air from the boat is filtered through that room. I tucked the cellophane into a crack behind some insulation. This wasn't for when I got home. I got blitzed four times underway on my off-time. No urinalysis tests underway on a Sub.

The sad follow up to this tale is that when we got back to Bangor, the urinalysis results from the surprise two-number pee test on the last day came back positive for two machinist mates on board. The command *had* known something, somebody narc'd them out.

Tim got his pot off the boat when we got back. Two weeks later he was caught selling some in a bar in Bremerton. I was the guy who had to do the paperwork to kick all three of them out of the Navy. Tim spent three months in the Brig before being put out, literally on the streets of Bremerton. I was sad for that, Tim was good guy. He and I had several adventures together, including some wild escapades in Seattle with sisters we met at a Valentines party.

Following accepted social convention, I thought it good to give my daughter a homelife and a full-time Father. Although I knew I didn't Love Lisa, I thought we would grow together and make a life, it was the "right thing to do."

I asked her to marry me, and in February 1989 we took a road trip to Nevada and got married in Reno. It was snowing terribly as we left Reno heading South. We spent our Honeymoon in Los Angeles and went on the Game Show Circuit. We saw Wheel of Fortune, Family Feud and got in the audience to hopefully be picked on The Price is Right.

We mentioned to a waitress at a Studio City restaurant we were hoping to get on the Price is Right and she told us how to do it. We showed up at 5am to sit in a gallery of benches under cover in a certain place at the studio. It is much different now, but then, a certain amount of people had tickets they'd written in for. Yet those ticketed people never filled the audience, so they would take the rest from the benches on a first-come-first-served basis.

We were some of the first people there and sat till 8am when they started assigning people. It was the ticketed people first, then we were in the first group of stand-byes. They gave us our name tags and told us to show up for the first taping at 1pm, same place. Lisa damn near pissed herself she was so excited. This was pretty fun stuff. We went to breakfast, then back to the Hotel to wait. While we were there, we watched that days Price is Right. We practiced and took note of all the prices and games.

At 1pm we were on those same benches with the other 300 plus people. They lined us up to file through a door on the side of the building. In front of that door was a roped off square with two people in it. One was on a stool wearing dark glasses, holding a notebook and pencil. The other would greet each person as they walked by.

I was wearing my Navy uniform and thought I was a shoe-in to be chosen. The greeter asked a question, you answered and the dark glasses lady would be writing things down. This is where they picked who would be called on stage. Lisa was a mess, talky, jumpy, smiley, I thought if not me, her for sure.

The whole place was like a High School Pep Rally. Everyone was super excited, the air was electric. Sadly enough, neither of us got called to play. But two of the games and prizes were exactly the same as ones we'd seen that morning on the program at the Hotel. If we would have been called up, we would have won those. Sitting next to us were a ticketed couple from Michigan, the Husband got called and won a Jeep.

That trip was the best memory I have of my time with Lisa. To this day I still like to sit down and watch that game show. Everyone is so gleeful, happy and hopeful. It all comes back to me and its nice.

This was also the year of my rotation to another command. I didn't have to leave the Alaska, but when your rotation comes up you are given choices. I decided to keep everything interesting and Lisa reluctantly agreed. I put in for a transfer and was assigned a boat under construction back in Connecticut at the shipyard across from Submarine School.

We packed everything up in the front of the biggest U-Haul truck they had. We had a new car and it was coming too. I also had a big Motorcycle to fit in there and still had my old Dodge. I took the truck the night before we were to leave and got a car trailer I'd seen parked at a used car dealership. I just pulled right up to it, hooked it up and left. *Yep, I stole it*.

Payback for an ongoing issue I was having with them about a failed car purchase. They kept what they called a "non-refundable" deposit. I kept what I now called, "my trailer."

The whole house of belongings fit in the front of the box. I put ramps from the trailer into the truck and drove both the new car and the motorcycle into the back of the truck. Then the Dodge went on the car trailer. We were on the road the next day and would be in Connecticut two weeks after visiting with family here and there across the country.

The prospect of watching a submarine being built was exciting for me. It sparked my deep-rooted mechanical interests. Here, being the junior in my division, my duties would be standing watch in the shipyard and furthering knowledge of my rate in the offices. There was a lot of off time also. I got to the ship yard a few months before launch and was there when it was both in dry dock and then launched into the water. This was a fast attack sub and a bow planes boat, the next iteration of the American fast-attack, I had another round of qualifications coming. Although fully versed in the Ohio class missile boats, this was a different genus of the same animal.

Fast attack subs have only one crew. There was also a wife's club which gathered weekly and helped each other out. This was something my wife was not a fan of. She didn't get along with a few of the wives in the Alaska wives club so she didn't participate. Here, it was something she was expected to engross herself in. I can't say that I blame her though, Navy wives typically take on the rank and status of their husbands within the club. She always complained the wives were snooty and condescending. Here in Connecticut is where my wife started to take a hard turn into her psychosis.

We lived in Norwich with a housing allowance to start off with. It was a bit of a drive into Groton to the shipyard but Norwich was a good place. We only lived in Norwich a few months before we got a place in Navy Housing there in Groton closer to the Shipyard.

I was spending a lot of time at the shipyard and in training. Lisa was pregnant again and left alone quite a bit. After a few weeks, she wouldn't participate in the wife's club and had no help there. I heard a lot about it from my superiors, it was a sore topic, I guess she got mad and told-off a couple of the ladies and acted manic a few times.

When Christmas came up, I found our bank account empty. I was getting paid pretty well considering we were in Navy housing, I had very few bills. It turned out she bought and sent out a raft of lavish gifts for her entire family and my daughter got a Christmas to remember. For me to remember that is, because to this day my daughter says she doesn't remember any of it. I thought all we bought her was a handmade Barbie sized doll house and a few other things. Yet, a few days before Christmas, boxes started appearing until the tree in the corner could barely be seen. I do think it stuck in the back of my daughter's head though, as an adult she has a penchant for those types of big doll houses.

That New Years, we went to Charleston, South Carolina to visit my Sister and Steve, He was now stationed on a boat there and wasn't that far away. My Sister arranged for a sitter and had reservations at a night club for the celebration.

We had a real nice table, elevated with a few others very close to the club's big Christmas tree. We ate and drank a lot; things were going ok until everyone had too much to drink. Steve was a problem drinker, as time went on, he became a full-blown chronic alcoholic, drunk all day every day, but at this time he was still trying to keep it together. The people at the next table were pretty loud and drunk also, Steve was giving them looks. One of the guys there was looking back. A chair was scooted too far back and hit Steve's chair and he said something. The guys at that table started talking to each other looking our way.

I saw what was coming so I turned to the girls and asked them to go get the car and meet us out front. They wouldn't do it. Steve stood up, the guy at the other table stood up. *It was on.* I had to have his back, that's just the way it is.

Steve jumped on the guy and the Christmas tree fell over, off the riser onto a table of people. More people were now mad and soon there was a brawl like you only see on TV. There were literally twenty to thirty people, men and women fighting like animals. Bouncers were trying to pick people up and throw them out but they were getting pummeled too. Chairs were being thrown, the buffet tables were flipped. The whole club was destroyed. There were so many people fighting....

I grabbed Steve, then walked on, and over people. Dodging blows and chairs, we ran out the door and down the stairs hoping the car would be waiting. But no, the girls were standing there waiting for us arguing with other girls.

We got to the car and Steve had to go to the hospital, he was hit in the head with a beer bottle and his skull was cracked and bleeding. I wasn't hurt except for a bruise or two. His injuries got Steve in trouble with his boat. Kelly said it was the beginning of the end for him. He was eventually kicked out of the Navy. My wife and I went home and heard nothing more.

As her pregnancy advanced, Lisa got worse and worse. Our phone bill was outrageous, into the thousands of dollars. In those days there were only landline phones and long-distance calling was *very* expensive. The phone was shut off, then she said it was all worked it out and it was back on. We were paying off the last bill in installments.

She was making prank phone calls to people we knew and they knew who was doing it. I was taking flak for that. Then two months later, very pregnant, on a Sunday, she answered a knock at the door.

I heard the door slam hard and her running up the stairs. The knocking started again and turned to pounding and yelling.

The phone issue she "worked out" turned out to be starting the phone back up under a false name with false information taken from our best friends, a guy I worked with on the boat. At the door with a two-thousand-dollar phone bill in his hand.

The Boat Command was not amused.
I was taken to Captains Mast *(Judgement and punishment)*. We worked out a plan to help her. I was to get her to Psychiatric counseling and stand junk duty on the boat for a while.

One day when dropping her off at the hospital annex for her counseling, she was very manic and did not want to go in. She had two cans of Diet Pepsi with her, something she certainly did not need being a wet 98lbs., but seemingly had become addicted to. As she got out of the car fuming, I mentioned maybe she should cut back on the soda, it might be a contributing factor. This lit her fuse and she shook one of the cans, shook it, popped the top and threw it back in the car at me. I quickly grabbed it and tossed it right back out the window. It glanced off her and she fell to the ground flailing.

Not understanding what was going on, I jumped out of the car and tried to help her up. She started yelling, *"LEAVE ME ALONE! HELP, HELP, HE'S TRYING TO KILL ME!!,"* over and over while flailing herself around.
There were other people outside and one of them, a patient herself, swore she saw me attacking my wife. The MP's came, I was brigged. This ended up in county court, the boat command understood, the County did not. That did not turn out well.

In July my son was born, I got the call at one in the morning while standing mid-watch on the docks. I got home, we rushed to the hospital and I was able to see my son being born.

One of the happiest occasions in my life. I can't actually think of anything to match. It was glorious.

I hoped things would finally calm down at home.
After she gave birth, her and I signed papers having her undergo a procedure to have her tubes tied so she couldn't have any more children.

The situation did not change, she continued on. The Command was finished with me, I was given a transfer to shore duty. Their honest wish was that somehow, lighter duty for me would be able to help. I was sent to Norfolk, Virginia to fill a spot at the Submarine Squadron 17 Operations Office.
It *Did Not* help.

With my wife's mental illness, and my honest intention to help and Love my family through it, there came a weight, a fog-like burden which somehow stuck to me. A piece of Ludd I would carry with me from that point forward.

I don't know how or why, maybe because now that I was immersed in it, I was starting to see incongruent behavior all around me. Not only was I living with my wife's mental illness abusing my children, myself and everyone we knew. I was noticing pieces of this behavior in others, and from this point on, it seems I became a magnet for people with mental skews. Separately and much later in life, three people I met even thought they were drawn to me by some divine outreach. They were sure I was meant to help them out of their mental issues. This is a very strange and sometimes scary situation which still follows me around.

Here in Norfolk, there was no wife's club to contend with, I didn't need to interact with my contemporaries outside of work if I did not want to. I could concentrate on my family.
.... *is what I was told.*

Within a few days of arrival, I was called into the Commanders Office. He wanted to go over everything happening with me. He pointed out that by looking at my service record, other than my family issues, I seemed to have put myself on a great advancement path. He referenced my previous elective trainings and willingness to volunteer for needed positions. "Always putting the Navy first," is how he put it. I made E5 in spite of many obstacles and he hoped I would keep it up. He would help me in any way possible to make things better both on and off the job.

It felt good, this was an unusual show of support from the brass. On board ships and even at the shipyard there was always a stern divide between enlisted and officers. It turned out he was softening me up as an introduction to the Warrant Officer Program. Even though I was in a sparse rate as a Submarine Quartermaster, the Warrant Officer program also needed billets filled all over the world, specifically Helicopter Pilots. The Quartermaster rate in the Submarine force was the fastest advancing rate in the Navy, I could be a Chief Petty Officer/E7 in eight years of service, only a few years away. This speed of advancement was unheard of throughout every branch of the military. From E7 I could apply for the Warrant Officer program.

Although he made sure I got all the required information and had me fly around with some great guys in the next few months, I would never get the chance to take the bait. I wasn't real-hot on helicopters anyway.

At that time, there weren't enough Nav/QMs to go around, so even when our time came for shore duty rotation, we were placed in a Squadron where we would fill temporary spots on Squadron ships until they got another. Because of this, I spent days and even weeks away from home filling roster holes in Navigational teams on submarines up and down the East coast.

This did not sit well with my wife. She was home alone taking care of our kids and was not mentally prepared for the job.

After being in Norfolk about three months, I came back from a three-day shakedown run with a ship after having some major work done. I was ready for a couple days off and couldn't wait to see my kids. My wife picked me up at the dock and had news. News that would be on my mind for the rest of my life.

My son had been having problems with ear infections since he was a couple months old. We were told this situation was not uncommon. There were antibiotics and ferrules in his ear drums to equalize pressure and drain fluids. I helped as much as I could with attention and scheduling of doctors, visits etc., but while I had been working and gone, my wife had not been keeping up.

This is not the news she was going to tell me, this is what the doctors and hospital told me later. Her news, given to me matter-of-factly as we drove, with very little compassion for the situation, was that my son's auditory nerves had died off and he was now profoundly deaf. There was no return, there was no help from here except to manage his deafness.

At that time, I cried for weeks, then later days. Then after a few years, only hours. Till I'm at the point now where the loss of humanity my son has experienced throughout his life is mitigated by our time together and my deep emotional ties to him. I now only cry occasionally, such as now while I write this. No-one can know the deep sadness of loss that situations like this can bring on unless they are personally immersed in them.

I have always considered both of my children my utmost responsibility. A responsibility to prevent a childhood like the emotionally blank and violent one I experienced. This news was a huge blow to my own ideas of personal ability to raise them as well as I could.

This jumps ahead, but as I write this, I have such a heartfelt satisfaction with my daughter. She is very bright and has realized the struggles we faced together. A beautiful woman, married to a great guy with her own daughter I cherish beyond my own belief. The image of her Mother at that age.

My son has grown to a perfect example of a human. All the failings and beautiful conquests at once. All the hardship he has experienced because of his deafness, has been taken in stride. He has been treated terribly over time, I know life has been *sooooo* hard for him.

Yet, to this day, unlike the rest of the world, when confronted with negativity, he thinks of positive first as a natural reaction. He has been my greatest teacher and continues to be. It is exceedingly hard to impart to other people, by talking or writing, the depths of life's mysteries that have been revealed to me through him, just by knowing him. He is here for me, I am here for him, without fail. Until I die, he is my favorite person on Earth.

Somehow, I survived that news and after a month or two, was once again called into the office for another deployment. This time, I would be flown to the Netherlands to take the place of a Quartermaster who had appendicitis and was removed from the boat for surgery and recovery.

I was given a hefty security packet for my carry-on and told to dress as a civilian, I would be traveling with another replacement crew member and two Naval MPs also dressed as civilians. When we landed in Amsterdam there was a driver waiting. He took us to the USS Hyman Rickover SSN 709 moored in Rotterdam. Once there, the MPs went back with the driver, I and the other guy were whistled on-board. I was told to report to the XO in the control room. I delivered the packet to him and was dismissed to the company of my section leader and crewmate, the lead Quartermaster.

He was anxious, and thankful my meeting was over.
"Bring your gear and let's get out of here, the van is waiting!"
We were on our way back to Amsterdam.

There were three days left before the boat shoved off for another week. There was no rack on the boat for me just yet so I was to stay in a B&B/Hotel in Rotterdam with ten other guys. Even though Rotterdam was quite nice, the crew were all having a great time on liberty in Amsterdam. I wasn't part of the roster yet so I got to spend two of these days exploring.

We went to the hotel to put my gear away, then back in the van, to the train and in Amsterdam within a couple hours. My section leader Daniel was quite an animal. All he and a couple others wanted to do was go pub crawling in the Red-Light district. I was at their mercy so I followed along.

We walked the brick streets checking out the girls in the windows. A pack of five guys, two of which were spending the entire liberty drunk, they needed to be herded. We went into three or four different places and had a beer in each. All were *"clam heavy"* as Daniel put it. That is; the ratio leaned heavily to the female side. Most, if not all of which were hookers or opportunists.

As we were tripping down the sidewalk towards another, a hawker came out of the shadows of an alcove. The neon above was flashing and wagging what I think was a sex scene but it was hard to tell since I was four strong beers in and some of the neon was out. The hawker was a heavier man dressed in a teddy and fishnets. Teased hair, makeup, spiked collar and platform boots, all bases were covered. He reminded me of the Rocky Horror Picture Show, Tim Curry would have to step up his game though.

He was speaking Dutch but changed to a thick, broken English. He grabbed both me and one of the other guys by the arm.

"Com in, you need see, all da best, you know. We have da show, you need see, da ladees like you I sure !!"

We all hesitated but looked at each other and agreed; *"what the hell, that's what we're here for."*
The foyer was a small poorly lit hallway with a window. Behind the window a sullen faced old lady took our three-drink minimum cover charge. I'd changed a hundred dollars for guilders at the airport and this seemed a little expensive.

It was all lit by colorful rotating lights, some slowly wagged, some spun quickly. Black light posters and shiny balls hanging from the ceiling which was a net. It seemed to me a very thick seining net stretched taught. There were many tables, some in the open, some in darker corners. Only half had people sitting at them, most there were dressed in a dark punk theme.

We took a table in front of, but to the right of a stage that had a screen showing men and women's faces in varying, flashing contortions of ecstasy. This place was wild, in my experience, completely different but right up there with a show I was once dragged into in Tijuana. We four stood out like sore thumbs. We were the only ones dressed as "normal" people and the only ones with short haircuts. If not an obvious group of U.S. military, American tourist targets for sure.

The ceiling was bowing down bouncing around in a couple spots. Under these areas, were tables of people looking up into the net. Obvious hookers were at the tables trying to get their attention also. After struggling to see, it hit me, there were people walking around on the net. I soon found out, not just walking. A couple walked across the net to above our table and started screwing right above us. On que, a couple girls came over and started talking us up. *Wow*, quite a sales pitch.

We all had a drink, one of the girls was in a lap across the table. I turned down a couple girls, I couldn't play these games.

It's fun to watch, but I have never been able to play the fake affection game. Sex workers have never appealed to me.

The song/beat changed, there were callouts in Dutch in a loud announcing tone. The screen on the stage went blank, trading with swirling multicolored lights. A guy came out on one side and was rhythmically dancing with a blank face.

He had nothing on but a watch and a gold chain around his neck. He made it to center stage and continued. Just when I thought this had gone on long enough and was kind of disturbing, the curtain next to the screen opened up and a woman came out doing the same. She was in a bustier' and fishnet garters, nothing else. She danced over to him and they started entwining themselves here and there. Soon she was on her knees servicing him. She seemed into it, but all he did was look around and check his watch. There was no finish. After a couple minutes, she stood up and they both robotically walked off the stage to either side.

After finishing our drinks, we all decided to disappoint the hookers and get out of there. It was a bit much for me. A sensory overload I never before experienced and would be wary of from that point on.

The rest of the trip was spent looking around Amsterdam and Rotterdam. The coffee shops with Marijuana menus were interesting. There was even a section of town with special access that allowed open air drug use, off limits of-course.

The last day there, I was on the roster and spent it going over charts and routes. From there we went North, took a left around Scotland and hooked into Holy Loch Naval Base. It was a short trip and a good one to get familiar with the ship's crew. Now that I was the new guy in rotation the short end of the stick was mine.

I was used to it though, that's the way it works. While we were there in Scotland, I was only able to get off the ship the last evening for a few hours of Cinderella Liberty. (*back on the ship by midnight)*

Another guy off the boat and I took a van into the Burg to a place he went the night before. Along the way, there were cars scurrying all over, many people were in an awful hurry and manners on the road seemed thin. The driver said it was a bad time to be out on the road.

Businesses were letting out and many people were in a rush to get home, get on their bicycles and get back to their favorite watering hole to watch that evenings football game and tip; *"many a pint." "Just wait till after the game and a few more, there'll be bikes wobbled over all along the way."*
He referred to it as "Drink Driving," the rules were tight and if a person was caught, could ruin your wallet and your year, even more, very strict.

On the way back to the boat that night about 10:30, we saw he was right. There were several men walking their bikes, a few weaving around and one was wheels up in a ditch. We stopped to see if he was ok and got a wave-off.
I would like to have stayed there a while longer.

It was the same for me as the ship headed South and stopped in France. I couldn't get off there at all. Next was Spain where I was allowed an afternoon at a Tapas Bar. Then it was off to an extended stay in Lisbon Portugal.

Lucky S.O.B.

Chapter Nine

Gramps was still awake and asked an occasional question but when I told him about going to Europe he perked up and wanted to hear more.

"I never made it to Europe. Betty and I talked about taking a trip or a cruise a few times but we never did, always too busy."

"Didn't you two ever take any vacations?"

"Not a foreign one. I've taken time off here and there. Hazel and Jacky and my Mom and Dad, we all took a month-long car ride all over the West, that was in '52. Maaan, it was hot and dusty down in Arizona, a lot of dirt roads, and there wasn't any air conditioning in cars back then. We went to Seattle too and visited with Otto.

Let's see... Then later Chris and I took an airplane to Cedar Rapids just to see what it was like and stayed a few days. That was in '67 I think, it was a new jet type plane. Betty and I took a few road trips to see people. We went to Branson a few times, we had friends who lived there. We came to Florida in the 80's and Seattle in the 90's, you remember that don't you? Other than that, we never left the country, we never flew. That one time with Chris was it for me."

It would be dicey but I could tell him some of what came next. There would be a part I might leave out, a part I've never spoken before. Maybe now would be a good time to get it off my chest. It's always made me sob when I've thought back on it since. Thoughts which sometimes pop into my head at the most inopportune times, spurned by the smallest of things.

I've woken up sweating with my adrenalin raised as visions quickly dissipate. I've been told I sometimes thrash and talk in my sleep about these things. I rarely remember any dreams, but I'm sure of what they are.

Now may be a good time to vent. It might sound callous, but part of my reasoning was that it wouldn't be too long before Gramps would literally take it to his grave. I wasn't sure how he would react, I needed to think about it first.

In Portugal is where my life became the most involving, dramatic and defining it had ever been. To me, it seemed like the next six weeks revolved around me. There were others who felt the same way, but not for the same reasons. Most of what would happen to me on this leg of my life would be a secret to different factions at different times, for different reasons.

Thinking back to my entire Navy experience, it now occurs to me the Navy spent a lot of time and effort on me that went unappreciated as I moved in and out of my own personal dramas. I was given a lot, I accepted a lot, but none of it ever came together as planned or expected.

In Lisbon It was my turn for duty the first day but the XO switched things up and asked me to supervise the juniors setting up in a Hotel. I could have the first day off, he'd straighten out the schedule and tell the Navigator. This seemed weird but I was a temp from Squadron so I thought maybe I was getting a little special treatment.

A little background:
There are 120+/- men on a submarine, but for the enlisted men, only roughly 40 beds. Underway, the boat runs on 18-hour days so a third of the crew is on duty, a third off watch and a third is having off-time *(sleep)*, all in 6-hour increments.

All this going-on facilitates something called "hot racking." The junior sailors shared beds, when one is on duty, the other was sleeping. When visiting a port, it was common practice to put half the juniors in a cheap hotel close by, supervised by a senior junior, a small perk junior submariners enjoyed.

When in ports, the boat went to a normal duty schedule measured in actual 24-hour days. I was to set these guys up, spell out the rules and make sure they got back and forth in time for duty.

We would be in Lisbon for an undetermined amount of time and the money for the Hotel would come from the U.S. Embassy. The guys could get back and eat all their meals on the ship, or eat out in town, whichever. In the mess decks the Embassy representative was spelling out rules, giving out maps with restricted areas and exchanging U.S. currency for local Escudos. We all then went to the Hotel in the Embassy Vans.

This was no cheap Hotel. It was a lavish Americanized Hotel in the middle of Lisbon, about a mile downhill from the Embassy. After everyone was settled, we all went our separate ways in groups of no less than three. In my group of four, we decided to go shopping and check out some local food. We hit the shops, I bought stuff for my wife and kids. When we got back to the Hotel, in preparation for the evening, we broke out the map of restricted areas.

"No uniforms tonight guys... follow me."
We went to a seedy area and found an Americanized bar. This area of Lisbon looked straight out of a National Geographic magazine. A couple of the guys were under age for the U.S. but there were no restrictions in Portugal for us.

The first bar had U.S. Navy ship patches on the bar-back, apparently we weren't the first. There were a couple whores eyeing us and after chatting them up, we turned them down.

One of them wouldn't leave one of the guys alone, so we left and went down the street to another bar a few doors down. After we ordered a round of beers, who comes in from the back? The same whore. We finished our beers and did the same thing again in a different bar, she showed up there also.

Hmmm tenacious, she really wouldn't leave him alone. From then-on, his nickname was; "Petty Officer Whorebait."

I had to be back at the boat before 8pm. The ships Navigator wanted to see me after dinner so I left these guys and got a cab back to the docks. I talked to the cabbie in broken Spanish and he understood, I asked him if Portuguese was similar to Spanish, I told him I thought it was and he took offense. I made the mistake of getting out of the cab, then thinking I would reach in and get my packages. But when my feet hit the ground, the cab took off with my packages, the motion forward slammed the door shut. Us *effin*' tourists Huh?

On the third day I was called back to the boat before noon. There was a message to the boat that needed my attention, I was to see the XO *(Executive Officer)*. After a manic episode, my Wife had been placed in the Virginia state mental hospital. My children were placed in temporary foster care. I had a couple choices but my Naval duties came first. I wasn't told what was to come, but I was told I needed to be on this ship by the following Thursday, it was Saturday.

The ships Navigator was a real nice guy. Him being a commissioned officer held more weight than I could wield so he was able to get others in the chain of command to pay attention. Within a few hours he planned an itinerary to get me back to Norfolk, take care of my business in one day and get back to the ship by Wednesday. I was able to use the military satcom phone system to call my wife's Father in Washington State, he would meet me in Norfolk on Tuesday, hopefully Monday.

I tried to call my Mother but she was blaming and not available, my Father was out of the question.

I've thought about this a few times over the years. In hindsight, this was a fork in the road for everyone involved. If I had asked my Father and his wife, I'm sure they would have said yes. They were even fairly close living in Savannah, Georgia.

I'm also sure my Father's reactions throughout the future concerning this event would have been exactly the opposite the way things eventually turned out. In my imagination, extrapolating the future from this alternate tine; going forward, all our lives would have been completely different, and not by just a little... completely. I literally would not be who I am today.

Within 4 hours, I was on a flight to Italy. Two hours after landing I was on a MAC flight to Germany. I waited 3 hours in Germany and wound up in Norfolk early Monday morning.

When I got back to the house it was empty, I couldn't sleep not knowing where my kids were and in what condition, my mind just raced. I only lightly slept on the airplanes and was very tired, but at 8am Monday morning, I was on the phone. I found my kids and they were brought to me at the house at noon.

Lisa's Father got there around 6pm. He drove his little Diesel Mercury Lynx straight through to get there and was very tired. I got in touch with squadron to tell them I was on schedule. Tuesday morning we all went (*Lisa included*) to a Virginia social services office and relinquished our parental rights to my wife's Father so he could legally take care of the children. He would take them back to Washington until I got back from my deployment and Lisa was out of the Hospital.

When that was over, I was a mental mess. I had to be back on a plane in 3 hours. I somehow got a little sleep, then was picked up by a squadron vehicle to be flown back to Portugal.

The whole trip was identical in reverse except the flight over the Atlantic was on a cargo transport, loud and cold.

I got back to the boat Wednesday evening mentally and physically drained, walking dead. I ate a little in the mess decks and was given the Docs quarters to sleep in. He was the one who took my place as babysitter in the Hotel. I slept fourteen hours and was woke by the watch captain. I was to square-up, get into a clean and complete uniform and report to the XO.

I found the XO, he wanted a small debrief of my last several days. After which, I thanked him profusely for the ships indulgence. He told me I was to take the parcel I brought with me initially from Norfolk to Rotterdam to another Boat in La Madelina, Italy. I was to get a bag with needed clothes and belongings together, the Embassy van would be picking me up at 1300. That would be twice in couple days I would fly back and forth to the Airforce base in Italy. There was a lot going through my head. I thought the security parcel I brought was for the Rickover but it turned out it was an advance package for me to deliver to the Pittsburg.

Occasionally there are things going on that can't be compromised. There are several ways to get messages across the world electronically, all have soft spots. To keep those who may be looking guessing, couriers are used also, sometimes as diversion. It's a shell game only those with a need-to-know are aware of, I was on the bottom rung. As far as I was led to be aware, there were two things going on, three if you count my family debacle. In reality there were actually a handful or more things and situations being juggled. This boat was about to do something which could not be compromised. The messenger knows very little.

When I got off the helicopter in Italy, I was met by two Airforce MP's in civilian clothes driving a standard issue civilian van truck with non-standard firearms on the floorboards.

I'm pretty sure there were other vehicles involved in our drive also. The passenger was talking to others on an earpiece that seemed to be following along. They walked me all the way to the end of the plank to the Sentry station on the Sub.

I was surprised to be whistled aboard and announced like someone important. The watch Captain appeared and took me to the boats XO who was waiting for me in the ships Control Room. It was a bit anti-climactic. I handed over the parcel, and from there I was given over to the lead quartermaster to be included in the ships underway roster as part of this boats navigation team.

I had no idea what was going on. I didn't know I would be expected to stay with this boat, but I did know I was to follow what I was told. There were just a few hours to go over the local charts before a navigational meeting was called for underway preparations. At this meeting I would learn another piece of what was in that parcel I delivered. We were going Southwest of Malta to launch Tomahawk missiles into Iraq.

We submerged the boat two miles off the Italian coast and flank speed was called. I and the Quartermaster on duty were at the plot going over our current route and the operational boundaries we had to maintain during this trip. This was the first, there would be another, and both routes had to be completely different. There could be no discernable patterns for anyone to notice. The ships Navigator popped into the control room and came straight to the plot. He looked at what was being done there, gave a compliment to the Quartermaster on duty and asked me to follow him.

Commissioned officers on submarines always had a grip of paperwork with them, they were always studying for qualifications or advancement. The stack the navigator had under his arm was hashed with blue.

I could see the forbidden acronym stamp under a folder meant to hide it, "UTS/Eyes Only." It was best to look away when you saw that. With a Top-Secret clearance, there could be no hint of impropriety, I pretended not to notice.

He headed towards the forward ladder and was skipping once he hit the bottom. This was officer territory, he opened the door to the Officers mess, looked back and ushered me in. *"Have a seat Petty Officer McNaney."*
I looked at the others sitting there dumfounded, only three were wearing underway jumpsuits, I met them earlier, I didn't recognize the other two squared off burly dudes. The NAV pushed a button on the coms panel, *"Captain, we're all here."* There was a two short-buzz acknowledging reply. The stack of files were split up and handed out to each of us. Even though I was lost, I knew not to talk. It was coming, something more than I already knew was about to be revealed, and for some reason, I was involved.

The Captain came in and took his seat at the head of the table. The plans were unfolded. The short of it is that there was a Seal advance team on board. Just before we left, they entered through the rear hatch and would stay in the engine room. On the way to our launch dime, we would surface for ten minutes, they would exit the ship, deploy into Syria, and I was the one who would take them there. A few days later, after the ships two payloads were delivered, I would also be the one to pick them up.

I guess I had a stupid look on my face as I heard what my involvement would be. The XO was looking at me with a shit eating grin. He knew this was a surprise to me and enjoyed it.

I was to go from here, straight to the engine room to be briefed, fitted with my wet suit and get familiar with my gear, we had five hours to get ready before being put on stand-bye.

I thought I'd sensed something else was in the air. I was already somewhat used to this. Quartermasters on ships navigational teams aren't allowed to discuss position and mission with others on the ship. Better than half the sailors on the boat were only there to keep it moving through the water. They had no need-to-know these things. Everyone on the crew knew the framework of the mission but none of the details.

As the Seal Team leader led me out the door, I wryly smiled and shortly nodded at the XO. I was vibrating, not scared, but electric. My body needed to evacuate. Team Leader waited outside the stall to make sure I was ok.
"You Good?"
"Yeah, sure, *101*."

It turns out I wasn't just a squadron messenger boy. I was the only one at squadron ops, now on the boat, with the navigational time-in, small arms, defense, open water and fitness training needed. All those Alaska off-patrol extra-curricular training courses were about to pay off for the Navy that granted them. This ship had two simultaneous missions. Get the Seal team on land, advance to a launch site, then get back to Italy. There would be two sorties, on the way back from the second we would pick up the team. Squadron knew what I was going to be doing when I left Virginia. That's the way it goes. You know, when it's time for you to know.
I had an hour mission briefing with the team, an hour to get familiar with my gear, an hour to set-up, and then as they put it.... a little time to shit my pants or jack my dick, my choice.

We had the equipment already loaded into the escape trunk. All dark and rig ship for quiet were called. I didn't really have to do much more than pilot the raft a short distance from land, then get back to the ship. As if this was usual, usually we would just let them out and they would swim in and return by themselves.

In this case there were Patrol boats and we couldn't get close enough. A sub can't get very close to the shores of Syria, or even most of North Africa. There are sunken cities down there, it's too shallow.

It happened quick. I was the last one out and the hatch immediately started to shut. The raft was nearly inflated when I dropped over the side. The water was shocking, but adrenaline took over from there. Up onto the raft I took a sight as the electric motor started to whir.

"Head, 165/full." The water was fairly smooth, this had been timed well for slack tide. The moon was at a quarter and would be behind us. There were five of them, very little talking. I kept taking sightings and calling out distance. At a quarter mile from land I called; *"Head 180/One Third."* I slowed the electric motor and the team readied themselves. Team leader tapped me on the shoulder, "Good work Yellow, one minute.... thirty seconds...... ten minus.... *Go.*"

I stopped the motor and all five let go of the raft, disappearing into the water. On the count of ten, I started and reversed course.

This wasn't a common boat type raft, more of an actual raft. Flat black with low sides and very heavy-duty, D-rings for carabiners along the edges, an aluminum mount plate for a very compact battery and submerged electric motor. Probably a special purpose raft for just the kind of thing we were doing. It wasn't speed-boat fast, but it did skip over the lite chop with ease. If the water would have been even more choppy, it would have taken much longer. The team had laid flat on it towards the front which held it down. They had two waterproof bags, their own field gear and rubber strap packs on their back, traveling light. On the way back to the ship, the rafts front was up and bouncing, I was afraid to be seen.

I was given no radio, no lights were allowed. The only things I had were a night vision sight pipe, dive watch, knife, and a sidearm strapped to me. I was to get back to where I started. No Small GPS devices in those days, I had to use traditional TDS calculations. A sonar transponder was tied to the raft, I was to put in the water when I got in position. The ship would surface again when they heard my transponder.

It all worked as planned, I was electric again. Even though a few guys came out to help and dropped a rope ladder over the side, the hardest part was dragging the raft onto the deck, getting it deflated and stuffed into the ship. When I let go of the ladder beneath the escape trunk, I felt very weak. I was *sooo* tired. The XO was there, he wanted a debrief.

The ship then went to do things that later I found would haunt me for the rest of my life. Twice we did it. Many on the ship were giddy. It's what every crew on every Navy vessel trains for and few ever realize. After the second trip, heading back to pick-up the team, for a while we were shallow trailing a wire-antennae which could pick up TV frequencies. The mess decks exploded with cheers as we all saw our Tomahawks skimming over Peter Arnett's head as he reported live from Syria.

Those guys on the mess decks wouldn't be at the debrief at Squadron Headquarters, but I would. They wouldn't see choppy nose camera footage of buildings full of people about to explode. They wouldn't see people on the ground look up before they died.

That made me re-think my life, my being in the Navy and what the hell we are all doing here. But that wasn't the half of it, that came later after we got back. I still had a mission to finish and hadn't yet been at the squadron debrief.

When I sat in that debrief a few weeks later, there would be a couple other things also pressing on my mind.

Worst of which happened later, Something I really wasn't qualified for. Something I never imagined I would do, be asked to do, or allowed.... or even Ok.

I could have, but I didn't try for EOD or Seal for a good reason. In my head, I wasn't that type of person, I knew I couldn't do what might be required. I wasn't blindly Gung-Ho, but still, there I was.

I had chosen to tell Grandpa what came next and a rush of dread washed over me. I started to hyperventilate and sob. I was using Grandpa to try and release some of the pain I have inside for the things I've done. Just the thought of the situation itself was enough to make me sob. I felt very small. I looked up and Grampa was looking at me in a way I'd never seen him before, he looked scared. He wasn't used to violent images running through his head. It made me sadder but it was too late now, I continued as best I could...

"It was the same as before, except there were eight ship crew helping me get the raft out of the ship. It had been prepped, rolled, strapped and the CO2 canisters replaced. It was heavy and unwieldy. We weren't as fast as the Seals getting it out but we were effective. I was to go near the same spot I dropped them off at and pick them up. A little closer this time, they would be on reserves.

As I think back on this, I now get a feeling of being scared and lonely; pushed off a boat into dark water in the middle of the night. I've long since lost my edge, but back then, I knew I wasn't actually alone. The Sonar Room in the Sub would be tracking me as a target. Those guys could track every bubble of a whale fart at ten miles. They knew exactly where I was, they were keeping track of everything in the water for 100 miles around the boat. There was a separate plot in the control room keeping track of the raft being fed positioning from sonar.

I also think of something which not a hint-of crossed my mind back then. The Sonar room on these boats were so good, they could also hear me get caught or die. I guess that's a display of life's change in perspective.

When I got there, I marked the time and dropped the transponder into the water. The team had a homer on the same frequency and would be there soon.
Only one showed up. Green had a messed-up leg, the three others stayed with him. Blue and I had to land and pick them up, all bets were off. They were waiting 100 yards from shore. We would land, blue would go to retrieve them and help cover. I would stay with the raft. I turned the transponder on and blipped the sonar room on the boat the signal for caution and stand-bye.

As we approached the breakers, both of us were in the water holding onto the raft, we could see sentries at the docks not far away. Blue told me to stake the raft and keep hidden behind a row of beached skiffs. "No-one can know we were here, no-one. ***He said it twice***. *"keep a watch down the beach, there may be a patrol, we'll be back in twenty."*

I sat there behind a skiff and waited, peeking over the top every minute or two. Looking both directions there was a uniformed armed patrolman walking up the path at the top of the beach, heading towards the docks. He was far up from the water so I hoped the raft would blend in. Nope, he saw it.

He wasn't alarmed though, he just walked up to the water edge and looked at it, then looked up and down the beach and back at it again. It was staked in 10 foot of water about 30 feet from shore, too far to walk out and get it, but he was testing to see how deep it was there.
I looked back for the team... nothing.
"No-one can know we were here."

He was intent on the raft as I crept up behind him. He was right handed. I got next to him and crouched up. Without thinking, I arm barred him, grabbed his throat and bent his knees at the same time. My right hand wrapped around his esophagus like gripping a broom handle. Pulling him down to the sand, I kept my grip, my body lying over him. It happened just as I was told, after doing just what I'd been taught.
It was "*text-book.*"

I laid there holding him down, the surf lapped over us, he stopped bucking, then I just laid there. I couldn't look in his face, we were entwined and I could feel his mustache on my cheek. He smelled of sweat, garlic and some kind of soap. I'm so sorry. I really am, I'd do anything else, just not that. *Please.*

I had to crab drag him further into the water, I couldn't leave him on the beach. I tried getting him to the raft but it was real hard, he was sinking. I panicked for a second, I wasn't going to let him go. I heard light splashing, they were back.
"What's the sitch?"

It looked like I was drowning to them and Red rushed over to me, then noticed I was being held down. He went under water and lifted the sentry up with me.
"What the? Blue, help me he's got one"
They lifted him onto the raft, I unstrapped his AK and it slipped into the water. They did the same with his knife and ammo belt. All five were on. Back to the ship.

Once the ship surfaced and the hatch opened, Red called down for a dive belt. Within ten minutes the hatch was shut, the sentry was sinking into the Med."

I've never written that before.... This was the first time I've ever mentioned it, I hope I never have to again. I've thought about it constantly for over 30 years.

I've constantly thought of all of it. The sweat, the soap. I can still feel his mustache. *I wish it would stop.*

Over time, I have often wondered what would have happened if I had not done that. If I just sat there and let things unfold in a different way. Would one of our team have died? captured? mission failed? World tilted a different way? I wonder if I had said no, and subsequently was put in jail or perhaps killed and this man saved...

Knowing how it did turn out, if it turned out different, the man now gone would not even know his life was spared, traded for another. That's how I've felt all these years, traded for nothing. Not necessarily for this reason alone, but certainly for the fake reasonings we were there in the first place.

I looked up again, Grandpas face was aghast. A tear running down one cheek. He reached over and touched my knee.

"Mike, do you go to church? Before coming here with me I mean. Do you really know Jesus?"

"I'm afraid I'm somehow ruined Grandpa. After everything I've seen and done, I can't believe in anything except what I've seen and done. My mind won't believe anything else."

His voice cracked and got stern. This was supposedly his wheelhouse, he had something to say.

"You need to repent your sins Mike. Don't worry, God will forgive you... Repent."

"That's what I've been doing Grandpa, all these years, it's all I've been doing."

I gave it to him in terms he would understand.
"I'm trying to be as Christ-like as I possibly can, everywhere I go I only help and try to make things better."

Grandpa's look slowly changed from one of stern matter of fact, to one of wonder, of epiphany. It was a look I had never seen from him before. It was a look of discovery. Now it seemed he understood something. In his mind, something had changed in a split second. From this point on, it was like I was his very best friend. He did nothing but pay his attention to me as I paid my attention to him. From this point on, our interactions were actually wonderous, it was like we had always been best friends.

After dinner I asked him if I should continue.
"There's not more I hope."

"Oh sure, none like that last, but I'm here aren't I? That was over thirty years ago, a lot has happened since."

"Ok, Yes, let's have some Pie."

"The ship went back to Italy to be fit with a standard payload. I don't know what they did after that. I was sent back to Lisbon and helped the Rickover get back to Norfolk.
If all of this wasn't enough weight for me, I had another small bag full of nonsense waiting for me in Lisbon. Then another large sack full of crap when I got back to Norfolk.

I was taken from Italy back to Portugal. A U.S. Embassy van was there at the landing pad and took me back to the docks in Lisbon. I went straight to the XO's quarters and reported with an unclassified debrief. He wasn't in the loop for that stuff, it's always a big web being weaved.

The XO wanted me to take up where I left off. The boat would be leaving in two days, Liberty would expire tomorrow. There were shore drills planned, then prep for launch which would occur at dawn the second day. I needed to have all the Hotel junior sailors on the boat before 11am in the morning. That left me the afternoon to do stuff and wrangle the herd.

I went to the Hotel and spread the word, they were already told but I left a note in everyone's room. Each of the rooms were trashed.

I went with two other guys and took the train up the coast to relax, we had dinner and were back by 10 PM. The next morning, I was up at 4 cracking the whip. I wanted everybody out front and in the van by eight. That would have everyone on the boat at least an hour early. And it nearly worked.

I went through all the rooms and had them clean up their messes. A lot of junior guys seemingly have no life experience at anything. For many, the Navy was their first time away from home and for most of them, their home training left a lot to be desired. It was six rooms, twelve guys. I had them in the hall ready at 8:30. Down the elevator and moving out the door, I was motioned to the front desk by the manager, I thought I would have to sign out or something.

He greeted me, and in a sloppy English asked me to sign and provide payment for the extras. My head cocked over,
"Extras?"
I looked at the sheet and it was basically a bill.... in Portuguese, with a *very* large number on the bottom.
It was in Escudos, but pretty easy to transfer the rate to dollars, *VERY* large.

These youngsters had emptied the honor bars in each room four times a day. There was pay TV on the bills, there was room service and concierge service on the bills.
A total of $7600.00. The manager looked at me smiling.

"We take-a all-a American-a cardsz."
I thought I would just present this to the XO and get a bunch of shit for this, certainly this would somehow be taken care of.
Uh... *no*.

They wouldn't let me leave the lobby. I was held hostage until the bill was payed. I called the boat, the boat called the Embassy, the Embassy Rep and the XO showed up at the Hotel at 2pm. Yada, yada. I didn't get back to the boat till after 2pm which made me technically late. Which also gave me the crap duty until we got back to Norfolk. The Navy is run on technicalities and technicalities are seldom let go.

So when we stopped in Bermuda for two days on the way back, I was made enlisted duty master. Also known as the wrong end of the shit stick. I couldn't leave the boat. I barely got out on the dock. I did actually get down to a corner store a block away for a few minutes to buy a couple sundries and got a small taste of what was to come. None of my cards worked.

As far as I know, the Rickover was on a stand-by Northern run. They may have done something before I got on board in Denmark. That wouldn't have concerned me so I wouldn't have been privy. Satisfyingly enough, being assigned to them even for the time I was, I would have been in line for any patrol achievement medal they were awarded. I was pretty sure I was in line for an action pin and perhaps even a bronze star for my involvement in the Iraq bombing and clandestine support service with the Seal team.

I'd taken the E6 advancement test and met all the requirements. When I got back to squadron 17 in Norfolk, I was going to be a decorated E6 bad-ass with a very impressive chest rack. There weren't many sailors in only six years with an SS Dolphin Service Pin, A full boat missile patrol pin *(9 patrols)*, and two rows of achievement medals, two of which were experts and a bronze star to boot. I was on a ladder up.

So... we are coming into Norfolk, the Commercial Pilot is on board, I'm part of the piloting team and am helping a junior get his qualifications plotting.

As we are put against the dock by tugs, things start happening to get us moored and the coms boxes are squawking with orders and acknowledgements. After he gets the word all lines are on shore, Chief of the watch, calls out "*Captain, the ship is moored,*" and the Captain leaves the control room. The Pilot departs the ship and more mooring communications and returns continue.

Within fifteen minutes all the standard hook-ups were called out, then we hear; *"Chief of the watch, the phone line is connected."*

This was an important one. The COW flips the switch on his coms box and doesn't speak, but taps to the Captains quarters. Within 30 seconds, the Captain appears in full-dress uniform. The Quartermaster on duty.... *me*, plugs in the telephone and the Captain stands on the Conn. He is now waiting for a call from the Admiral, congratulating him on completing his mission and commending him on being a credit to the United States Navy.

These are billion-dollar boats which by themselves can level a city or even power one. Truly, the pride of the U.S. Navy. This acknowledgement from the Admiral is a *VERY* big deal.
We wait...
Within a minute, the phone rings.

After the call, he will get on the ship-wide announcing system and tell the entire boat how proud he is of his crew and what a great job they did. What a credit we all are to the U.S. Navy... *yada, yada*. He will then leave the ship to be congratulated in person by the Admiral at Squadron 17 Headquarters.
The phone rings again.

The Captain is *sooo* proud. With a big smile on his face, he picks up the phone, puts the receiver to his ear.... His face drops. "*What?... Who?... Who is this?*

He looks around the control room and his gaze falls upon *ME.* "*Petty Officer McNaney*, he reaches the phone out in my direction, "*It's for you.*"

Ships in the Navy are assigned to stations and piers. Each has a phone number. Big ships have a switchboard. Submarines have a phone in the control room, that's it. If you know the phone number and the Sub is in port, you can call the boat directly. The control room is always manned and sometimes you will hear the coms speaker throughout the boat calling for a sailor to come to the control room for a call.
At least that's the way it used to be.

This call was from an officer of my bank. He had been calling the boats phone number every 30 minutes for a week. My wife defrauded the bank and he was trying to get hold of me.
This did not go over well... not well at all.
This may go down in the annals of the US Navy as *THE* fastest fall from grace ever experienced.

The next day, I had to go to the operational debrief of the Syrian mission. I was escorted there by MPs. I then spent three hours with NIS discussing what I did on shore in Syria. When I got back, I was confined to the ship. By the end of the next day I was put off the ship and quartered in the Naval base stockade until this got straightened out. The Command wasn't sure at first whether I was involved or not. I was supposed to be free of my temporary assignment to the ship then continue on at Squadron 17 but the Captain of the Rickover would not have it, he would not sign me over.

In two days, I was let out of the stockade and given orders to be at the ship every morning by 0800. At home, no-one was there, my mind was a mess and I was very lonely without my kids. Within half an hour a police detective was at the door. He told the neighbors earlier, if anyone came home, to call him. My wife had escaped the Mental Hospital.

A short time later I found she emptied our bank accounts, defrauded the bank of $3500 with a fake deposit, cashed in six thousand dollars of savings bonds and not heard from since. By the looks of the house she had been home but there wasn't a suitcase or any clothes missing. As I think back from here... *That* was a full day.

Two days later I came home from the boat early in the afternoon to find the car in the driveway and her going through the house gathering things. I was told to call the cops if I saw her, so I did. At this point, I was thinking I was finished with her.

She started yelling and throwing things at me as I left out the back door. A neighbor in back was also in her back yard and watched as my wife kept yelling, throwing things at me and stomping around. At the very least, I had a witness. I was talking with the neighbor through the fence when the cops came around the corner. They asked where she was, but I thought she was out front.

There, the rear doors to the car were open but she was gone. I talked to the police in the front yard for a few minutes and as I was looking down the street, saw her darting between bushes in someone's front yard. The police called others and they scoured the neighborhood but never found her. A few days later I got a call from her with a demented gloat. She got on a bus to Washington and was gone.

That afternoon I was sitting in the living room watching Tv, my mind continually spinning, I heard a truck out front beeping and jangling. After a few more minutes there was a honking. I went outside to see our car on a tow truck.

She had been in charge of the bills and the car payment hadn't been made in eight months. It was being re-possessed. Later, I found neither had the phone, electric, gas or rent been payed.

When I eventually moved out, I found dozens of full pill bottles and stacks of late and final notices piled and thrown under our bed. It was a raised bed with drawers and an end cap that covered a void in the middle, it was full of all this stuff.

On about the second week, I was called to the ships Officers mess, the Captain and the XO were there. On the table before them was laid out my entire Naval history from intake MEPS scores to my involvement off the ship in Portugal, culminating in the incidents since.

They saw I had exemplary scores my entire time in the Navy. They had the reports of my wife's "mischief" at all of my duty stations. They knew of every little thing I had done wrong and right. The XO and I talked back and forth lightly about my service history. The Captain sat there quietly listening. Then there was a pause and the Captain spoke.

"Petty Officer McNaney, I must say to start off with, the Admiral seems to really like you. I wanted to immediately Mast you and take a stripe. He asked me to reconsider. You did your job on my ship well. I understand you had no part in the debacle with the Hotel in Lisbon. Your advancement records are solid and here on this table is your advancement package to E6. I am told you will be receiving the finest of recommendation from your off-ship assignment while we were in Portugal.

All in all, you seem to have the makings of one of our finest sailors with a very bright future. What I also see here is that you also have a VERY big problem. There have been registered occurrences and complaints from every duty station you have been assigned. All of which concern your wife.

I will go no further into this, this is all your personal business. I will only concern myself with how it affects the United States Navy, and after what happened here, I can let it go no further.

This is not an official Captains Mast, none of this will be recorded, but I am going to give you three choices. The Executive officer and myself will do our best to expedite your choice of any of these three. You will have three days to make your decision.

Choice one is for you to separate yourself from your wife. Choice two is for your wife to not be in your company and to return to wherever she may and to not interact with the Navy, any Naval base or Naval wives club ever again for the entirety of your Naval career. Choice three is for you to leave Naval service under an RE3 Naval discharge. That is a hardship discharge, not a dishonorable discharge. If you take this choice, I will have no choice myself other than to demote you, and considering your position and service involvement, clean your service file. You can give your answer to the XO within three days. That is all. Dismissed."

Short and concise. I thought about this seriously for about the count of two. There really was no choice. After what went on the past couple months, I was already heavily leaning on getting out. If not applying for an RE3 discharge myself, certainly not re-enlisting again when my time was up. I thought I might be able to get my wife some help if I was home and we were living like a normal family. I couldn't bear the thought of not being with my children.

In two days, I knocked on the XO's door and told him my decision. Two days from then I was at a Captains Mast. The Captain did not appreciate my decision and was visibly upset. I was stripped of my rank, demoted back to E3 and put in confined detention until discharge. They had me picking up garbage on base. Five days after that, MP's came and got me. I had ten minutes to gather my things. They took me to an office in the Squadron building where I signed a stack of paperwork.

The MP's then escorted me off the Base. I called a cab to pick me up from a payphone down the street.

It usually takes a minimum of 90 days, sometimes as long as six months. The Captain kept his word, this was expeditious. Probably the fastest anyone has ever been kicked out the gate. I was out of the Navy.

Lucky S.O.B.

Chapter Ten

"What kind of discharge was that? RE3? We didn't have that when I was in, at least I never heard of it. Did that ruin things for you in the future? I think it was good you thought of your family first. Not a lot of that happening these days."

"There was no way I was going to leave my kids behind and rarely see them while I'm off who knows where in the Navy. Not my kids... *no, no, no*. It really hasn't affected me throughout my life though. An RE3 discharge is still a type of honorable discharge. I mean look at me now, all shot up, half crippled, I have a Navy disability pension even though this happened here in the States. I can't complain, but it does give me pause."

"Pause? why is that?"

"Taking part in all the killing over there is the only reason I was able to get a pension. It's like trading their lives for mine. Don't get me wrong, I appreciate it immensely, I don't know how I'd be getting along right now if I didn't have it. It's just uncomfortable to know because all those people died, I get a pension to take care of me till I go."

"Oh, we can't think that way. You had an obligation to your country, these things are mitigated in Gods eyes. You're alive, we won, you are righteous in whatever comes after. If not, God wouldn't have allowed it. You shouldn't feel bad about that, it was Gods will."

Looking down at the floor, lightly nodding...

"Yeah, that's about what I tell myself, it doesn't help much.

Just enough to forget about it for a little while, it always comes back. Doing these things strains our minds, I don't think we are here to kill each other. I know the Old Testament is full of killing and death, even directed by God. Yet, right there with it is "*Thou shall not kill.*" That's a confusion that doesn't sit right."

"We just have to follow, obey and believe that Jesus died for our sins and through acknowledging that, and our continued faith in God, we get to spend eternity with him in Eden. It's our faith that leads us to heaven. We must believe Jesus died for us and payed our sins debt. YOUR sins debt Mike, you have nothing to worry about if you have accepted this."

This is about as far as I was willing to go in discussing these things with Gramps. I already know what all his answers to every question or statement are. I know where they come from and all the reasonings. It's much easier for him not having a world education and being a servant of authority his whole life. He simply had no basis for understanding other than relaying the standard religious angles. For him, all secular paths lead to Hell. For me, I've been singed and forked to the point, I'm pretty sure I'm in Hell. At least it's all easier for me now, I have a much broader understanding than most everyone I meet, its own kind of Hell.

It seemed by now, the issues he was having the previous Summer and early Fall were gone. Gramps was "enjoying" less old age bodily anguish, but still pretty weak and tired most of the time. Looking at his arms, it seemed there was only bone under the skin. He could barely pick up a coffee pot to pour. I was needed to help him stand but he could scoot around pretty well with his walker.

He hadn't been to Church in a long time. Not that he couldn't make it, I'm pretty sure he just didn't want people to see him like this.

Some type of church ministry was now on TV most hours of the day. I even found his own churches video feed on the internet and put it up on the TV screen on Sunday mornings. His critical comments on the service were pretty funny sometimes, stuff he would never say when actually there. This church had a more modern approach to its service and there were quite a few younger people there. He could never get over having a full band playing during the service with a drum kit and all. There were four things he quipped about fairly often, to him, it was all Hippie stuff:

- *Drum kits behind the pulpit*
- *Brunch*
- *Men with long hair*
- *Most of my shirts*

Ever since I showed up, his mental state was something to think about. In the Autumn of his 104th year, he was sharp as a tack. He had no cognitive issues at all to worry about. Some people seem to fade a bit as they get older, dementia and Alzheimers are a big problem now. There was none of that to be seen with this guy, and I was looking. By consciously evaluating him all the time, I guess I was actually gauging what may be in-store for myself. Yet the other side of my family is riddled with dementia and Alzheimers. On that side, it seems nobody gets out sane.

I think he was constantly evaluating himself also. More and more, he wanted the mental stimulation of being prodded to remember. Now, he would ask me to sit and continue telling him more about my life so he could follow along and ask questions. This would often lead to questions of my own for him. Considering the situation we were both in, it was a welcome entertainment for both of us.

I was noticing he now ran on sugar. When his blood sugar got low, he slowed down or fell asleep.

Luckily, sugar was one of his vices. A couple candy bars per day and desert with lunch and dinner had been a life-long practice. Now, with every bite of a Milky Way, his attitude would improve. With every bite of pie, another hour of awake time. It became standard practice to sit and talk in the afternoons over pie, ice cream or even just a candy bar.

It had been a few days since we sat like that. It was the first of the year, cold outside, blazing inside, he liked it very warm. I sat in the chair next to the patio door with it cracked a bit so I could get a cold breeze to offset the constant inferno coming from the heater vent above.

He liked to say alamode'. It was the only foreign word he knew. He would say it with dramatic flair like it was special. Most of the time, he would tell me: *"You know what that means don't you? It's French for Ice cream."*
Gramps knew nothing of any foreign language and it apparently made him happy to say "with ice cream," and poke at me a bit. I would occasionally say something in Latin or Spanish, any phrase in a foreign language and it would eventually lead to alamode'.

" Mike, its one o'clock, how about some of that pie? This time, make it.... a... la...mode'. You know what that means, right? and coffee, get yourself some and come sit..."

"So where were we?....

I guess we're up to the late 80's, early 90's. What were you doing back then Grandpa?"

"Oh, me? Ok, let's see... the 1980's...

There's not much there besides serving the Lord, but you probably mean other things huh? Well that's when I met Betty, I finished studies at Moody and got ordained as a minister.

That let me minister to churches in the area, I did that quite a lot, it kept me busy for sure. My church family grew all across Des Moines and the County."

"Tell me about Betty, she was very nice wasn't she?" Grandpa looked to his lap and lightly shook his head.

"Oh... Betty was the best. A better wife I could not have asked for. The Lord blessed me with a true gem."

"Where did you two meet?"

"Well I knew her and her husband from a church I pastored down in Indianola. One day I was getting my car washed and she was there in the waiting room. We talked a bit and I found out she had lost her husband a few months earlier. Before she left, I asked her to coffee and it kind of went from there. It was about eight months before we got married. That was 1982, It was about a year and a half after Hazel died.

Betty was a great follower of Jesus, She died in 2016, I can't wait to see her again with Jesus."

"Yes, I remember she was quite ill when I visited that summer... Can I ask you a question that has occurred to me more than once? It's about Grandma Hazel."

"I guess so, but these were two different women Mike, Very little similarity at all."

"Oh yes, I'm sure, but what about Grandma, do you think she will be in heaven with you?"

"Why would you ask me something like that?"

"I'm just interested. This is not an unusual circumstance, being widowed and remarried. I've always wondered and I don't think I've ever heard any Christian views on it. Will they both be your wife in heaven?"

"We'll just have to see."

"Do you think she is in heaven right now waiting for you?"

"I don't know."

I could see this made him uncomfortable. Short answers about anything religious was not his style. There was something else there and I was pretty sure I knew what it was. Grandma wasn't as gung-ho on religion as he was. If he held her to the same standards as everyone else, I'd bet he thought it would just be Betty and himself basking in the glory. The answer "I don't know," was a tell. The very first time he ever backed down. He couldn't bring himself to say it.

After he retired in 1989, he and Betty were "Pastor and wife," something he and Hazel never were. He and Hazel were always at odds when it came to religion, he and Betty never were.

At this point, I steered the conversation away, and then back to me. I already knew the next 25 years of his life up until now. He served the Lord.

But in November 1992, now out of the Navy with no prospects, I spent another month in Norfolk kicking around. I decided to wait out the house eviction notice till the last day. I had my last two paychecks which was plenty. I made good friends with Alana, the neighbor who saw my wife's backyard outbursts. I'd noticed her several times before without any special interest, but now we spent that last month together as I tried to figure things out. I eventually headed towards Savannah, Georgia. My Father was living there, he had a business of his own and offered me a job.

When I first arrived, I stayed at his house. Both inside, then in his old travel trailer in the yard. I stayed there until I figured my next move. The first night I showed up in Savannah, not surprisingly, the military was there also.

In company at the dinner table were Captain obvious and Commander hindsight. Although he always knew better than to push his brand of nonsense on me, I never heard anything from him having to do with my life. Now amongst the canned peas and fresh ham he certainly knew I would not eat, he would get his say. He made sure to set another negative baseline for our future interactions.

I went back and forth to Norfolk a couple times to see Alana, she came down to visit me once or twice after I'd moved into a place of my own. But on her last visit to see me, I knew it was the last time I wanted to see her, I really had no deep feelings for her. She was the kind of woman who traded on her extreme good looks and they were soon to fade. She was 10 years older than me also. That wasn't what bothered me, it was the attitude sure to result from the loss of her trading stock. I was already getting small tastes of what was soon to come. I appreciate a good-looking woman, but I wouldn't be held hostage by one.

I spent my days learning my Fathers business and worrying about my wife and kids. Eventually I was able to talk Lisa into coming to Savannah with the kids. I went back there for a visit and brought them all back with me.

Steve was out of the Navy now, he and my Sister and their kids moved from Charleston to Savannah. Steve also got a job with my Father.

My wife and I rented a nice house and she got a job. We tried our hand at a normal family life, it still wouldn't work. It didn't help we were being held down tight by all of her credit card bills stretching all the way back to Groton. She completely alienated my Father and his wife, as well as my Sister and Steve. In a year, she was fired from a couple jobs and was now working at a department store soon to be fired again.

One day I got a call from her, my daughter was very sick. I rushed home and found Megan limp and unresponsive. We rushed her to the hospital. In a very long hour, the Doctors pumped her stomach and saved her life. She had ingested several of her Mothers medication pills. And there was another issue; *Her bloodwork tested positive for cocaine.*

I was knocked over and had to sit. The police came in and read us our rights. My son was taken from me and both of my children were taken to a halfway house for foster care.
I looked at Lisa in disbelief, it wasn't me, it had to be her.

I insisted on an immediate blood test and urinalysis for both of us and another for my daughter. They weren't going to do it, then I mentioned the lawsuit that was forthcoming, and the news crew that would soon be there. We were going to find out right now before it was too late for these tests to be viable.

We were all given tests and both my wife and I turned up negative for all illicit drugs. They wouldn't tell us the results of my daughter's test. We were released, but my children were kept. This would not do, I would not have this. I raised hell for two days until a Judge was willing to see me in his chamber. The same Judge who signed the emergency order taking my children, I was not hopeful.

When we entered the Judges chamber there were five people already there, we also brought an attorney. Introductions were made, after we all sat, the Judge spoke;

"We would like to start by saying that we are deeply sorry."
Huh? I didn't understand but had an old feeling arise, the air was clearing.

In three subsequent tests, Megan came up clean and they traced the issue back to an accidentally switched blood vial. The positive test was someone else.

Lisa, *FREAKED OUT* and showed them just who she was. A ranting outburst which turned out to help me in the future.

In a fit of rage, she cleared the Judges desk towards the Doctors and Hospital staff. She was screaming at the top of her lungs. She would soon own the Hospital and they wouldn't be able to get a job at McDonalds. Just *waaay out* accusations and fervor. I had to try and calm her down outside. Our attorney walked away when my wife couldn't be calmed, she was starting in on him. The Hospital administrator came out and apologized again. He offered an amount of compensation for our trouble. We would go pick up our children immediately and be in his office in the morning.

We followed a social worker to the half-way house to pick up our Children. As we stood in the foyer, I could see my daughter sobbing face down on the dirty floor. My son was toddling around in a diaper so full it was nearly dragging the floor. This vision is one I had wiped from my mind until I deeply thought about it recently. I was horrified this happened to my children. Lucky enough neither one of them consciously remember it.

But I do, and at that point in time I also knew the core of who was actually responsible. I later found out my wife knew Megan had taken the medication (*if not actually given it to her*) I think she was hoping to be called home by the baby sitter so she didn't have to work that day. No concept of reality, none.

The next day we were at the Hospital sitting in the Administrators office. After more manic behavior, the Hospital's lawyer offered us $3500. I didn't think that was nearly enough, I was thinking more like $20k and a long, legally vindicating letter of apology.

They hemmed and hawed and finally Lisa grabbed the check off the table saying; *"just take it, let's leave."*

As we were sitting in the car discussing it, she couldn't keep her eyes off the check, she had to hold it and keep it. I told her if we waited it out a couple weeks and started the proceedings, we may get even more than 20k in settlement, she wasn't listening. Since our car was repossessed in Virginia, we only had the old car I'd bought for myself to drive. She hated this car and wanted a new car of her own. Her face was gleeful, it was like she won something and her plan had worked. I literally felt sick, it was disgusting.

We cashed the check and within two days were sitting in front of a used car salesman, ready to buy her a late model used car. The price was $3200 all-in. She had the money in one hundred-dollar bills and gave it to him. We went out, got in the car and before we pulled out of the lot, the salesman ran out and yelled to us. She only gave him $3100. With a sly, sheepish grin, she pulled a hundred-dollar bill out of her pocket and gave it to him. That guy was looking at us like shysters.

For the next couple weeks, I tried to get her back on her medications and back to seeing a doctor. She acted as if I was an enemy. I kept going back to how Megan got hold of her medications and found out more. We were arguing about this and other things one day at home when I noticed her carrying her purse around the house on her shoulder. She hadn't said she was going anywhere. I thought she soon would, but it became evident something was up. I got back to the bedroom and found our pistol was gone from its hiding place.

I went back to the main room and said I was leaving with the kids. She wouldn't allow this and I knew it. Jumping ahead, she went through the front door first. I then backed up and locked her outside with the gun. She threw herself to the ground and immediately started screaming and kicking the door, yelling as she had done before in Connecticut;

"Help ! Help! He's trying to kill me !!" Throwing herself to the ground and thrashing around.

The neighbors were more than willing to immediately call the police. As one might imagine, they already disliked us. The police showed up and surrounded the house. I could see her outside talking with them manically spinning tales, the neighbors were there telling their side.
Just like in the movies, the police yelled at me to come out of the house with my hands up. I yelled back out the window, they were in danger;
"I locked her out on purpose, she has a gun in her purse!"

They put her against a car, searched her and found the gun. A cop came inside to talk with me. My story and the neighbors story matched. *Thank You Mrs. Kravitz.*
Lisa was taken away for mental evaluation.

I was at a loss, I didn't know what to do. If I was the one to have her committed, there would be no chance of any kind of reconciliation if she ever got better. I was told by her doctors that she could manage and eventually would get better. I now personally think they either knew better for continued insurance compensation or were actually delusional in their own training and abilities. Either way, *to this very day* she is absolute proof of the opposite.

She came home a few days later in a continued, zonked out stupor and stayed on that medication for a couple weeks till she stopped taking it. Then one morning, I woke up and her and the kids were gone, no note or anything.

I could tell there were a few clothes missing but that was all. She didn't take the car, probably because there wasn't enough money for gas to get where she was going. I called the social worker, who notified the courts and a warrant was taken out on her.

Detectives found she boarded a Bus with Washington tickets, taking the kids and two garbage bags of belongings. The State of Georgia was not going to chase her. If she got caught doing something else wrong by the police anywhere in the Country, they would decide what to do at that point.

She took the kids back to Bremerton, left me in Savannah and there was nothing I could do about it. On paper, her Father still had legal custody of the children. To get custody back was on the list, but I had a lot to deal with and Lisa wouldn't help with that. I guess she figured it was an Ace she held.

I stayed in Savannah working with my Father. Steve and I had a big fight over his drinking. When he came back from a job one day and I smelled it on him, we fought all over my Fathers front yard. He and my Sister left and went to Tampa where my Mother was.

My wife's Father guaranteed me the children were being taken good care of but I missed them terribly. I got my own place which was smaller and cheaper and went through a few girlfriends. One was an ex-marine who worked with me and drank a lot of beer every night. She smelled like Budweiser when she sweated. I must have been nuts.

This is also the time frame when I divorced Lisa and had to claim bankruptcy. There was over sixty-thousand in bills and nothing to show for it. I was slowly finding out what she'd done with all the money and it was completely wacko.

The strangest was having a psychic on retainer to find out what I was doing in the Navy. The Psychic was in Norfolk and had been dinging one of our cards I didn't know we had for $400 a month for over a year. I thought I had two credit cards and one bank account. It turned out I had eight credit cards, a loan, and bad checks following me from three bank accounts, all Lisa's doing.

The bankruptcy thing really chapped my ass. I worked hard and was very responsible with my credit ever since I got my first card at 19. I wasn't paying attention as Lisa ruined everything.

Most people today don't know, but credit reports and credit scores weren't a thing until 1988. Before that, credit to buy houses and cars was face-to-face and you built up a reputation with card issuers who took an initial chance on you. Things are entirely different now. Those were like the wild west days of credit. There has been a steep learning curve in the industry since then because so many people can't control themselves and there have been so many ways to commit fraud. There are still ways, but now they are all electronic, back then there was no internet. Personal computers were for weirdos and cell phones were carried around in a bag. *(I had both an early computer and eventually a bag phone)*

Back then, something else was easier also, starting a new credit file, that's something which can't be done today. I doubt it is the same today, but back then, there was a way to start a new credit file, and as long as you didn't intend fraud, it was perfectly legal. I won't go over how, but that's what I did. Within a year of going bankrupt I had another file started and two credit cards. That credit file carried me through my life, my future business and through the 2000's. Thank goodness for the "good ole' days."

While my wife, kids and myself were on separate coasts I flew back to see my kids every 6 months. An incident that happened the last time I went, solidified in my mind the urgency of needing to move there permanently.

It was Washington State Fair time and I was visiting. Lisa and I made plans to take the kids to the Fair. We were all in her car, I was driving down the highway at regular speed with quite a bit of traffic.

I asked my daughter a question. Looking at her in the rear-view mirror, she was obviously distraught.
I asked her sweetly what the matter was and she whimpered.
"Mommy said I can't tell."

I looked at Lisa in the front passenger seat.
"It's Ok sugar, what's the matter?"
"I don't feel good, I'm sick."

I looked at Lisa, "She's sick? why are we going to the Fair?"

Lisa looked at me like the jig was up and immediately turned to my daughter in the back seat and screamed at her. She knew I wouldn't take Megan to the Fair sick.

"NOW SEE WHAT YOU"VE DONE? YOU RUINED EVERYTHING, NOW WE CAN"T GO TO THE FAIR BECAUSE OF YOU !!"

Megan burst out crying and I tried to console her with words as I looked forward to the next exit.
"It's ok baby, we'll get you back to the house, you'll get better."

Lisa was fuming. I told her we'd take Megan back to her Dads and see what he had to say. Lisa Freaked out and grabbed the steering wheel, yanking it hard right. The car almost flipped over but started spinning. I was trying to counter steer and slow down but she kept grabbing the wheel.
I back handed her and pushed her over to her side of the seat.

I got it straightened out, we turned around at the next exit and headed to Keyport where her Father lived. All the way there, about 30 miles, she was hanging out her window screaming to cars that I was killing her and other horrible things of the such.

When back to her Father's house, she opened the car door before we stopped and jumped out in front of the driveway. She tripped and fell onto the concrete face first. Screaming at the top of her lungs, she went inside and started on her spin to her Father.

He and his wife didn't know what to think but Lisa's face was scraped and bleeding from her fall on the concrete so I didn't look too good. She told them I beat her up and did it all.

I'm sure they had an idea of reality but the current situation did not look very good. Ever since she left Savannah, her Father allowed her to keep the kids with her. It turned out later he had an idea of her condition but did not know the extent. Later, after I returned to Savannah to save money to move back, he paid better attention and found the depths of her mental illness. He eventually took both children to permanently live with him. There were a couple incidents I heard of, and if there were a couple, there were definitely more. What I don't know of what happened to my kids in those months has always haunted me.

The couple I did hear of always made me imagine dark things of what I'd do if time and distance weren't a factor. She once pulled a box off a shelf in Kmart onto my son sitting in the shopping cart. He was crying and it set her off. Then when the crowd appeared, she turned the table and blamed the store with such venom, blaming them for the falling box, they paid her off to shut her up.

Another similar occurrence happened at Burger King where my son fell off a bench as he was standing at the table not using a child seat/high chair. She blamed them and they paid her also. I heard all this from friends and family who were with her.

The final straw was when she bought several gift certificates at a local High-End Bremerton restaurant with a bad check. She wrote hundreds of bad checks. A week or two later she called in an order for pick-up and sent my daughter *(8 years old)* into the restaurant with one of the gift certificates to get the food. The bogus certificate was confiscated and the police called. Her Father being the legal custodian of the children got in a bit of trouble for that one.

Something else happened with Lisa I was never told, but he finally had enough proof for himself and enforced his custodial rights. Megan was now living with him and his wife. Gavin was living across the street with his Aunt and Uncle. I had the feeling I needed to be there before things got even worse. I still missed my kids terribly and they were now living in Keyport, Washington, twenty miles North of Bremerton under their Grandfathers eye. There will be more about my first wife's family as this all unfolds. All in the sobbing-regrets column of my life.

My Fathers church sponsored a woman, her children and Mother, as refugees from what was then former Soviet Georgia. She claimed asylum from the civil war there and my Father put them up in his house. None of them spoke good English but they all caught on *very* fast. It turned out she was a trained linguist and already spoke four languages. After a few months, my Father gave her a job to help her get by and we ended up working together. Long story short we also ended up romantically together. She was a beautiful, smart and exotic woman, and somehow beyond the odds, we were in Love.

She and hers got an apartment, I had my house, we settled in to this life. After a while, she worked part time for my Father and full time at Savannah's first Coffee Shop / Espresso bar.

Her undefinable accent and exotic beauty brought in a lot of customers. At one point, ZZ top was in town for a concert and Billy Gibbons came into the coffee shop. He made several passes at her over a three-day period. I wanted to drag his ugly ass down the street by his beard. She thought it was funny and later told me his look disgusted her but she liked I was jealous. *Pfft*, women. That actually boosted me up a little.

One day when I was going down to the coffee shop to see her, there were flyers in the windows of all the shops on the street.

They were attention notices informing everyone of streets being shut down for the filming of something called, "Forrest Gump." There was no explanation of the movie. Until the movie actually came out for viewing, most people in Savannah thought the name was something completely different and had no idea what a Forrest Gump was.

There would be other call-outs for people in period garb and period vehicles to pass-bye during filming. It was quite a thing. Marika and I would go stand and watch the filming of different scenes nearby. We were not 20 feet away the whole time they were filming the bench in the park scenes. It has become one of my all-time favorite movies. Not only is it a great movie hiding a Love story within the life of Forrest, it is also a rose memory for myself and a time in my life I cherish.

My Fathers company was making good money, I was making decent money. He often dangled a carrot that I would have my own division and that this would all be mine someday. He imagined a situation where I would finally see his ideals as the way to go. I would come around to the conventional happiness he was laying out.

Except, through a couple grave instances, I was coming to consider my Father's avenue to success despicable. I was privy to a couple situations where he took blatant advantage of people and purposefully did the wrong thing because no-one was looking or would find out. And like all situations, if there was one, I'm sure there were more I didn't know about.

He also took jobs from the County throwing people out of their homes under eviction. After the first one, I was disgusted, I wouldn't do it again. That was just one objectionable aspect. There were a few shady circumstances I won't go over which sealed the deal for me but it's enough to say I didn't think this kind of stuff was right, it always left a bad taste in my mouth.

In the meantime, I was saving money and put an offer on a two-story house on a corner lot with an apartment above the garage, it was forty-two thousand. That was average in Savannah at that time for such a house. It wasn't new and it wasn't in the best part of town, but it was a pretty good start. The plan was for us all to move into it and then when I left for Washington it would be rental income. They turned down my offer of $5k down. It was going to be a default house and the current owners were hoping for a bit more because the down was supposed get them out of arrears with a bit of cash to leave. I took it as a sign.

I had long conversations with Marika and her Mom about the situation. One day Marika told me that through her family, they knew someone in Seattle with a rental house for us to stay if we went there. I called my Mom and told her about how I might move. She told my Sister who was now separated from Steve, he went back to his childhood home in Colorado. They all wanted to go to Seattle too.

Soon the plan was in motion. My Mom and Sister moved to Savannah. All of us, rented a big (*huge*) old house so we could pool our money and save for the trip. It took about six months for us all to save enough for the trip and a place to stay once we got there as well as interim money while we found work. My Sister had a place lined up in Bremerton, the rest of us would rent a house Marika's family friends owned in Bellevue, Washington on the East side of Seattle.

I quit working for my Father a few months earlier. We never could get along, always oil and water. I'd gone through a few jobs and was working for the Toyota Dealership in town as a line Mechanic. I'd previously bought Marika an old used car in great shape and she learned to drive. She never needed to drive her entire life so she'd never driven before.

A month before leaving for Seattle I took advantage of my employee benefits at the Dealership and bought two used trade-in vehicles at cost. One I turned for a thousand-dollar profit in one week. The other was a Dodge Caravan I gave to Marika, it would help us make the move. We sold her car for a cool profit and soon we were very close to the needed amounts to make the trip. By the time we left, we had a lot more than we anticipated needing.

When we left Savannah in May of 1996, it was quite a scene. My Sister was driving a 20 foot fully loaded moving truck with her kids, pulling a trailer with her car on it. The car on the trailer was fully stuffed and items strapped to it. I was driving my pickup truck with a camper top, fully loaded, pulling a trailer with a car on it also fully stuffed. Marika was driving the Caravan fully loaded with things strapped to the top, pulling a fully stuffed small car with a tow bar.

It was like the Grapes of Wrath extraordinaire.

Lucky S.O.B.

Chapter Eleven

While my mind is in Savannah, I'll go-on a little about what I loved about Marika. She was a corruption of all the best attributes. Strong and stubborn to a fault, yet somehow naively vulnerable and soft. We fit together this way. Both able to take what's coming, good or bad, then ride the roughest of waves to a temporarily calm beach. I saw me in her. Able to cross the World and make her way. Make a blank future out of the toughest of circumstance work for her. This is how we clicked. She knew I saw this in her. She was the strong one who made it happen, I was the calculating one who knew how it worked. I leaned on her, she on me.

The trip across the Country in this wagon train was torturous for Marika, her Mom and kids. She and her Mother were very brave and trusting of my abilities to make it all work, it is absolutely amazing to me she did it. I mean after-all, she'd only been driving less than a year. From the driving aspect, she was truly frazzled. Yet, she hardened quickly after experiencing huge cities with twisting highways packed with inattentive and rude drivers speeding all around, paying no attention.

She was angry at me on more than one occasion as I lead the way, unthinkingly driving like those around me. Not realizing how hard it was on her. That used to be one of my blatant failings. Imagining if I could do it easily, others could do it easily also. I've graduated from that ideal, I now think back to what it took for me to get where I am. I can't expect that of those around me. But Marika was tough, she did it and put up with me at the same time. I loved her more for that.

Her and I were so very different, from opposite cultures, but somehow it seemed to work. The moment it came together for us was at Christmas 1994, two years before we moved to Seattle. I gave her a Jacket. In style, it was a throwback jacket. A style held in time which conveyed our mutual metaphor.

It was a black leather jacket with straps, silver snaps and buckles. The look of a tough biker, yet made of soft flowing kid leather. The look of what she imagined of herself, the touch of what she really was. I imagine she still has this jacket without ever wearing it or telling anyone where it came from. A reminder of our decade together. At one time, we were the bravest, the hardest, the softest. The move to Seattle gave us a solidarity which lasted quite a while.

We moved into a nice quiet cul-de-sac on the far East side of Bellevue not far from Lake Sammamish. I was able to get a job at the local Dodge/Plymouth Dealership within a week. I became a line mechanic and started on corporate mechanical qualifications. Within a year I had all the highest industry qualifications. I made open industry ASE Master technician quickly and was taking the courses for Chrysler Master Tech when an incident occurred prompting me to quit working for that Dealership.

I openly questioned a decision which was patently unfair concerning employee compensation for one technician who got screwed. The Service manager did not like I was questioning her decision. I was called into a meeting with the dealership echelon to be embarrassed openly for my ideals of fairness. When done, she asked me in a condescending way if I could now keep my mouth shut and do my job. I hesitated, thought for a second, and replied; "*yes, I think I can.*"

From there, I put my ducks in a row quietly, then two weeks later, at the worst possible premeditated time, I went into her office while she was having a meeting with management.

Many of the same people were in this meeting as were in the previous, with one exception. The owner and potential new owner were in attendance. I just opened the door and walked right in. I interrupted who was speaking, smiled nicely to everyone sitting at the table, then turned to her and told her I changed my mind. I would not shut my mouth, I didn't appreciate how she treated her employees, I quit.

Thinking back and clicking through all the instances, this was probably the start of my disdain for the selfish and money-grubbing attitudes which eventually drove me nuts in Seattle. Previous to Seattle, I'd always had people around me of a more moderate temperament. Always trying to get ahead, but not stepping on others to do it. Here, the pace was such that it was the norm. It seemed everyone was a wannabe Bill Gates and running a game or willing to step on other people to get there.

With this Service Managers attitude towards the mechanics who paid her salary, I was happy to look her in the eye as I left her in the lurch. I'd already spoken to the management at the Chrysler/Jeep corporate dealership down the street, the management there was happy to give me a position in the shop. I was able to easily continue with my qualifications and made full Chrysler Master Tech within a few months.

Auto Dealerships used to be very cut-throat about quality service personnel; they would steal them from each other on a regular basis. Many of the best Techs are paid very well, given performance bonuses and put on work contracts for this very reason. I was in line for this same treatment at the Corporate Chrysler Dealership but something came-up that precluded it.

Within a year I was making excellent money, I'd made Corporate Master Tech and team leader. One day the Service Manager called me into his office. I thought they were going to tell me it was contract time but it was something else.

There was a Northwest Chrysler performance review going on. I and another guy from the Dealership had been chosen for accolades due to our performance records. I had the fewest return incidents in the Northwest division for Techs. They promised a raise and a contract, but first I would join all the Chrysler and Mopar Performance management in the corporate suite at the starting line at that years Northwest Nationals Drag Racing event at Seattle International Raceway.

It was pretty great, there was a ton of swag. I met all the race car drivers and Corporate Managers, shook everyone's hand, talked shop and made a good impression. So good in-fact, early the next week I got a call at home and was offered a job as the Mopar Performance Northwest Customer Satisfaction Representative. I would work for Chrysler corporate but have an office in the current Dealership I worked at and a significant raise, a salary position.

Long story short, that was the worst job I have ever had. Everyone with complaints about their cars were sat in front of me. My days were 14 hours long and it never ended. Within six months, I was completely beleaguered.

Then one day the service Manager came in and asked me a favor. It was 3pm and a customer had just come back with a complaint we would need to fix under warrantee but needed it done asap that day. I ended up replacing the rear differential on their Jeep. Not as big of a job as it sounds but it would take a few hours.

At 7pm, with the customer waiting up front, I was almost done. All but the re-filling of gear oil and testing. I left the Jeep in the air on the rack and went to the rest room. When I came back, the Jeep was gone. The salesman had taken it. As I ran out the bay doors, I could see the Jeep leaving the lot. There was no-way to get them back.

The next morning the vehicle came back on a tow truck. It ground to a stop on the highway with no gear oil in the differential.

This was deemed my fault and I was told the next axle assembly would come out of my pay. I was in the clutches of the service account bonus scheme. If they couldn't take it off my balance sheet, the cost would have to come out of the Service Department operating account. An account that paid bonuses to those who didn't use it. This was the third Service Manager hired since I started working there and he was another typical shyster on his way out.

My bosses at Corporate wouldn't help. Their input was that I wasn't a line mechanic anymore so I shouldn't have done that job in the first place. There was one saving grace, I was never put on a work contract. I was a corporate employee but being paid by through dealership, somehow it had escaped them.

I was starting to feel relief, I knew what was next, within two days I resigned my job. I hated that job, it felt good to quit. I gave no notice or anything. They were appalled I gave no notice, but I considered it a situation where I was firing them as my employer. If they were to fire me, would I get two weeks notice? Of-course not.

By this time I had quite a few friends in Seattle Automotive circles and a little money saved, I started thinking about starting my own repair shop. I started rebuilding transmissions and doing other high paying work in my homes two-car garage while trying to get the business situation together.

After a short time, a friend who owned a couple gas stations with repair bays called and offered a job managing a four-bay repair shop in one of his stations. Getting my own repair business together was turning out to be a big pain-in-the-butt so I accepted.

While I was working there, another of my industry acquaintances came in to visit. After I talked him into having his cars repaired at this shop, we would make a little trade. He talked me into doing side-work for him on a personal basis. He needed help repossessing and selling cars turned around in his Auto Pawn business.

Robert was the founding King of the Auto Pawn industry in the U.S, he actually started the entire idea. He was previously sued under the RICO act for banking violations but took all the legal hits, paid all the fees and fines and rode the learning curve which eventually led to what today is a thriving Nationwide Pawn business revolving around vehicle titles and ownership. He had four locations, one of which was based in Bellevue on Seattle's East side. There were managers handling his other locations in California and Arizona.

His personality and conniving ways are an entire book of its own, he was a pretty greasy guy, but my part would be to repo cars and get them ready to sell. The repo part was semi-easy since part of the Pawn deal was that he had a set of keys to the cars. Each Friday afternoon I would get paperwork and keys for the weeks' repos. I would take a friend with me and we would go find and take the cars. They would be driven to a warehouse and sit there for disposition.

It wasn't always straightforward to get these cars though. Most people who ended up in default knew what was coming and would hide them or disable them somehow. Less than half would be easy to get, the rest took extra effort.

I once had a girls unwitting boyfriend jump on the windshield and ride down the block screaming. His girlfriend never told him about her title pawn deal, he thought I was stealing the car. I would sometimes have to follow people around or go to families houses to find cars.

I was threatened with bats and pipes and guns. At times it was quite exciting. One time I flew to New Mexico to repo a new Jaguar and drive it back.

There was a guy on the program named Jawaan Oldham. He was a Former NBA Basketball player on the Seattle Super Sonics 1978 championship team, but at this time was just a very tall dude with no prospects. Back in his day, Basketball players didn't make millions each year and what they did make was spent on glitz and lifestyle. He had his Italian made, gull wing Sbarro Mercedes on the Auto Pawn deal for years. It was an outrageous custom-made car to fit his seven-foot frame. Jawaan had been in default on occasion and was able to catch-up a couple times, he even got it out of Pawn but then returned later to do it again. This time, the car was missing for over a year and Robert couldn't get in touch with him.

We just got back from New Mexico with a newer Jaguar, but while cleaning it, found a lot of drugs and paraphernalia. The car had interior panels askew and things just weren't right. We decided to call the local police, turn-in all the stuff and ask them to check the car further. It had been used to ferry drugs across the Mexican border so it might have had secret compartments, etc.

While the police were doing this, Robert produced a flyer with a picture of Jawaan's car and offered a finder's fee if they ever found it. One of the officers worked a second job in a high-rise apartment building in downtown Seattle and immediately said he knew where the car was. It was on the 4th basement level of the building where he worked, sitting in a corner with a cover on it. *Bingo.*

The next night, Robert and I went there. It was a completely secure building, only keypad access. There was no way to get in so we waited for the garage to open for an outgoing car and snuck in on foot.

We soon found the car right where the cop said it was. It took till 4am but we got the car. It ended up sold three months later at a National auction to a guy in North Carolina.

Roberts business had a seedy underbelly even worse than its seedy topside. He regularly took cars as collateral for money used for drug deals and other nefarious use. I one time picked up a glitzed-out BMW, then the next morning a very dangerous and angry dude was at the door looking for his whip. He stood in front of Robert with his coat open showing a pistol in his belt. His woman was with him and on que, she opened her big handbag. He reached in and paid his arrears with stacks of 20's wrapped in cellophane.

I wasn't in the room, but had let this guy in. The office door remained open and I waited outside. I was ready, we had land lines and early cellphones at this point. I also knew there was a shotgun behind the door in another office. Not to mention the large caliber pistol, pointed at the guys groin, bolted to the underside of Robert's desk, another in the drawer.

There were also guys using the money to speculate and short sell in the stock market. One such guy lost a Ferrari *and* a Pantera in the deal. One of the benefits of my job with Robert was that I got to drive the cars, within reason. It was like having a company car. I always had a nice car to drive daily and could use the expensive ones for day trips with permission. I was driving Ferrari's and Porsche's, Mercedes, Rover, Corvette's. You name the twist needing money and those cars were being used as collateral.

Marika was a Real Estate agent by this time and one day she mentioned something that struck an idea. Her office was being approached by an internet company to make personal agent web pages. I took this idea one further and enlisted a friend we had that worked in the tech industry.

We would do the same thing for Doctors and Doctor offices of all kinds except there would be a feedback component for patients to leave pluses or minuses. These were the first days of the internet and things were expanding exponentially. It was only 1999, these years were the first couple stairs of the internet. Later I would come to realize this idea was actually a precursor to Yelp and Angie's List. I'm not claiming to be an innovator or anything like that, these ideas were a natural progression, but I did have them early-on.

Our friend worked for Oracle and had access to some of their newest databases. I had another tech friend making tons of money by retrieving email addresses and selling them. I enlisted him to skew his web spider program a bit to also get mailing addresses. It took four months but Referadoctor.com was up and making money. I was in charge of data entry, maintaining the website and mailings. This itself was a very big job and I was still managing the gas station auto repair shop. All this made for sixteen-hour days.

Our tech company came to an impasse, it was time to make a grand expansion. We were seeing big tech companies buy up small tech companies all around us and we needed to expand to join the ranks of buyable small tech. My partner knew tech minded people from his Harvard days. He approached them about capital investment and we all had a meeting. Two days later, I was offered 1% in the restructuring or to leave. The only actual reason for my slap was that I was not a tech guy and had too steep a learning curve. They'd rather me leave and hire a couple real technically trained guys to expedite things.

This was all true, but did not sit well with my sensibilities at that time. There was a big dusting up between all involved and since I had other means, Marika and I were two thirds of ownership and my ego was severely bruised, I chose a "screw-you" move. I shut it all down.

Truly, thinking back from the industry advancements today, it was a stupid move, I was very naive to what would soon happen in the tech industry. It was typical blue-collar thinking, I admit it. Dumb. I could have taken a pay-off and been done with it, but no. I closed the doors and sold the equipment. I made a deal with another tech company for our data and paid off all our debt. In six weeks, it was finished. My partner tried to sue me but that didn't work out well for him. I went back to 10-hour days at the auto repair shop.

By this time, Robert sold his Auto Pawn business and I wasn't working with him anymore. I tried to slow my life down a little but Marika was still in the basement of high-end Real Estate and needed to be kept in nicer cars and clothes. We had her Mom and Father living with us as well as her best childhood friend who came to visit for a few months but ended up staying. With all the cars and a boat and house and family expenses at every turn, our monthly expenses were outrageous. It kept piling up but we really were just spinning and not really getting anywhere, just further into a hole. The more we made, the more we spent.

Marika and I started a Property Management Company. She was able to reel in Russian Investors from Vladivostok. They would buy houses in the Seattle area and she would handle the sale. I would rent them out, do all the accounting and maintenance. Then when the houses appreciated enough, she would handle the sale and the investors could continue on.

That was a fabulous business plan and worked great... for a very short while. This worked for the first couple houses except new Government regulations were enacted. All money coming into the United States now had to have a declaration of origin as to whether the Country it was coming from knew about it and had properly vetted and taxed it.

This was a problem since our investors were oligarchs buying houses with suitcases full of American hundred-dollar bills. They did not want this money traced, hence, our business died. We had just a couple houses that hung around my neck for a few years till they were sold. At least for those couple years those houses generated a decent side income for us as rentals. Otherwise it was a bust.

But something is so-far missing isn't it? I've gone over a lot of what I did since moving to the Seattle area, but what of the actual reason to get me there? My children...

Well, starting the very same weekend we arrived in May of 1996, I saw my children *every* Sunday. For the first few years I didn't have enough money to challenge my ex-wife's Father for custody. When I first arrived, he suspected I would try and take them back so he put up a legal front knowing I initially had no money. What I did was to buy legal insurance. I used a lawyer to send nasty threatening letters forcing him to go into a legal visitation contract until I could get them back. I saw them in Keyport all-day every Sunday and they came over to my house for holiday visits and even weeks during school breaks and the summers. I have great memories and also great sadness for these times.

Thinking back on all this really chaps my ass and makes my ears burn. I think now of things I might have done to change things but really, at the time, I was locked in, *and out*, by circumstance and balancing temperaments of my ex-wife's family. They were extensively spread out on the Olympic peninsula and were the kind of people to hide and move around young kids out of spite. I was threatened with that a few times.

One nice Summer, my Children were staying the weekend. They were young, my daughter nine, my son seven.

We had a good Saturday, yet my son was unusually quiet and withdrawn. That night before bed he asked me for help. At 60 years old, remembering this question haunts me. It makes me fall apart. It ruins my day and sours several after.

Gavin said he didn't want to be deaf anymore, could I please help him. *Please, please daddy please.*

My son and I have always had an especially close relationship. The same principles of existence that kept me safe, free and "Lucky" my entire adolescent life have actually been doing the same for me since and throughout. In some circles it might be referred to as being protected by a guardian angel. Whatever it may be that keeps me on a path of enlightenment, the one thing I know for sure is; of its existence.

I have had many opportunities to die and kill in my life. I've brushed near many forms of negativity which have trapped others, but I keep going back in my head to that time in the driveway in Ochlocknee, hearing from the tree branch above, "*You are one lucky son-of-a-bitch.*"

My son has been without my protection for several spans of his life. Within those spans he has been treated as horribly as any human ever has. Out of jealousy, ignorance, hate, stupidity, disgust and other animalistic ideals of hierarchy, he has been grandly abused. I'm sure I only know of a portion, but of those I know, I am tortured.

He has been lured into a tree to be purposefully pushed out from 30ft. Shot with a bow and arrow through the side. Slapped and beat up by his Uncle. Left deep in the woods, left 200 feet below the surface in a mine, left on the highway in the middle of no-where. Used as a toy, used by his Moms side of the family as validation for alcoholism, methamphetamine abuse and his monthly disability check.

The list goes on. Basically, treated as no person should be treated under any circumstances.
All he wants, all he has ever wanted is acceptance and Love.

It is true, I am perhaps the luckiest son-of-a-bitch that most people will ever know. Lucky, because there was time and distance between me and the people that did these things to him. None of them realize how life-changing their own luck has been because of this time and distance.

Except for one time which I deeply regret, I have always pulled back before going too far. I've already gone over that, but even in the darkest of my thoughts, I would never want to purposefully kill any person. I would though happily make them pay and remember their day of penance for the rest of their lives. I would maim and disfigure. I would suffer these fates on their closest family. I would suffer upon them the human ideals of empathy and compassion. I would give them something to remember, something to think about the rest of their days.

Because there has been the gift of time and distance, I have stayed out of jail and perhaps even the electric chair. To my last breath, I will be the protector of my son. I failed him once, and that failure cost him his place on Earth. This will torture me the rest of my days. I will not fail again.

All of this aside, not only have I been a protector and teacher while we have been together, he has been one of the most important people in my life. I have tried to instill in him as much freedom as I can without control. Always waiting in the corner and letting him experience everything on his own.

When he was very young, six or seven I think, there was a time the whole family went out to lunch at a restaurant. While we were eating he asked if he could go to the rest room and wanted to go alone.

I could see the rest room door so I told him sure he could. I watched as he went in and kept my eye on the door and everyone who went in and out. He was in there for quite a while and I started to wonder what was going on. When I went in there to look, Gavin was standing there against the wall holding a $20 bill. He was asking everyone if they had lost it and was waiting for the person who dropped it to come back and claim it. That's how innocent he was, and still is.

Any time something potentially bad arises, to this very day, he always thinks of the good side first. He has to be shown the bad side of everyone first before he will believe it. Conversely, I am just the opposite. I need to see a glimmer of good before I believe good exists in people. I will always give that chance, but have seen too much bad to be taken-in without warning.

I am sooooo sorrrrry.... oh my god.......
No, my precious little boy, I am more sorry for this than any person can be. I can't help you hear, but I will live this with you. I will be by your side until my last breath.

Throughout my time in Seattle, my saving grace and weekly mental relaxation were my kids. Lisa's Father would not easily relinquish custody of them. I had no money for a legal fight to start with and then as I advanced, it seemed there was always something in the way. It was a resentment that added up in the negative column of my relationship with Marika. She would have accepted the kids with open arms but with all of her and my life issues, we had no space and no money for even more. I hated this situation.

Gavin was living with his Aunt and Uncle across the street from Megan, she was living at her Grampa's house. They were being taken care of physically, but I loathed their environment. These were people of "lesser intent." There was no drive or ambition there.

All of these people were shysters on the dole and always willing to lie, cheat and steal for the smallest of perceived value. It was a dark and mundane existence, and although in a small town, in a nice area, my kids were also lacking positive emotional stimulation.

Their Mother was on her 5th husband and spent time in both the Mental hospital and the State women's penitentiary for fraud and Identity theft. Their Aunt and Uncle were derelicts and sponged off their Grandfather. No positive examples were being given.

For ten years, I would get up at 5am on Sundays and go to the Seattle/Bainbridge Ferry. Then a 20-mile drive to their house in Keyport, pick them up and spend the day, then reverse the trip home to get back by 8pm. I only missed two Sundays in ten years till they finally came to live with me. For a while, my Sister and Steve lived in that area so all the cousins could get together occasionally, but other than that, we explored every facet of the Olympic Peninsula and everything we could possibly do.

Going back on the Ferry each Sunday, I would lean on the railing and stare at Seattle as it grew bigger. Over and over I would ask the Universe; what did Seattle need I could provide that would help me change all this? How could I get ahead here in this money grubbing environment?

At the Service Station I was working at in Bellevue there was a Hotel next door with a bar. The bar had a Happy hour from 5-7pm with free finger foods and dollar beers. Several of the guys at the shop would go over there after work to wind down. I was invited a few times and for a while, I went there after work also. I got to know a few of the regulars. One of them was a guy named Leon, about ten years younger than me, he worked all day cleaning and repairing roofs.

He would always complain about his boss and his pay. His boss was making a lot of money and Leon wasn't happy with his share. I chatted him up about the operation. It seemed like a decent business a person could build up to make a good living.

I made him a proposition.
I would buy all the equipment needed to start out with, he would do the work. We would both drum up business and would half the profits. If he stayed busy, this would double his current income, but he would have to also hunt down jobs.

Long story short, I sold my old Dodge GTS and used the money to start the business. I bought a truck and full rig to do the work. I soon figured out a great way to get jobs. After just a couple months, I was able to buy another full truck and rig and started doing this myself. No more car repair.

A few months after that, Marika and I officially got married. Admittedly, we did it for all the wrong reasons, it wasn't a very good choice. We were growing further apart and thought getting married would help us stay together. Our wedding at the Bellagio in Las Vegas was quite an event. We were starry eyed for a while, but in the end, we were still living two very different and separate lives.

One event which happened in this time was worth noting. I started making pretty good money and bought a Jet-ski for us all to enjoy at the lake. It was a good family relaxation move. We would go picnic with my kids and Marika's kids and family and play in the water. Occasionally we would have friends with us also. One of these friends was in the Georgian immigrant circles with Marika and her family.

It was a very proud situation that the Seattle Supersonics Basketball team just drafted a new recruit from Marika's home Country of Georgia.

He was welcomed into our circle and everyone was very happy that Georgia was being represented locally by a sports star. His name was Vladimir Stephania, seven-foot tall and spoke very little English. He was actually what we here in the U.S. would call a "Country Hick," within his own country. A naive person now in the big city on a national stage. He was a pretty good guy with honest intent, but one of the other Georgian immigrants in our circle was not-so-much. He was a hangar-on and would buzz around Vlad like a cartoon character, trying to involve himself as much as possible within Vlad's life as a pro Basketball player.

Vlad had his family coming to the US to visit and this guy asked for me to lend them all our jet-ski to use at the lake house Vlad was living in. I agreed, I saw no issue there. I went there, met them all, showed them all how to use it, had a nice day and left it there for them to use for a week.

When I went back the next weekend to retrieve it, it was literally destroyed. It no longer moved. It had been run aground and bashed against the pier till every corner was gnarled. It was torn, scratched and chipped every inch. I could hardly believe this was my jet-ski. I gave it to them in perfect condition. It was quite expensive and I take care of my things.

No one was home when I picked it up so I called the "friend," who set the whole thing up. Somehow the situation was skewed to be my tough luck. I would not let this pass, the repair bill was nearly four thousand dollars. In the end I had to sue Vladimir Stephania. I couldn't believe that a person making that much money would be so stingy but of course it wasn't really all his idea, most of it came from the hangar-on "friend."

Something funny to note is; after I filed suit, I was contacted by the TV show, "The Peoples Court" and asked if I wanted to appear with this suit on their show. I told everyone involved about it but I declined the appearance.

The day of the court appearance we were all there standing around ready to go into the courtroom. The team manager walked up to me and apologized. I was given a check for the full amount by the Seattle Supersonics. This would hit the newspapers if it went to court and they wanted it stopped before that happened. I used to have a picture of that check but it has long disappeared, inside a stolen laptop computer.

This seems like another good place to wax nostalgic about my life and marriage in Seattle...

It has been many years, but I still think about Marika on occasion. We spent so much time together and overcame too many obstacles for the memories to fade. We laughed and cried, lost two children together *(nuff said)* and were each other's mentor for the finer points of life and Love.
Yet we still loved and lost.

For awhile, I thought we were just too different. She didn't think in English; it wasn't her first language. I know this is like saying she didn't understand me, but not so. Much smarter than me in many ways, she understood plenty. Everything except I wasn't cut-out to realize the conventional dream-set.

People across the world are shown the American dream as a shiny representation to set a disparity in what they themselves have or have not. Whether they ever come to the U.S. or not, they know it is here. Some of them aspire, and when they get here, start-in on the *"American dream"* not realizing these ideals can be hollow and what it actually takes from your personality and character to achieve them.

As many people who struggle separately do, we grew apart. We ended up with two different lives, living each in the same house. Her moving towards that conventional dream set, me shunning it and moving away.

Me resenting her for liking it, her not understanding why. At the time, I didn't actually know why, it was just in me, clouded with Ego.

I found living a life of money, status and acceptance of peers within never-ending struggle and maintenance was too uncomfortable. She accepted it as a goal realized and was satisfied in that way. It was what people are "supposed" to do. It was what people "dream" of and there could be no wrong in realizing that dream. Except I found the dream hollow and the realization was that it was a game not to be won, only played. There was no end to the game, it just went on-and-on with another goal realized, then another goal waiting with fresh bitters to swallow.

And the people... our circles were full of shysters and wannabees thinking and talking only of money and shiny things. There was no substance to any of it. It was all so painfully fake. Maybe I was just tired of sitting still. There was another very disappointing realization. Even in these monetarily higher levels of society I attained, there was Ludd.

Later, after being apart for several years, there came a realization of what the American dream can be; pounding on Marika's front door. In this we became simpatico.

Marika's mother lived with us and as such wanted a job of her own so she could contribute. Early on in Seattle she got a job as a Nanny for a very nice family. She raised their two children as her own and the family showered her with acceptance and love. Then came the knock.

The mother of this family worked in Seattle. One day she was at a meeting and needed to go out to feed the parking meter. Gloria was no shrinking flower by any stretch, she was a type-A woman, so when the car-jacker demanded her keys, she refused. Gloria was shot and killed for her car keys.

This horrified everyone and was of-course a defining moment in all their lives. Not much later, Marika's Father had a stroke and all involved thought it better he leave the United States.

In my heart of hearts, I believe this is the best thing anyone with enduring human conscious can do. This Country is a cesspool of runaway imagination and disingenuous intent. Only those willing to look past or partake in the environment have any kind of chance. And even then, they will slowly lose pieces of their soul until spat out at death.
Harsh? Yep, and true every word.
I get to say that... keep reading, *you'll see.*

About a year later, after her and I being together for ten years, I moved out to a shared rental with my business partner Leon. Hard as I can, I can't remember how I justified that. I'll bet I was a hard-nosed blanked out fool though, still living my accepted bad examples.

Leon was a single guy and lived a bachelor's life. He drank and caroused. Being around this constantly now, I did too. We had a great house with a big deck and hot-tub. I knew people in local Seattle bands, I got back into playing the guitar. We had big parties, did a lot of drinking and a lot of drugs.

We also had a small side business. This house had a very deep Garage. I sectioned it off, we bought all the equipment and started a perpetual pot garden hidden away unnoticeable from any angle in the garage. This was before marijuana was legal in Washington State.

I took a trip to Vancouver, B.C. to a head shop run by a guy named Mark Emory. He would later become famous in the U.S and be arrested by the FBI for selling pot seeds by mail into the US. At least I got mine direct and didn't have them mailed. His recommendation on how I should bring them into the country worked. Rub them into the carpet of the car, no problem.

A pot garden was something I thought about many times since that old Abbie Hoffman book when I was young. It was a pretty sweet deal that brought us in another bag full of cash every month. We only sold bulk once a month to one guy in Seattle so our exposure was limited, things worked out well.

Along the way, Leon started drinking a lot more and working a lot less. The quality of the work he was doing was slipping and he was at the bar talking himself up, and me down. His bank card drained our account several times while buying the whole bar several rounds. He was getting out of control.

One day after work I got a call from the client he was working for that day and they complained about him. I talked with him that evening and he copped an attitude, leaving in a huff. Off to see his girlfriend in North Seattle he drove like a crazy person. I knew this by the next phone call I got. It was from a guy complaining that one of my company trucks with logo and phone number was careening across the bridge and nearly ran him off the road.

I was *real* nice to the guy, we talked for a bit and I promised to get retribution for him. Four days later, this guy's wife called. She was a procurement manager for a huge property management company that owned several apartment complexes and dozens of houses all over Puget Sound. She invited me to bid on an Apartment complex job.

I made sure I got that job by going so low, we barely made any money. From there we did every complex and house they owned on a yearly basis. From there we were recommended to other management companies. From there we were recommended to County and City municipalities. We were working for five Cities and four management companies and residential out the wazoo. Rolling Heavily.

Leon thought since we were doing so good, we should get a fleet of flashy trucks but I was more frugal. He didn't like that at all. We settled on a company car he could drive when he wanted, a late model Mercedes. He would be at the bars spending hundreds each night telling everyone he was the Boss of his own company, I was his employee and making up all kinds of weird stories. His self-esteem could not be boosted by our success, it was a bit nuts actually.

Finally, we had it out. On paper, Marika and I were two thirds of the company and asked him to leave. He said he would take a rig for himself and go. I agreed but we had to do it as the corporate paperwork laid out, we had a buy/sell agreement. He was actually due a third of everything. The next day he didn't go to work, he moved all of his things out of the house, ruining many walls and floors. Later I would lose the security deposit because of this. He took a complete truck and rigging and would not answer his phone. It kinda sucked that it ended that way. I tried to give him more but he was crazy drunk and his girlfriend was very dramatic and filling his head with bazaar notions. Soon I didn't hear from him again for over a year.

Problem was, he emptied one of the company bank accounts of much more than what he was due. Our lawyer advised me of the proper course of action. Since he didn't follow the corporate rules in the agreement he signed, I reported the truck, trailer and rig stolen.

I had to close down the garden and move from that house. I found a nice, small house on Mercer Island, centrally located and sans garden, carried the business on by myself. I bought a couple more rigs and hired a few guys. It was nowhere near easy, but within six months, I was high rolling on my own.

Word was that Leon moved to Oregon and was working there. I had no ill intent towards him, I didn't worry about him, good for him.

Then one day a year after, I get a letter in the mail that one of my trucks will be towed if not moved from a street in South Seattle. It was the truck Leon took.

I went there and brought it back. The trailer and rig weren't there but I had the truck back. Not actually owning the truck, he couldn't tag it. He soon would have been caught and jailed for driving a stolen vehicle. A few months after that, a mutual friend of ours told me Leon was back in town and had the trailer and rig behind his own truck. He was at the bars again mouthing off about how he was going to take over the business again. Completely off-the-wall with no foundation and no hope, he was again out of control. This friend of ours knew where Leon was living.

I called the police and met an officer there to repossess the trailer and equipment. That was over ten thousand dollars' worth of equipment. I made sure there were plenty of people there he'd been lying to, to see him forced to legally give it up. The officer read the complaint out loud in front of everyone and I declined to have him jailed. All I wanted was the equipment and his embarrassment for being a lying drunk. Done. I never heard from Leon again.

I could no longer work having to baby sit my workers and follow-up on every job. I was back to 16-hour days for a couple years. It was torture of the soul, a mindless, blank time of life.

With jobs going all over the County, I did a lot of driving and baby-sitting employees. I would go to Estate sales and ran into quite a few money-making opportunities. I once bought, and then sold a record and stereo equipment shop. I ended up with a side business of buying low/selling high.

Driving around the Counties, I'd listen to the radio. One day, the radio station started a promotion calling for all aspiring comedians and wannabe chuckle heads in the Seattle area.

It was sponsored by the radio station and included Jerry Seinfeld. The gist was; since the Seinfeld show was now over, he was moving on to a new show and putting out the word for new talent to fill the shows roster. There would be an open call on a particularly apropos date, April first, at the radio station in downtown Seattle. They played this come-on quite a bit, at least 20 times a day. The more I listened, the more I thought.

I'd always been able to make people laugh, I was funny-ish, my wife and friends were always entertained....

I talked myself into it, when the day came, I showed up early. I was one of the first in the door at 7am. Myself and a couple others were sitting around waiting when a producer came in and asked us for our "package." A list of achievements and a professional Headshot, kind of like a resume'. I of course didn't have one of these and didn't even know I should have one so I begged off to get one. I figured I could get it all done in a couple hours and be back in time to continue.

I did all that in record time with the help of Marika and was back by 9:30am. When I got back in to the waiting room it was packed. They'd gone through a dozen and there were at least 20 more waiting.

When called in, you had three minutes to a little comedy something to impress Jerry Seinfeld who was live on a monitor in the radio booth watching as you did your bit on live radio.

Well, I didn't make the cut. Being late to the game, the morning show was over before I got in. But the producers let the last six of us that didn't make it, go in to the booth to see and hear the end result directly from Jerry Seinfeld.

There were the two morning DJ's, a couple others and us six all talking and watching Seinfeld on the monitor in the corner. Everything was jovial and I resigned to thinking it was fate and apparently was just not to be.

So, the famous Seattle DJ finally gets to the part where he asks Jerry about who he thought was best and who would get consideration. Jerry talked shortly about a couple of the performers and then the conversation turned to the DJ and his previous jobs. One of which was a time when he interviewed Jerry after a particularly stinking performance.

The DJ's eyes looked off into the mist and agreed. He remembered that time and remarked on how far Jerry had come.... *Aaaah, wasn't it great?*

Then Jerry's tone changed a bit and he voiced just how much he didn't appreciate that interview. Then he had a few choice comments, a few expletives and a wish for the DJ to have a good April Fools Day. The monitor went blank.

The DJ and the control room personnel were aghast and us remaining six were quickly rushed out of the booth. The next week, the DJ was fired and soon after, the station went to "Jack Radio," a canned syndicated radio station format. *Fuckin' Jerry Seinfeld - April Fools... Bitches... whew!*

Gavin came to live with me the night of his 16th birthday in 2006. This did not sit well with his Mother's side of the family. After-all, they would lose his Social Security check. They moaned about his disrespect of them giving him a place to live all this time and just up and leaving. When Gavin came to live with me was when I finally heard directly from him of what he put up with the whole time he lived there. He told me stories that made me want to sneak over there in the middle of the night and burn down their house with them in it. Truly, their terrible daily lives are my best revenge, screw those people.

Megan stayed there until she graduated high school the next year but attitudes changed toward her also. They knew she was leaving as soon as she could.

When she did finally come over, I helped her get a job at the new Bellevue Whole Foods and she started on her own life. She lived with me for a year then moved out on her own. I am so proud of her recognizing the whole situation and putting all that behind her. She completely agrees, screw those people.

One night, one of my good employees called me. Tanner was a good kid and I rarely needed to worry about him at all. Him and two of his friends worked for me. I'd known all of them since those days back in the gas station auto repair situation. Tanner called and asked me to go out and have a drink, maybe bar-hop a little. I couldn't, even though it was Friday night, I had a lot of business stuff to do, I begged off.

The next day, while on the road going around the County doing estimates, I got a call from another of my guys. Tanner had been found dead in his bed that morning of a heroin overdose. I was knocked over, if only I had known. If only I had gone out with him that night, if only.... I never had a hint of an issue.

Some of his friends said they had hints but it seemed a mystery how it had gotten this far. Someone for sure knew. This played heavily on me and a few of the guys that worked for me. This was 2008 and I was mentally torn apart by the business, this situation and other of life's dramas.

I decided to temporarily downsize the company and look for a buyer. Someone to take it and run it just like I had and then go from there. I had four guys try on separate occasions but none of them had it in them to learn the job or handle the work. I tried to sell to other local companies but they figured to get my clients for free when I closed down, why buy me out?

By the fall of 2009 I was turning down 80% of work offered. I was down to myself and one employee. I was making as much money with two as I had with four trucks and six employees.

I was able to cherry pick the work but was still not enjoying anything. My life was full of work and not much else. On top of that I almost fell off a roof twice and was starting to feel like this work was getting too much for my age.

I made plans to let it all go. I would do all the preparations to quit working in the Winter of 2009. I liquidated and let my last employee go. I worked by myself for the last few months.

Lucky S.O.B.

Chapter Twelve

While getting ready to leave Mercer Island, I was selling all the stuff I'd collected but there really wasn't enough time. I ended up having to put quite a lot in a large storage locker and paid its rent two years in advance.

My last job was a week before Christmas 2009. I had a small feeling of relief, but there was still a lot to do before I would be able to pick-up and go. I had to sell off the vehicles and equipment separately and just stop.

A start-up company from Vancouver Canada came across the border and bought all of my equipment. There were three trucks left but I would be keeping the newest one. The other two sold easily within a few weeks.

I kept my eye out for an RV that would be a decent livable size and still be small enough for my truck. I found one just a couple years old in like-new condition, a 24-foot fifth wheel. I bought a fifth wheel hitch and installed it in my Dakota. Everyone said it would never work and the trucks V6 motor and small transmission would blow-up in a matter of months. Having an actual mechanical background, I knew better.

I installed proper upgrades and was religious with required maintenance, it never broke down once. At this very moment it is sitting outside my home waiting to take me and haul stuff anywhere I want to go. Although, with way over 200 thousand miles, it deserves the light duty it now gets. It has been the best vehicle I ever owned.

Once we were ready, Gavin and I hit the road. As we left Seattle behind, I had a true feeling of relief.

We were backed by a large bank account, no bills and no worries. The rat-race was not for me, from now on, I was a free spirit. I didn't know why I had such an urge to leave all this so-called "success" behind me. I often wonder if this was what is called my "mid-life crisis," manifesting in a profound way. I never really even thought of it at all. There was just something in me that would not accept the terms of what my life had become, none of it seemed right. This seemed right, a feeling of unencumbered freedom. I also felt like I was giving my son a gift, a gift of wide-open life.

Gavin was ok with this as far as I could explain it to him but like most young folks, he really had no idea of the future. I knew it all felt unstable to him, but as long as there was money and some semblance of comfort, he was ok. One thing he did know was that his Dad was a doer and things got done, he was on board with that. Besides, we actually had an action plan and he was the star attraction.

My plan was to buy low/sell high, make a little money here and there, maybe 15-20k a year and with my current bank balance, never have to work again. That was for myself, Gavin was another story all-together. I, and to an extent we, had a grand plan to make Gavin famous among his peers and set him on a path that would continue to blossom and open up as time passed throughout his life.

By now, I understood how hearing people and deaf people differed, I understood how adventure worked and how marketing yourself worked. I planned to put these all together in an adventure business called *"Deaf Trek."*

Two weeks before we left, I had the RV wrapped with Deaf Trek markings including website, Facebook and YouTube addresses. I bought a full kit of web-ready cameras and software. Gavin and I were going to travel the country and see ALL the sites.

As we visited them, we would learn all about them, script them and then he would teach other deaf people via video and text discussion on the internet. When we gathered enough of an audience, I was going to sell this to ASL classes and Deaf Schools throughout the country by personalizing it for them. It would be monetized on the internet with advertising. It was a good business plan in the same way my previous internet start-up had been. That one had been proven, just not by me. This time, I would be in control of the tech and purse so it hopefully had a fighting chance.

We mapped out a route across the US, but first we would stop by Las Vegas and see my Mother and Sister. They were living there and we hadn't seen them for some time. From there we would head into Arizona and start with the National parks.

We started with the Grand Canyon, then went into Utah to Zion National Park. It was just outside a couple nicer small towns. This would be a good place to use as a center point.

We decided to make St. George, Utah our hub. We found a nice little RV Park tucked away, next to a lot of interesting scenery. It had a clubhouse and considering my Sister and Mother were just 140 miles away, could serve as a home base. I could never use Las Vegas as a center point, family there or not. Las Vegas is a pit of negativity from many angles. I can barely stand visiting for a few days.

The RV park wasn't actually in St. George, it was in the nethers a few miles North, actually just on the other side of a small town called Hurricane. Famous during the Rodeo season for the Hurricane Barrel Races. Even closer to a little one-horse town called Leeds. From there we went to all the Parks in Utah and did our thing, it was working as planned. In a month or so we were heading East and stopped in Iowa to see family. Here is where things took a turn for Gavin.

Some of his old friends, and a few others on the message boards were giving him grief about traveling around explaining everything he saw. Typical high drama internet nonsense he wasn't used to. He was young and this was his first time putting up with haters on the internet. He felt he needed to answer them all and things got to be a little too much for him.

Sometimes as we travelled, I would pretend to be deaf also. Just us two deaf guys traveling around the country. We would go into a restaurant and I wouldn't say anything the whole time. We would openly converse only in sign language, I would only gesture and point to menus. I would write things down and pretend not to hear anything.

Don't get me wrong, honestly, most-all go out of their way to help or be compassionate in some way if needed. But there were also a few people who would treat us like nothing more than dirt on the floor. Saying things out loud they would never say to your face if you could hear them. Trying to cheat and steal from us. Taking small advantage of a person who can't hear their disrespect and personal character flaws in action. That sounds awful doesn't it? *It was, and it is.*

It's hard to imagine the ignorance and stupidity of people in the world around you until you give them an opportunity to prove themselves. Luckily, Gavin couldn't hear the disrespect of the world around him. But I could.

I would call them out for it and get aggressive when it happened. A couple people were startled and embarrassed after they said something off-color, then I looked them in the eye and clearly told them of their failing. One time, I walked up to a family in a restaurant and told the two children their Father sitting there was wrong. We weren't dummy's, "*Deaf people are people too, and just as smart as everyone else. Please don't grow up to be as inconsiderate as your Father.* "

He stood up and looked hard at me but had nothing to say as we walked away.

Ultimately very sad, yet the overwhelming majority of folks were neutral to nice. That the negative side still stands out all these years later is just another example for me of how negative memories overshadow the good. Many times kids would come up to Gavin and try out some sign language they learned, that was always fun.

From Utah, then East. Niagara Falls into Canada, Montreal, New York and South. By the time we got to Georgia I stupidly decided to go see my Father. Gavin was still fending off nonsense on the internet and getting more frustrated with the entire situation.

My Father did not then or ever, understand anything about deafness or deaf people. He always treated Gavin as an unknown and never accepted him. I'm sure he somehow equated Gavin with his Mother. Gavin knew and felt this and was uncomfortable there. Within days there was conflict.

I asked Gavin not to drink or get high while we were there. He left the house a few times and went off and did it anyway. My Father noticed and started on a "proper parenting" lecture. It was the same old thing, except this time I would abruptly stop it and admonish him openly. When Gavin would no longer acknowledge him, he recommended to me, I should send him home to his Mother... Yeah, *As If.*

Here is where Gavin and I had our worst "fight." I was worried he had gone and done something my Father would freak out about and I had brought Gavin to a house in which he was given no respect... from his own family. He already had his fill of that and I had subjected him to more. It took me awhile to realize that, but when I did, I apologized and we made up. We haven't been terse with each other since.

It was at this point I realized, at another depth, this situation was all my fault. Why did I keep coming back? Convention, it was what I was supposed to do. We are all supposed to put up with whatever our parents dish out then forgive them and make nice.

Yet, this was an epiphanic moment, I realized that if my Father were just another man on the street and I met him in passing, perhaps ended up in the same circle or crossed paths in any other way throughout my life, I wouldn't allow him to be my friend. I would separate myself from him. I have run across several people I avoid or just never respond to over time who have displayed their characters in unacceptable ways to my sensibilities. At this point, I'm just glad he didn't kill me or my brother and am happy he found acceptance somewhere. If this sounds bad, I'm sorry, but we all reap what we've sown. My days as "sucker for punishment," were over.

Gavin and I packed up and left abruptly, we headed to Atlanta. This was just another worry on Gavin's mind. Between the internet dramas and his disrespecting Grandfather, he was losing self-esteem fast, it was becoming too much.

In Atlanta, he disappeared for four days. He wouldn't answer texts, I had no idea where he was. I had the police looking for him and spent the days and nights driving the streets asking everyone I saw if they'd seen him. It was the deepest fear I ever endured.

He showed up on the fifth day. We talked for a solid six hours straight; I was completely drained. In the end, we decided to stop the *Deaf-Trek* business and just continue on as "regular" people traveling around. The new plan was to continue travelling, but this time, we would just have fun amongst ourselves. We slowly headed back to the RV park in Utah. When we got there, we spent several weeks hunting, fishing and exploring.

Here in this park, was a perfect little spot for the RV under a tree, everything fit perfectly. I paid a yearly fee and reserved that spot for us. Anytime we came back, with two-weeks notice, that spot would be ours.

We joined a Gold Prospecting club, I bought all the needed equipment and we spent a lot of time in the wilds. We went back and forth to Montana, Nevada, Colorado, California and Oregon. We hunted, fished and Prospected.

We stayed there in the RV park a few weeks to relax and while there, I went into St. George one day to the Barnes & Noble bookstore to sit with coffee and a magazine. After looking through the magazine, in the back-advertisement section there was a little entry looking for submissions. It mentioned that if I liked the genre' of the magazine and had writing experience, they would accept a few paragraph submissions for review.

I looked at a few more magazines and found similar come-ons in the back of them. Later, I took a little time and wrote a few paragraphs for each publication. A few weeks later, I was accepted to write and submit articles for three magazines.

We headed to the Feather River in Northern California to use the prospecting club membership and spent a few months digging, panning and exploring. We found gold, fished, had a run-in with a Bear and a Mountain Lion. Dens of rattle snakes, abandon mines and several sketchy, backwoods weirdos were all in the mix.

One time, while heading back to camp from Oroville, we were driving through the Mountain valleys and passes and a group of three-wheel motorcycles passed us. All three bikes had two people on them, they zipped around us and continued. Not seeing those very often, Gavin and I were commenting on them and as we rounded the next curve there was a dust cloud on the side of the road dissipating.

It seemed weird and then one of the three wheeled bike was heading back towards us. I realized what just happened. We stopped, backed up and looked over the edge to see the colors of the people's clothes, and the bike in the trees half way down in the ravine below.

The other two bikes showed up and those folks were shocked in disbelief. We called the State Patrol and I got a long climbing rope out of my truck. Tied off to the truck, I descended the cliff to see if I could help down there until official help arrived. It was a very steep and deep loam over the side, they were down about 150 feet. The guy was aware and attentive but one leg was bent backwards and obviously broken. He was cut-up and bleeding but would be Ok. His passenger was hanging upside down in a nearby tree, purple with a blank stare, she was gone.

I stayed with the guy until the fire department came, then climbed out and eventually left the scene. They were tourists from India who had rented the bikes for a day trip through the mountains. A small but very strong blip in our time in Northern California, a devastating and life changing time for those folks.

Otherwise, Gavin and I had a great time. I wrote about most of it and was published in a few magazines. This was all great for the Ego but ended up much more trouble than it was worth, it didn't pay much.

In the meantime, the plan was evolving. We would continue to travel till our feet fell off. Next phase would be out of the U.S. I was looking around on the internet for a volunteering situation out of the Country which would suit us. Most were actually quite expensive and were out of our wants and needs. Then I found a situation in Nepal where we could go for five months on a sign language and deaf life teaching program. It was in the city of Katmandu. We would live with sponsor families, help and teach at a local school.

It was relatively inexpensive compared to most programs I'd looked at and seemed tailor made for us. I applied for both of us, we were accepted and paid the fees. I got the schedule and bought the plane tickets, all we had to do was wait. We would be leaving in May of 2013. Until then we would bide our time, I would once again start on the liquidation of stuff we'd gathered along the way. We headed back to the RV park in Utah. The plan was to stay there and keep busy till the following May when we would leave for Nepal.

One day in early November I got a call from a friend I'd met on the road in California while prospecting there. He and his wife would be in Las Vegas for a few days and we all wanted to get together. When the day came, I headed in to meet them.

It's a two-hour drive from the RV park to Las Vegas if you do the speed limit and just relax. Problem is; the drive is very engrossing with scenery and crazy-ass drivers going to and from Vegas. I've seen more terrible wrecks and nuts on the road on that stretch of U.S. Interstate 15 than anywhere else I've travelled. It winds through a beautiful high wall canyon and miles of open desolate desert. It also has a lot of traffic. Best to pick a speed, put on the cruise control and relax.

That's what I was doing. No matter what speed you're going there is always someone going slower or faster. I would just try to not touch the brakes and scoot around and down the road. Cruise control set at 2mph under the speed limit, I was passing a slower car, when an old van came up from behind very fast.

Getting back in the slower lane, this van passed me with both the driver and passenger yelling and giving grand hand and finger gestures. Quite upset, apparently they had somewhere to go in a hurry. They raced on, but traffic would not allow it. They weaved back and forth, in and out, slower, faster, till others blocked them off, they ended up behind me again.

Traffic was heavy and typically, other folks were upset and playing with them. There was some weaving and yelling out windows... not me, I was watching everything in the mirrors.

We ended up in the same situation again, they were behind me again as I was passing a couple cars. As I got back into the slower lane again, this time they passed with pistols in their hands, got in front of me and slammed on their brakes.

I got on the phone and called 911, but on that barren stretch I was between districts and passed-off to three different dispatchers. After the third pass-off and a long silence, I hung up. These guys had me in their sites and I was now a target. I decided to get off the highway and let them continue on without me. I took the next exit late but they went off the road to follow me. They went half-way into the ditch, through the scrub and back up on to the exit tarmac.

This did not look good. I got my pistol out of the door panel. In a few seconds they were behind me at the stop sign. No use in running from here, I just sat there.

They stopped a few feet behind me and the driver jumped out. The other one was out of the van picking up rocks and throwing them at the truck. I could see in the mirror he had no weapon. He kicked my truck, punched my window screaming and shouting in Spanish. These were two Mexicans high on Meth. I just looked at him through the driver's door window as he screamed and tried to open the door. He punched the widow again, I raised the pistol so he could see it.

His eyes got big, he took this as a challenge and yelled more as he turned and ran back to his van, but he didn't get in. I could see he was reaching across the driver's seat for the pistol his passenger was handing him. I opened my door, crouched, shot his door twice, the windshield twice, the radiator twice.

He jumped into the van and was not hit. I wasn't trying to shoot him, only to scare them and disable the van.

I got back in my truck and tore out and up the highway ramp on the other side as fast as I could. I heard several shots coming after me but none hit the truck. He couldn't follow, his windshield was shattered and radiator blowing steam. What a terrible day. It ruined my visit in Vegas, I couldn't stop vibrating.

Guns, violence and Drugs have played a huge negative part in mine, as well as the lives of Americans all over the country. I've been involved and noticed it around me my entire life. I ran that whole scenario through my mind for weeks to try and think of a way it could have ended differently, better somehow... but there was even more of this coming my way. I would soon be forced to forget about this crazy road rage incident for a while.

This next piece was the primary turning point in my life. An upcoming event so wrenching, so profound, I consider this the half-point of my life. An actual before and after situation. As a matter of fact, it has been a definite turning point in thought for everyone I know, or even knows of me. My life is now defined as "before Utah," and "after Utah." A fact steeped in irony, being that my main life's focus has always been to try and define my life by the next thing that I'll do. Not to sit around in a vegetative state and re-live fond memories of my past. In my current life post-Utah, the best I can now do is to try and balance and meld the two distinctly different halves.

One afternoon, while sitting on the couch in my RV reading, the door was thrown open and in jumped a man with a shotgun. This man gave no warning of his intent, he didn't knock or call out. In-fact the only thing he said at all was to yell; *DIE DEVIL !!*

He was in a methamphetamine induced trance as he shot me four times with the hunting gun.
The whole fiasco was over in the matter of fifteen seconds.

When hearing of this, people often ask:
"What? Shot four times with a shotgun and you lived?"

Yes, I "lived."
Of course, this needs a little more explaining. Nobody just jumps in anywhere and starts shooting for no reason, do they?

I must have called his mother a filthy lying whore, or at the very least, ran over his dog. I must have extended a lifelong torture on the souls of his family, a new found depth of the poon-ji mind screw he was intent on freeing himself and his loved ones from.

Well, let's see... it goes like this...
From the time we entered the RV Resort in early November 2012, it was evident this person was trouble. He accosted my son on several occasions in a drugged up and manic fashion. He'd been a nuisance to everyone in the RV Park in this manner. Everyone in the Park, including the employees, had a story to recite of how this person was a drugged-up nutcase. My son pointed him out to me on one occasion then told me how erratic and weird his behavior was. We agreed to try and avoid him at whatever cost till we left the Park. Not easy since he was sitting in a lawn chair most of the day two RV spaces away, chain smoking outside his Fathers trailer. He was visiting his father who lived there as a permanent resident in his RV.

Gavin was gone to visit his Sister for Thanksgiving and was to return for Christmas in Las Vegas. I'd just returned after visiting a day in Vegas for Thanksgiving, this incident happened the day after. Luckily, thanks to advance planning and happenstance, Gavin wasn't there.

I was relaxing in my RV, reading a book in the early evening around 6pm. There was a rustling outside and then overly hard knocking on my door. When I looked out the window, I saw this guy standing there nervously fidgeting. When I opened the door, there he stood, obviously drugged up and hyper.

Grinding his teeth and twitching, he asked if my son was there. When I told him no, and why, his glazed look changed a bit. Without missing a beat, he cocked his head sideways and demanded I give him a cigarette. I told him; "*Sorry, I don't smoke*," then abruptly shut the door.

When the door shut, he immediately growled like an animal and started shouting obscenities while smacking the side of my RV. So hard, it was enough to make the whole trailer shake a bit. He stomped away cussing and yelled at nearby tenants. This was both the beginning, and end of my patience with this guy. I knew by smacking the side of my RV hard like that, he definitely left a big dent in the aluminum sheathing, I got on the phone and called the local sheriff.

Soon finished with my complaint and assured they were on their way, I sat down on the couch again intently listening to the goings on outside. I'm not an overly aggressive person and this guy hadn't been known *(to me)* as an actual danger, so I didn't think of getting a gun out for protection. He was not a big guy and wiry or not, I could easily pick this guy up and toss him around if need be. There was no possible way he could tussle with me and win, I would be more worried about hurting him and getting a charge of my own. I gave him no more weight than an obnoxious drunk teetering around the park. My son and I had seen plenty of those types in our travels.

There was a bit more noise and yelling outside as other tenants stared on. After a minute or so, I heard nothing more.

All of this happened in the span of five to ten minutes.

As I looked back to my book for a second, waiting for the authorities, I heard paced footsteps on the gravel in front of my RV. I thought it was probably the old guy parked next to me coming to talk about this guy, but within a second, the door of my RV was thrown open and in he bounded. At this point, he was no longer just some idiot drug freak causing problems.

This fool went back to his Fathers RV where he was staying, retrieved his Fathers shotgun, loaded it, then retraced his steps back to my RV. On his way back to my trailer, he traveled by foot carrying a shotgun, and even though several people saw what was happening, nobody yelled. Everyone ran without so much as a sound.

All these people who sit around campfires with guns strapped to their sides postulating on scenarios of violence. All of these people who dream of being a "hero," with their guns, spewing what they would do and how they would do it... they all *RAN* without a sound. Apparently, a drug fiend carrying a shotgun back to the place he just made a scene doesn't raise concern enough in modern America.

When I first saw him coming through the doorway, it was the shotgun that caught my eye. I thought of the type and its capacity. I thought of where my closest gun was, easy to get, but first I would have to turn around. My next thought was to turn around and get it, but there was no time, he leveled the shotgun at me and racked it within a half second.

Somehow, instinctively, I jumped towards him, first moving left then lunging to the right as he racked the gun. I skirted to the side and grabbed the shotgun by the end few inches of the barrel.

As I was taught many years earlier, this movement kept him from pulling the trigger as he tried to keep the long gun pointed at me.

We struggled for a second, I leapt ten feet and was leaning forward off balance, he had a leverage advantage. The butt of the gun was wedged against him and a protruding wall immovable. In the struggle, within milliseconds, the open end of the shotgun barrel found its way to my left eye socket. As I turned my head and pushed the barrel away, he pulled the trigger and a piece of the back of my head was blown away.

This spun me around onto the couch to which he immediately racked the gun again. Stepping forward, he put the gun in my back pulling the trigger again. I was writhing as I felt the barrel touch my spine and moved just enough to where the blast went through the back of my right elbow, effectively severing my arm in two.

Mind blurred, I struggled halfway to my feet again and heard him yell *DIE DEVIL!* as the shotgun's action racked again.

I somehow jumped out of the way and was able to yell, ***WHAT ARE YOU DOING!*** as the next blast ripped through the chair next to me, also shredding pieces of my clothing.

Again, I heard the gun rack. I was able to jump out of the way, falling onto the dinette table suffering little more than "pepper," to my legs.

As I heard the guns action rack once more, I thought this was surely my end. I was thinking in packets of compressed experience which expanded into deep, meaningful all-encompassing visions I had been a part of. What a terrible end this was for my family, I couldn't believe I was to die like this.

I waited there for death, this was a five round gun and there should have been one shell left. I was now very weak and couldn't bring myself to move again.
I laid there prone and broken, a sitting duck, I was fogging out.

A loud *CLICK!* was what temporarily broke that fog.

Hearing the gun's firing pin fall on an empty chamber gave me a "second wind" of sorts as a mind-numbing yell in my head shouted, ***"JUMP FOR YOUR GUN !!"***

I struggled up as fast as I could reaching across to the void beside the couch where the pistol was. I reached with only the action of my right shoulder as I saw what remained of my right arm hanging limp in shreds. Without hesitation, I quickly reached for the gun with my left. Standing there with my back turned to him I yanked the holster snap off with my teeth. Spinning around I took a bead on his now wide-eyed head from ten feet away as he moved to jump out the door. I was able to pull the trigger and nearly hit him... I would have hit him easy... time for two... but intensely concentrating and spinning around, I became faint with these last desperate movements having run completely out of blood.

I was floating in a cloud as I turned to shoot and slumped to the floor in staccato slow motion, still able to see for a few minutes longer but now, completely unable to move.

In the next minutes, the Sheriff finally arrived. A uniformed officer appeared in reflection coming in the RV full bore, quickly asking blank questions. There were muddled sounds and shadows of fading responders dancing across the pools of blood I was lying in.
I could barely gurgle ....*help...why?... why?...*

Breaking free, I floated to the ceiling, I could see myself on the RV floor. Covered in blood, akimbo, staring at the baseboard with a blank gaze. My consciousness changed from inside the RV to hovering in the tree above the gurney I was placed on outside. The crowd was wrought with looks of horror, people were pushing and running in circles. Someone was holding the shotgun, it seems bent. The paramedics lifted me into the ambulance and the scene faded away.

The scene changed again; I hovered at blade height on the highway out front. I was being taken off the gurney and placed in a Medivac helicopter. A nurse's face was horrified, brow furrowed shaking her head with a look of little hope.
Then, my previous Earth's consciousness was gone.

It is very hard reliving that time and those circumstances over and over, again and again. I have spent many years on this subject. Here, it is enough to know it happened.

Some months later when looking through news coverage of the event, I found a picture taken by someone at the very moment I remember hovering at the helicopter. The picture isn't sharply clear, but I always look for a visage of my soul somewhere there. I recounted that scene to people many times before I ever saw that picture. From the time I came back, and for a long time after, I was trying to make sense of things. I was confused for quite a while about the conditions of my death and return.

Two days after the incident, I woke in a Hospital bed at University Medical Center in Las Vegas. It took a few minutes to get my bearings. I felt very clear, literally as if there were no roof. No top to my head, no ceiling in the room, no roof over the building. The bed with me in it was below, the room I was in was below, the building that room was in, below. It was almost like looking down from Google Earth, in a tunnel descending. All very clear and crisp. Everything was positive, everything bright.

My right arm was in a traction device waiting, it was severed and barely attached. Before coming to, I had a couple small strokes, but on that second day, I woke up, clear as a bell.

I looked around the room and settled on a dark corner. Everything else was bright, this darkness drew my attention.

A person was sitting in a chair in the corner, it was my Father. I thought to myself, *"you don't belong here."* It felt as if his presence was interrupting my experience. I looked right at him and in a judgmental tone said; *"What are you doing here?"* It was automatic and seemed correct.

I do realize that was harsh and cold, unfeeling and perhaps even seems mean, but it wasn't meant that way. I didn't even think about it, I said it quick and automatically, it was what our previous interactions had produced. I felt as if someone not qualified to be in my new presence had found their way in to my room and it was time for them to unequivocally know. You should not be here. It was a strange feeling, like I was a King on a throne.

This is an example of what I mean when I say this was a turning point for thought in my life. I now thought of my Father differently than just a week before. There was an expansion of thought processes and more to pull meaning from.

Just a week before, I thought of him as a lifelong asshole, a pain in my ass as well as anyone that gave him their time. I was thinking of him in terms of how he affected my thought and our extensively negative time together.

Now, I think of him as an average human plodding around Earth with no purpose. Someone following along with the conventional thought they've been given, not knowing where they are going and basically living a life of never-ending frustration and futility. Not a situation they consciously think of, or even realize, but a baseline condition they never rise above or move away from.

I realized; I was now different. Throughout my life I was always reaching out for something else. Looking for something I could never find. Feeling there had to be something besides the standard circles humans live their lives in.

No different now than a thousand years ago save the baubles. Our thoughts and actions are the same, completely centric. Now, somehow my mind was open to something else, I felt closer to something those around me can't understand. From then forward, this would always be in the front of my mind instead of hidden deep in the back. It would still take me a few years to believe the differences were real, but eventually I proved it to myself.

That was the last time I would see my Father. He said nothing and left quickly, very few people knew he was even there. As I write this, I write it in the tense of a future time frame, he has not yet passed, but I doubt I will see him again, I have no place at his funeral or at his gravesite. I realized in that moment he was a donor for my body and had nothing to do with my mind other than being a lesson for me to pick the negatives from. Solidifying those negatives as a place to which I would no longer return. He served his purpose, anything more was useless. I do nothing more than thank him for his contribution. Throughout our lives, we were never endeared to one another.

Like most, he is steeped in self-serving convention. He was at my bedside out of convention, it was what he was expected and prodded to do, therefore thought he should. I'm sure he had his own emotion tied to being there, but these were emotions put there by example of convention. I thank him for his part in my life, that is all.
Truly, without the dark there is no light.

Now, nearly 15 years after the fact of what I consider my "awakening," I am *VERY* different than I was. A completely different person actually. I am *very* different from most everyone I will ever meet throughout the rest of my life. The freshness I experienced in the weeks after I woke up has faded a little, but I still see everything in a very crisp and finite way.

I know where the light is, yet am fated to walking in circles through this brimstone until we touch again.

I was lying in a hospital bed hooked up to machines and devices. The trauma Surgeon only tied off my damaged arteries, refilled me with blood and restarted my heart. They weren't going to fix me yet, they wanted a couple days of observation, it didn't look like I had a very good chance. I'd been flatlined, completely out of blood for over an hour before they were able to get me off the roof, into the building and get me going again. No-one was sure of my state. The Heli-vac team did their best, many were surprised my heart restarted. Now they wanted to wait and see if I was going to die again before moving forward, no sense in spending all that time, effort and money on a lost cause.

Two days of tests were run, Doctors and Nurses came and went. I was in good physical shape when this happened, things were looking up. I was put to sleep and taken in for three separate surgeries. I later found out the five Surgeon team had taken a vote on whether to remove my arm or not. Only the vascular Surgeon voted to remove it.

I'm so thankful he lost out, I'm not sure whether I could have stood being a one-armed person. I know many are... I just don't know for myself, and thankfully I don't need to worry about that now. All these years later, I am typing this with one-and-a-half hands. If there ever was such a thing, it's a miracle my arm works at all. By all accounts it shouldn't, but somehow, I now have slight use of it.

There was a trough in my skull to repair. My arm was reattached and rebuilt with titanium and a twenty-degree hinge for an elbow. My leg was the least damaged, part of it was used to fix my arm. Amazingly, by the virtues of modern medical science, my body would be Ok.

In the next few months of recovery, I would find that my mind was a much different story.

I was told a lot of things in prognosis, most of which I've risen above. Getting to where I am today was a long road, but unless I tell people, or they see me without clothes in some way, I look, act and move relatively normal. All in all, I must say, considering what they were working with, everyone involved did a great job. Heartfelt and eternal thanks to all of them for putting me back together.

Yet my mind is so very different. Not the same at all, it's like I'm a different person. A *MUCH* better person as far as I can tell. There were, and are, things going on in my mind useless to try and explain. There is no point of reference for other people to understand. It took me several years to figure it out, but now I know, and it is still too much to explain. There isn't actually any reason for explanation, it just is, I just am. Now that it's all over, I'll have to continue.

When people hear of this debacle, I often hear things like; *"Well at least you were able to sue everyone involved." "I would have sued the pants off everyone involved." etc....*

But No, that is not how it worked.
It is true, shortly after I woke up from my surgeries, I entertained a somewhat long list of lawyers with the tale of events. The problem with all of it was that it happened in Utah. If all of this would have happened thirty miles away in Nevada or Arizona, all would have been much different. Utah does not have reckless endangerment laws. Or any laws that would afford me satisfaction. No Utah Lawyers would take the case and no National Lawyers would challenge the Church.

That's right, not the Laws, or the State... The Church.
Utah is entirely run by the Mormon church.

In Utah, personal responsibility means you avoid those of lesser intent. It is not for them to not do bad, it is up to you to avoid it. If you get stuck in the middle, the church will help you; if you are a Mormon. Otherwise they will work against you.

One might imagine there would be a company of legal firebrands to challenge this, but again you would need to know more. Everyone of any sand in Utah is a Mormon, everyone in the Utah Government is a Mormon, All the Lawyers in Utah are Mormons. They won't go against the church, and if they do, the Mormon Church cannot be outlasted. They actually do have "more money than God."

When all the people holding all the top offices and courts in the state are in the church, the rules of the church are upheld. It is the church that runs the state. The consensus from everyone involved, on every legal angle presented, towards all the entities that failed, is that I needed to forget about it and move-on. The wagons were circled and I was on the outside of that circle. I did get a heartfelt apology from my attackers Father. He worked for a church controlled media company and brought me a truck bed full of food from the Mormon Deseret Industries Food Bank.

He said his son had been trouble since young and he wished I had been able to kill him when I had that chance. He thought that would be the only way to end the pain and suffering his son had caused his entire life. He was sure there were "demons" involved.

Craig M. Bennett Jr., the man that shot me, spent a few years in jail and was let go. I don't purposefully follow him so there is no telling what has become of him.

When I got out of the Hospital, I stayed at my Mom's apartment there in Vegas, she was a big help. Yet, my Mom was used to living alone and her apartment wasn't very big.

After a month, I seemed to be doing alright and it wasn't long before it was time to go.

We went back to Utah and retrieved my trailer. It was a horrific event for my family, but while I was initially in the hospital, they cleaned and sanitized the entire RV. Most all evidence of the ordeal had been erased. The only remaining signs were shot pepper marks and some missing interior panels.

By February, 2013 the Hospital had a court order to freeze my bank accounts and find all my assets. Within two weeks I had no money, they left me with my RV and my truck. Even my children's college funds were taken. I had a hidden box of $5k in hundreds tucked away in the RV, that was all I had left. A real-life example of why health insurance can be useful if you have it. I did not have any health insurance, I was screwed. My life was yanked back twenty years to a negative square one.

A friend of mine I met in that RV park in Utah sent me a message. Knowing the management personally, she worked there off and on. Occasionally I played guitar for the guests during weekend potlucks and get togethers in the clubhouse. Her and I would sing a certain duet now and then.

Nickel was always bright and shiney. She had her own Karaoke act she performed there also, a real fun and likeable person. She was back at her home in Arizona now and offered me a place to stay while I recovered. I mentioned everything about my current predicament. She offered free of any charge, glad to help me in any way she could.

Arm still bound and prescriptions full, I hooked up my RV and headed to; of all places on Earth, Tombstone Arizona. I didn't realize it yet, but there, I would be facing more "demons."

I arrived in Tombstone the last week of March of 2013. Not being fully healed, I was enjoying a course of daily inebriation via the "pain management" medication oxycodone.

It was good to see Nickel again. She was always smiley and cheerful. I parked my trailer beside her house and lived in it for a few days until we had the unlived-in side of her adobe duplex full of storage items dealt with. This was my home till October of 2015. A long time to suffer the indignity of that town.

A full 6 months lost, being totally zonked out on oxy. I was finally able to say to myself; *enough is enough*. For some apparently, physiologic reason, I've never had an addiction temperament. It's always been easy for me to leave behind things like drugs and routines which seem to trap others. Even though I had a never-ending prescription from the "Pain Management" facility in Vegas, I stopped the oxy when my most recent bottle ran out. I then needed to find something to do with myself.

I started walking the town and looking around. Right then, and to this day, Tombstone is as big as it's ever been, Tombstone proper seems hardly a square mile, about 6x13 blocks.

I explored everything and learned pretty much all there was to know about Tombstone, including its history and how it got to be where it is today. Actually, not very exciting stuff, most of Tombstone's story today is a fuzzy, purposeful lie. Concocted, built up and maintained for the tourist trade. Most of the town's *actual* history is based around profiteers and no-accounts. The most interesting thing I found there was the fact that out of all U.S. towns of its size, it holds the death and destruction record by far. Most small towns rarely have any incidents of gun play, Tombstone prides itself on it.

I met a real nice guy there named Leroy, he lived there for many years. He was an usher at one of the main tourist attractions in town, the Birdcage Theater. He was one of the few people in town who didn't carry a gun on his side, he had a folding Buck knife on his belt.

He was shot dead in the street two blocks from my house by an idiot over a woman who didn't really like either one of them. I heard noise and commotion one day around noon then walked out in front of my house. Leroy was laying there askew in the street until someone put a blanket over him.

I was walking through town the next day and heard one of the mindless street hawkers talking to a UPS man about the event. It was her contention it was Leroy's own fault he got killed, primarily because he didn't carry a gun. That's how twisted that town is.

Tourists regularly shot holes in the ceilings of bars. Two people, including a tourist were shot a week after I left during one of the daily fake gunfights. A local drunkard stooge in the street show had real bullets in his gun. It is my personal contention; no person with half a wit has any business in Tombstone, Arizona.

Gavin came to Tombstone to "take care of me." The whole town was another adventure for him also. As things turned out, he seemed to be there to play a bigger part. Not unlike the major role he has always played in my life.

Typical of the type of things that happen to Gavin as he mingles with the "hearing world," two near death experiences were thrust upon him there. He entered the circle of people his age that lived there and as always initially happens, the girls were interested in him. This is a usual situation for him, but what comes with that is jealousy from the guys.

Once, a group of them took him into the strictly off limits abandon mine shafts. Tombstone is honeycombed and riddled with mine shafts that extend down to 400 feet and are filled with water at the bottom. None of them have been in use for a hundred years and all are very dangerous, especially without any prior knowledge.

These guys ditched him down there at about two hundred feet with only a lighter, it took him two days to find his way out. Another time, one of them spiked his beer with an overdose of some drug and he fell face down in the middle of the main street. Paramedics had to administer Narcan, he was passed out for two days. Luckily the local Marshalls knew both of us and were keeping an eye on him or I'm sure more would have happened. They kept me informed on all they knew. After a year of this, Gavin left Tombstone for Seattle and stayed there for a while. That was never much better though.

While he was still there in town with me, one day I came home and found a book on the dining table. Curious to it how it got there, I picked it up and just casually turned to a page. The first sentence I read said something like;
"This book finds those it is meant for."

Later, I learned my son had put it there. Someone coming through town he didn't know gave it to him. People have always been interested in Gavin. Many meet and spend a few minutes conversing with him, this was one of those people. The guy told him he thought this book was for him. Gavin wanted me to tell him about the book. I explained it to him but the book wasn't for him, it was for me. It started to explain what was in my head. *It found me.*

The entire time I was living in Tombstone, I never dressed the part like the rest of the town. I was in Beach Resort Cabana wear the entire time. Shorts and a bright button-down short-sleeve shirt, flowers or paisley, wearing sandals. Everybody knew who I was as I walked around, I was the guy that didn't belong there. I'd walk right through the middle of town to go sit in the library and use the Wi-Fi. I fine-tuned two books written there, helped Nickel with her stage show a few times and made friends with the best people in town. The couple that owned the Rock Shop were a real nice couple.

I eventually got so bored, I documented, then applied for a patent on a piece of RV equipment I previously made and had been using. Many people in RV parks all over the country had commented on it in the last few years. I thought maybe I could re-coup a bit of my losses... but no, it didn't work out. It could have, I just had no help. I got as far as the provisional patent being approved but didn't have the wherewithal for the rest. I wasn't used to my new physical condition and finalizing a patent is quite expensive, more lessons learned.

After a while I couldn't stand Tombstone or most of the people who lived there. I would leave town and explore other places. I particularly liked Bisbee, another old mining town 20 miles to the Southeast. It had a progressive Hippy side of town designated the tourist area. The other side was a dilapidated conservative side.

Soon, I had a book signing in the only new book store in Bisbee, I was putting up posters all over town a week before. While doing this, I passed the only other book store in town, a used book store. I looked in the window and saw a very interesting looking woman working in there. I went in and turned on a little charm asking her to put my flyer up in her window. A flyer for an event being held at her competitor. She couldn't believe my audacity, but she did it, and it wasn't long before we were good friends. She was the owner of that book store, we ended up spending a lot of time together.

I would hang out and look through the shelves. One day when I was there waiting for her to close so we could go out, I sat in a chair in the back. I started looking through the books right in front of me. Exactly at eye level in front of my face was a book that changed everything for me. It was another book that found me. Inside that book explained everything happening in my head since I was shot.

Not a book for general consumption, if it's for you, you will find it, but to me it was like the grail had found me. Allie didn't know about the book or care what was in it. Very strange in itself since she curated all the books in her shop. She made me pay full price, I had to want that book, and I did. I've read it a dozen times now, and... I *AM* that book. It was written by someone exactly like me.... for me. There aren't many of us, and there aren't many of those books floating around. For that book to have been there at that time in front of my face was like finding the proverbial needle in a field of haystacks.

I also thought for some reason, like the book, Allie might be for me, but ultimately, she wasn't. She was a beautiful messenger whom I will always treasure, I have deep affection for her. We would go on weekend trips to nearby towns and explore. Later, I'd meet her someplace she was across the country, she'd come meet me someplace I was.

I really liked Allie as a person and good friend. She was living her life within the ideals of a circle of women if have termed, "The Impermanence Dolls." That being, aware women who shun attachment. Over time, I have known many. Although it's not a club and none know of each other I am aware of, we all are/were in the same wide circles for a while.

There were a couple other women in Bisbee and Tombstone I would like to have known better, and almost did, but they turned out to be in situations I've come to know a lot about. I like the woman but not the situation. I didn't want to get stuck in a situation I ultimately didn't really want, merely for some temporary intimacy. I can handle it, but most women our age would like more. I knew I was getting out of Tombstone as soon as I possibly could and didn't want to be anywhere near there ever again, for *any* reason.

I finally got my chance.

When I first arrived in Tombstone, I applied for Social Security Disability Income. After a year and a half, it was finally approved. Once the money started coming every month, I started paying Nickel rent and for her help. I started looking around for anywhere to go. I would have preferred somewhere out of Arizona but accidentally came across info from "somewhere" for an intentional community North of Tucson called Wind Spirit Community. I emailed back and forth a couple times and made plans to head that way.

This place would turn out to be another of these strange things which have now come to be normal in my life. Bad things brush off and fall away without leaving residue, good things find me and become part of me. Those books I ran across helped me with the reasoning and understanding why. I could have only found them together at the bottom of that pit.

I figure there was very little reason for a person recovering from being shot-up the way I was to move to such a violent and gun ridden place like Tombstone. A much denser person may have had the mind to double down, but I'm not dense.

Sure, I had an invite from a friend which was hard to resist, but I also had several other opportunities. I could have gone a hand-full of other directions, but I chose the hell-hole. Not for a clear reason, but for a subconscious one. I believe I was drawn there, the wheels were turning. It wasn't an attraction to Nickel as one might think. There was plenty of opportunity, and I'm sure that's what she had in mind in the first place, but we were never together. Other things were coming together in my head. Memories of situations unfamiliar were beginning to make sense. Everything I had ever done in my life led to this place and now the next.

Tombstone was a snake's belly in a wagon rut, the lowest of low. No place to go but up, and now, I found my way out.

Before I left, I did two things that were nagging. I was still clinging to pieces of my old life. Old life situations tend to ruin new. We leave old ideas and ways behind for new places and experiences, but bringing with me last life's stuff was like not shaking off the ludd. *Gotta shake-off the Ludd.*

I contacted Marika and initiated a divorce. I don't really know how she felt about it, she was very tight lipped and matter-of-fact about the whole thing. The idea of hurting her, hurt me, but I knew what she was on the outside, a hard-nosed survivor. I'm pretty sure she already moved on. By now, I know she has for sure. Time heals, relationships are replaced with another. Sometimes fond memories are enough, sometimes not.

I did something else which still hurts to this day. The loss became a part of me I had been missing. I sold my last guitar. Playing music had been solace for me for many years. Picking up a guitar always calmed me and immediately changed my head space. I had a visceral feeling of calm when I picked up a guitar but it was time to let it go. With my destroyed right arm, I could no longer play. It just sat there and frustrated me. Now when I tried to play it, it would make me cry. I can still feel a twinge of this previous calm as I write this. I truly miss that sensory feeling, the focus and release, the attention and admiration from those listening.

I consider it a cog in my life which made its last turn. Another cog would take its place. The realization I was done with it, hit hard, and somehow still does. If I transpose this feeling, likening it to drugs and alcohol, even our long-term relationships, I can empathize with these things. Many years later, recovering drug addicts and alcoholics still have that twinge. Lifelong lovers can still feel the arms of their loved ones embrace. My guitar was an old lover, I can still feel her embrace, even now, this many years later.

It was much more than just a beautiful day when I was finally able to kick over that Tombstone. When I looked back as I left that crappy little town, why was I crying?

When I left, I felt so good, like I couldn't be stopped. Just to leave that town is a story worth telling.

Lucky S.O.B.

Chapter Thirteen

"You know, when you came through here a few years back, you told me all about how that happened to you. None of it ever came together till just now, I'm glad I heard all that. I wasn't much good for company back then, Betty was so sick, I didn't have much else on my mind. It sounds like you never made it out of Purgatory, you've got another chance, you have to be sure and use it. Faith in Jesus."

"Oh, not really, I consider this point just the opposite. It's true Tombstone was purgatory if any place on Earth is. Except there, one can choose to leave. Those folks never choose to leave, it's a terrible place to live. But I did choose to leave, I could hardly wait. I left there and basically went to the Garden of Eden. The Intentional Community I went to was the best place I've ever lived, at least for a while."

"Was it a religious place or some kind of cult?"

"Well they didn't make me shave my head or wear special underwear, anything like that. But the people I found there at that time were some of the best folks I've ever known. Truly a great place."

"Was there any kind of church or Spiritual leader? Did you have to give up all your stuff?"

"No, it wasn't that kind of place at all. Just a place where everyone intentionally tried to live together peacefully and help each other. No religion at all, but if someone wanted to, they could go into town to a church if they wanted, no-one would have cared.

That was part of the intention. Free to do what you want, and not imposing ourselves or our previous lives on one another. The first couple years there were the best I've ever known...."

I left Tombstone at 10am on a Thursday Morning, I was surprised and quite happy to show up at the community around 1:30pm. I was thinking it was much further than it actually was. I found the leader, Don, he directed me to a second driveway, then to a spot for my RV. It was a real nice spot, tucked into a small clearing under a tree. Next to a small garden and a laundry shed.

After I was settled, I took a rest, and after an hour or so, there came a knock. I opened the door and was greeted nicely with a big smile. It was one of the people in the community inviting me to come sit and relax with a group of others.
A big happy greeting, then the first thing Jerry asked me was
"Do you smoke?"
"Not cigarettes if that's what you mean."
"Cigarettes is NOT what I mean..."

Eight of us sat in a circle with bird feeders, suncatchers and sparkly-jingly things dangling from crisscrossed cords above our heads. Happy dogs were lying next to their masters. Dozens of hummingbirds were darting around us feeding and giving us a wonderous show. The sounds of a desert Oasis were unknown and uncommon to me but oh, so welcome. When I finally went to bed that night, I didn't know who or what to thank, such a beautiful confusion.

The land itself was utterly amazing.
Sixteen acres of gardens, trails, trees and vegetation. The whole place was square in the middle of a valley desert area but fully irrigated by a three hundred foot well. A huge, fully equipped Kitchen with an outside gathering area beside it. Permanent hut residences and several trailers and buses set up on the back end for full-time and temporary living quarters.

All of this among fruit and nut trees. Plums, several kinds of oranges and grapefruit, pecan and pistachio, peach, lemon, mulberry and a large olive grove. Much more, but you get the idea. It was a fantastic place, the proverbial, yet literal, oasis in the desert.

It has been there since the early 1970's when started by a group of Hippy types, back then for some reason, it was called Christmas and also much bigger. It evolved over the years but as money became tight, parcels were sold to what are now neighboring homesteads and small ranches.

My first impressions of this place were very positive.
It felt so relaxed and peaceful, all the people living there were so nice and thoughtful. A stark and welcome difference from Tombstone, it was like being slapped with a good hand.

I spent the Fall and Winter getting to know the land, the area and all the people both at Wind Spirit and on the 8-mile, dead end dirt road it was on. The whole situation was paradisiacal. The weather was very mild for what Arizona previously offered. At 4800 feet, it rarely went over 100 degrees and would actually get chilly at night, there was even a dusting of snow that Winter.

Time was spent in maintenance of the land and readiness for the next season. Whether it be growing, swelter or retreat season, there was always something to do. Over the Winter a lot of people came for temporary visits. Some had never been there before and some were return guests who came to get away for a week or maybe a month.

In February a woman making a circle of the US showed up. She was from Montreal and wanted to see the communities and communes in the US open for visitors. She had just come from a month in the strawberry fields of Plant City, Florida. There, one could volunteer to work in return for room and board.

Lucy was a very nice woman, just a few years younger than me. Slight and coquettish, just as I always imagined French Canadian women to be. Typical of what I would see over time, she was traveling and taking notes to try and open her own property in Canada. She was very energetic, both a looker and a worker, she did not sit still. We hit it off and when she left in March for her next visit to a place in California, we made plans to get together the next month in Utah. She wanted to see all the National Parks there. It worked out well, she had a camper van and I had an Unlimited National Parks Pass. I had already been to all the parks in Utah a few years back with Gavin, I knew just what to do and where to go.

After our sojourn, I got back to Wind Spirit and Lucy moved on to Dancing Rabbit Community in Missouri. From there she would go to the Oaks then head back to Canada. We had a great time, I asked her back to Wind Spirit, but she reminded me her heart belonged to a man in Canada who worked on a cranberry farm. She was hoping to start her own new property with him.

I would find a lot of this attitude within this communal lifestyle. People who knew the difference, and separated mind and body, love and emotion, a very satisfying life. I was jealous of him only because he had her heart.

In the next month, the community hosted a few retreats. One of the ways the community made money was to host events and retreats. Each Spring and Fall there was a schedule for different kinds of Yoga and Spiritual getaways. We even hosted the Dances of Universal Peace. All great fun and a way to meet a diverse group of people, many would become great friends.

During the Winters and especially the hotter and more uncomfortable Summers, many of the permanent residents would take short trips.

Over the years I was there, I went to San Diego several times to visit my Uncle and house sit while his family went on vacation. I went back and forth to Florida to visit my Mother, Brother and Sister a few times, I spent a few weeks in Key West, Seattle and Mexico with friends putting around. I even stayed several times with a friend in Sedona who made her living as a spiritualist. In actuality, she wasn't very spiritual. On other occasions throughout the years, people I met on my journeys would come to see where I was living. Allie from Bisbee came and so did other girlfriends and folks I'd met along the way.

The time I spent at Wind Spirit would have been a true respite from my previous life; if I'd ever gone back to my previous life. As it was, it was a re-direction to a better way. With the exception of only a handful of people I met there, most who filtered through were using Wind Spirit as an extended vacation or were merely playing along with what they thought was a game. many were always hoping to somehow jump back into the ways of regular life and "get-ahead." The other more serious types are the ones I really admired, they were mentors and positive examples I still fall back on. None of them stayed longer than a week or two per year. Usually only during the retreat season.

Time there helped me put humanity in prospective and to explore the contents of those books I came across in Tombstone and Bisbee. I actually used a lot of my time in Wind Spirit to prove the contents of those books. One of the ways I did that occurred early-on, and helped to solidify my mind in its new space.

When I got back from the parks trip with Lucy in my first year, the Community hosted a couple retreats, then got ready to settle into an Arizona Summer. I used this opportunity to head into the wilderness of the United States with no intent other than to prove the ideals I was trying to come to terms with.

I would practice and prove, a walking meditation.

Donning a backpack, I waved goodbye and started a three month walk around the US. I would hitchhike, catch rideshare via the internet and occasionally the bus. It served to prove the values of a mindful existence. Accepting the environment as I found it, depending on nothing more than the positive energy I brought with me. It worked much better than I expected.

It worked out *very* well. I ran into many negative situations and breezed right through. Some I was immersed in, but came out better than I went in. I met a lot of great people, saw a lot of previously met friends and most importantly, proved to myself time after time, the ideals of our humanity are positive, we taint ourselves. I will spend the rest of my life living within these ideals. My life has, and will continue to turn out great. I feel as though I've subliminally known this way since I was very young but was butting my head against a wall. Following along with all the bad examples freely given all around me.

From now on, I would be the light in every room, I would be the positive example for others to notice or follow. From now on, I would be invincible. Better than ten years later, I still am.

I wrote an entire book about that Summer trip. *"A Curb Caste Experience,"* there are a lot of interesting things that happened so I won't go over the whole experience here. A lite overview will suffice.

Stolen cars, shoplifting derelicts, sleeping in the bushes, scabies scare, helping others, meth whore, hitch-hiking, renegade truckers, meth-den party, kidnapped for gas money, drunk driving, running out of water in the desert, old intimate friends, new intimate friends, pie of greatness and getting back to Wind Spirit unscathed with a great big goofy smile. I have been many places, but that stands as the best trip of my life.

Wind Spirit was my home for five years. I built many features and buildings there. I rehabbed many more gone derelict from the environment and needed attention. I stayed busy and lived an easy life. There was short time spent away, but it was my hub, I always came back. Each time I came back, and even sometimes while I was there, things would change. People would come and go. They would take positive and sometimes leave negative. There was always a drama of negative being dispelled. People who didn't belong there or have the right mind-set would try to weedle their way in and exert their own control. It seldom worked for very long but sometimes it would take hold for a while.

The average and boring way of people being people. Dragging their old life baggage with them trying to start something new in their sallow life of old baggage. It is what can be expected. It's a very hard prospect to find a group of people all on the same page for very long, peoples lives evolve.

While I was there, Gavin came to visit twice and stayed for a while each time. He really liked it there and the people there really liked him. He helped us beat down a brush fire heading towards the property and one of our people, a really nice guy named Pierre, died of a heart attack with the effort.

It stuck with Gavin to see Pierre fall and never get up again. Death strikes Gavin pretty hard. When his Grandpa in Keyport died in 2009 before we left Seattle, he took it very hard. He disappeared for two weeks. When Pierre died, he was terribly upset for a week before he could come to terms with it. Gavin and I are no longer Father and son, we are best friends. It hurts me deeply thinking I will one day die and leave him.

In 2017 Social Security kicked me off the roles when they found out I was a Veteran. I was told I would never get any benefits when I was put out of the Navy.

It was part of the paperwork I signed before leaving. Social Security made me apply for Military benefits anyway and wanted a turn-down letter if I wasn't entitled. I applied and it turns out that because of the situation of a portion of my service being in a conflict zone, I do get benefits. Now I have a disability Pension and health care benefits, a lot more than Social Security was giving. Another Silver lining within my life provided by the powers that be.

One day in the Fall of 2018, one of my good friends at Wind Spirit, Mark, came to me with a proposition. He didn't like the direction the community was going and wanted to get out. In his words, *"I can't stand the constant influx of crazies and Don letting them stay, I'm too old for this now."* I agreed about the situation but we both saw many ups and downs, I thought it would turn up again.

Mark was now in his seventies and had been on the property for thirteen years. He was an illegal immigrant... from Canada. Wind Spirit was a saving solace for him as it was for many of us there. He tripped onto the property at the lowest point in his life. He was on his way to Las Vegas to blow his life savings on wine, woman and song, then commit suicide. The land and people there at Wind Spirit saved him from that fate.

He proposed to buy my RV and I would take his hut. He had enough money saved and maybe I could get him a spot in the Trailer Park where I previously stayed in Tucson.

I took his offer, it worked out well for him. he really enjoyed the change. I guess he was feeling the ludd.

In late 2019, The pandemic was starting to take its toll on the community, some there became reclusive and paranoid. There were new rules for going outside the community some didn't like. Half there wanted to be in complete seclusion and the other half wouldn't even wear a mask when in town.

By the turn of the year 2020, things at the Community changed quite a bit. Many of the regulars were still there but there was a new guy living there now who started as a temporary visitor. He wanted to be a permanent and was buying his way in.

Right away, he and I did not get along.
He left his wife and young child in Phoenix, took up with a wannabe Hippy girl and was growing his hair long. He would sit around in a loin cloth and work at his job via computer in the kitchen. He worked for Lockheed Martin, a completely anti-community type company. At one time, he wouldn't have been allowed to stay as a visitor, let alone apply to be a resident. He and his "girl" would call to each other like Tarzan and Jane from opposite sides of the property. *Sooooo* very annoying.

His midlife crisis was imposed on us further with him trying to start a Dome building business for the bus-side permanent residents to make money. He of-course would be the Boss. A step worse, our primary Don, had been looking for a way to be left alone in his age and defer some of his leadership responsibility for quite a while. He decided this guy elbowing his way in might be a path to that.

I did not participate in any of the situations being presented. I was also quite vocal and straight forward about what I saw going on. The community in the last year had turned into a retreat for people with overbearing physical and mental infirmities. It was becoming a difficult place to live. Sob stories and money were now the bar to meet for entrance criteria. I was against that grain and it didn't take long for the tables to turn against me.

I and one of the mentally unstable girls they'd let in had a falling out and it was decided by the new guy that a community meeting was needed to deal with my non-partisan attitude. The less monetarily liquid and mentally infirm people were easy for him to control, those were his people.

During the meeting I laid out my points and many people agreed, but in the end, the promise of money overshadowed the communities previous committed lifestyle, I had to go. I was effectively voted out.

While in my habitual morning quiet space, it came to me; this placed had served its purpose, I shouldn't fight for a losing cause. It was indeed time for me to go. The turn the community had taken was playing a purpose in my life.

I had a great open feeling when I left, not hesitant at all. A little strange, but I knew this was just another chapter closed and eagerly awaited the next. This situation, as many in my post Utah life, was a just-in-time situation. Conditions turned much worse after I left. A few months later, brush fires forced the evacuation of the property by the authorities and the whole community was disbanded. In a twist of luck and satisfying validation, I was not there, I side-stepped that turmoil.

The new found attitude I have since being shot, killed and brought back to life started slow. It took a while to realize I was meant to be different. I feel I've been guided through, *and to*, this life I now have. My new found attitude attracts people from all walks of life. I've never had so much attention from people who want to know more. From people who feel something themselves and get a glimmer of hope when in contact with me. I have a confidence which cannot be shaken, and it is contagious. And women... I've had quite a time wading through that part. I've had to learn how to avoid becoming entangled. It's a very strange situation which makes me feel as if I control everything around me. Now I realize, *I actually do.*

I'm now able to separate people's actions from their intent and see how much humanity they let in. I do not allow people to take advantage of my good nature, or other people around me if I can help it.

I will always help others without expecting any reciprocation. Yet, I would rather someone learn how to help themselves and am willing to show them if they are open to it. I will under no circumstances personally kill anyone or anything ever again. I will die first if it comes right down to it. I am though, willing to teach hard lessons and stand-by while hard lessons are taught.

This is the attitude that stuck to me. I would take this with me from Wind Spirit, from Tombstone and the end of that shot gun. It turns out, being shot was the best thing that ever happened to me. When I left Wind Spirit, it was over, I had graduated Shotgun therapy. *Flip the tassel.*

By this time, it was May of 2020, in the middle of the Covid 19 Pandemic. I took my things to Tucson but had no place to stay right off hand. I went to see Mark and made plans to go visit my Mom and Sister in Ocala, Florida.

The landlord at the park Mark was in was gracious enough to offer me a place to rent for a few days till I lit out for Florida. She was pretty nice and was doing all the coordinating for her husband. By that time, Mark was doing all the maintenance in the Park for them and had become a trusted employee/tenant. He mentioned she asked a lot of questions about me before she rented me the furnished trailer for a week. I thought that a bit strange since I'd rented there before on two occasions and we were already familiar with each other.

Mark was not surprised I was pushed out of Wind Spirit. He got an I-told-you-so moment and spent a couple days hovering on what he'd been noticing at the community for quite a while. All of what I experienced was the very reason he decided to leave after thirteen years of living there. He was right, it hadn't been a quiet and peaceful place for over a year and had no signs of going back.

Gavin and I went to Florida to visit my Sister and Mother.

The entire Country was shut down, there wasn't much else to do. I maintained the yard and did some additions to my Sisters house. Did a ton of maintenance on my truck and twiddled my thumbs quite a bit. It was painfully hot and humid that Summer, I couldn't be outside more that 15 minutes at a time during the day.

Gavin was bored stiff and had been texting back and forth with a girl he met at Wind Spirit. She was gone from there also and was now in Northern California living in the woods with a band of folks near Mt. Shasta. That sounded good to him so he took a flight to Sacramento where she picked him up. The Covid era airline prices were nuts, an Ocala to Sacramento ticket for $85. He was off on an adventure of his own.

Him doing that kind of stuff was hard on me but I knew he needed to get out and do things like every other person. All I could do is keep my fingers crossed and my phone close. I knew he could take care of himself in general and I trusted in the kindness of others to help keep him safe. Besides, part of the situation would be him working as a Marijuana trimmer. That paid well and those folks mostly sat around high all the time, not a lot to worry about.

In July, my friend Allie from Bisbee got in touch. She would be visiting her parents in Venice Beach, Florida and wanted to hang out Camping in the State forest there. I packed up my things in Ocala and met her in Venice Beach. We spent a couple weeks together traipsing all over the area then went up the coast to spend time on the water at a Park near Port St. Joe. It took a little while, but she finally got tired of me so I headed back to Arizona.

On my way back to Arizona I purposefully drove along the water through the panhandle to see the devastation of Mexico Beach from the hurricane that went through a couple months earlier.

The devastation was literally hair raising. Traveling west, 200 yards from the beach, there were acres of pine trees snapped off half way up their length. Huge boats were perched on top of them. Nothing but snapped pilings on the left where the beach houses used to be. Pieces of homes and lives strewn everywhere. Topless semi-tractor trailers being filled with debris were everywhere. It was hard to imagine someone carrying on after such an event.

As a teen in Tampa, we would have hurricane parties in cinderblock houses and blast "Rock you like a Hurricane" in a short rotation. There were never any direct hits while I was there, only parties. Sometimes the power would go out and things got a little scary, but when it was all over, all we had to do was pick-up the yard. Here in Mexico Beach after a direct hit, it looked like Hell came to visit.

When I got back from Florida in the fall of 2020, Mark was doing great as the trailer park maintenance man but was having a hard time with his health, his breathing had become labored. I started renting monthly there again except this time I would live inside the owner's compound in a furnished trailer which was covered and behind gates.

I eventually got a new girlfriend, did some more back and forth to San Diego house sitting for my Uncle and was living a basic existence again. After a month or two, Mark came to me and asked a favor. Would I take him to the airport in a couple days, he was going to fly home to Canada. In a few short months, his health had really taken a turn. His breathing was now so bad from a lifetime of smoking, he could barely walk 10 feet without stopping to rest. He couldn't get healthcare here in the States and didn't want to die here.

I of course took him and we said our final goodbyes. Mark was a great guy and a good friend.

I sold the RV for him, sent him the money and we emailed back and forth a couple times. A couple months after our last email, his brother sent me a message informing me Mark had died. At least he got to see his home and family again. Mark was a beautifully troubled Soul. I think about and miss him often, I'm so glad to have met and known him well.

I was now the maintenance man for the trailer park and the other houses the Landlord owned. The actual Landlord I initially knew, *(husband*) had recently died and his wife was now taking over all the responsibilities. This guy had been in his mid-eighties, she was in her late forties with their two children and she was taking on quite a load. I could tell, she was looking for someone to share the responsibilities with.

I found out the reasoning for her asking Mark all about me. She was looking for a partner at the very least, and I was a candidate. She was quite forward and I'm sure would have been more overt except for the fact I already had a girlfriend and she knew it. My friend Kathy came over to my place quite often and I'd seen them giving each other the hairy eyeball.

Although she was an exceptionally good-looking woman, I kept her at arms-length, I really liked Kathy and I had no desire to live out my life doing maintenance on houses, stuck in Tucson. I didn't know what was next, but I couldn't lock myself into this heat scorched place.

A week or so after finding out Mark died, I got a call in the middle of the night. It was a girl in Northern California, Gavin had her call me. He needed bus fare to get him out of there. Things had turned for him. Some of the guys in the group he was with there in Shasta robbed him and left him on the highway in the middle of nowhere. He made it to the closest town and met this girl at a coffee shop. I went the next day to wire him some money, the girl took him there to get the cash.

Then he called his old girlfriend from the woods to pick him up, she agreed to take him back to the camp to get his remaining things. The same thing happened again. They took his money and left him on the highway. At least this time he had his backpack and belongings.

I waited two painful days to hear something from him. I sent money enough for a ticket and a new phone. He knew my number by heart to text me but the call I got was from a guy who picked him up on the highway. He was a pot farmer and was very interested in the whole situation. He turned out to be a pretty good guy. He gave Gavin $300 cash, bought him a plane ticket to Tucson and took him to Sacramento to the airport.

This is how the World treats those unlike themselves. You get two extremes. Hate and harmful indifference or Love and caring. The middle ground the rest of us live with is a very hard situation to come by for functionally different people.

All I can come up with in response, is gratitude and a mental fog that keeps whispering my saving grace.
Time and distance, Time and distance.

The heat and violence of Tucson always preyed on me. A person could only dart from one air-conditioned space to the other in the Summers. The Fall, Winter and Spring were actually pretty nice but the negativity overtook the environment. If it wasn't bolted down, it was stolen, traffic and crazy driving was constant and the daily murder toll was mental torture. I think the worst part was how all the nicer people who lived there had become accustomed to it and thought nothing of it like that was the way life was supposed to be. Living scared of your environment.

Not me, I started saving money and within a few months had enough to get out.

My daughter was my timer, she was pregnant. When she gave birth, Gavin and I would leave Arizona for good.

My Granddaughter was born in late February, 2022.
Gavin and I took two weeks to get ready and pack-up then headed off to Seattle. When there, we stayed a week looking over the baby. The most beautiful little girl I'd ever seen. Except that is, for her Mother. She is the spitting image of her Mother, nearly identical.

Gavin and I visited old friends and went around looking at all we had previously known. Typically, things had morphed so much it was hard to recognize what had been. The Seattle area had become outrageously congested, no longer livable by my standards.

From there, we meandered to Iowa to start the first chapter of this book.

Lucky S.O.B.

Chapter Fourteen

The Spring of 2024 was a continuance of the same for my Grandfathers health. Although he tried not to let me see, I could tell he was slipping.

He had me take his watch to get a new battery, and while I was there, I had them remove a link from the band. It was so loose on his arm, it would slip nearly up to his elbow. Although he had a couple other watches tucked away with adjustable bands, he really liked the $20 watch he had been wearing for several years. It had a button on the side to push for a light feature which made it easier for him to see at night.

In April, a week before his next birthday, he had me take him for a haircut. This was a routine he enjoyed, he was excited to get out into the sunshine and fresh air. It was a short trip to-and-fro being just a few blocks away. When he got up to pay, reaching in his front pocket he had a look like something was missing. It looked to me he had forgotten his money so I offered to pay, but his face was odd.

"I must have lost my money clip."

He was patting all around his pants until he found his wallet. Then a realization and a look of embarrassment came over him. He hadn't used a money clip in many years. It just came to him as he lightly shook his head mumbling.

"I must be losing it"

That was the first time I saw a full-on glitch, it stirred me a little because it lasted for a minute or better and by the look on his face, he was lost.

His 105th Birthday was a pretty big event. More so for those who attended over the three-day weekend than him. He asked me a few times if I could just forget about it, somewhat selfishly, I could not. It seems as we get older and live into an extended age, along with that comes unwanted responsibility. That of celebrating, and putting up with that celebration.

He mustered all his strength and we hosted dozens of people. I contacted everyone that ever knew him or knew of him. The Iowa State Chiropractic Society assumed he had already passed and were thrilled to hear all about the beginning of their Society from the first President. He got a birthday announcement and accolades in their quarterly publication.

He withstood well-wishers for three hours per day, and even stood for pictures with friends and his big cake. All the conversation and pats on the back tired him out quite a bit.

My Grandfather's 105th birthday was his final turning point. A few days after, he started to get very weak and slowed down a lot. A week after that, he needed help standing and moving around, he could barely get out of bed. He had fully regressed to the point he was at eight months previous. One of these mornings, I called the VA Hospice team Lead Nurse. After another evaluation they recommended he be put in the Hospice unit at the VA Hospital.

Two others showed up, they were preparing to bring an ambulance. I didn't want it to be like this, this isn't what he really wanted. He already voiced his preference to me a few weeks back. He had it in his mind God would take him in his sleep. All he had to do was to go back to sleep, and he wanted that to be in his own bed.

I was a bit relieved though. I was cleaning and sanitizing the bathroom and bedroom every day now. I really hadn't been prepared for this, I was very naive to the facts.

I pulled the nurse aside and told her I would take him to the hospital. They all helped get him in my truck, the ER folks would help me get him out.

Gramps and I took the long way through town, we drove past old places and made historical comments musing on days past. The fifteen-minute drive took us nearly an hour. Thank goodness it was a bright sunny day. We both had to wear sunglasses, my eyes were leaking a little bit. Windows down with a light breeze helped keep my cheeks dry.

First an ER room, then admitted to a regular room, there was a crowd around him at all times. It was a strange thing, all the congratulations and overt respect they were paying him. They kept him over-night for observation and in the morning my Mother and I helped take him through the Hospital to the Hospice unit in the furthest wing. He knew what was going on. As he was wheeled into his room, he looked around and made a pitiful statement.

"So this is where I'm going to die."

He didn't say it to anyone, barely said under his breath, but I heard and kept my hands on his arm and shoulder as things were readied around him.

He was treated as Royalty; I was told he was the oldest World War Two Veteran who had ever been in the Hospice unit. People came with commemorative hats, blankets, blessings and well wishes. I got in touch with everyone still around and for the next week or two there was a steady stream of visitors, family and friends. I visited every day for at least four hours.

For the first week he would beg me to take him home. His mind started to fade and after another week he couldn't be understood. I would read the bible to him, occasionally he would nod and ask a barely intelligible question.

While I was there, in what turned out to be his last week, I made a decision to tell him something else I had never told anyone. Something so very personal and profound, I chose never to mention it. Very few people would believe it or give it any weight. I'm sure most would add-in their own imaginations as to its meaning and worth. A truth, I've held all these years, protected from the mockery of the World.

Grandpas eyes were closed but he would still respond occasionally with a slight nod or hand squeeze. I asked if he could hear me and he squeezed my hand.

"Grandpa, there is something you never asked me. I always thought you might, but you never did. But now, I think it's time you might like to know. I can give you this small benefit.

Everyone is scared about going home, we all imagine something different. Yet when our time comes, we all get the same as we leave. There is nothing to be afraid of, absolutely nothing. I don't know what's on the other side of the curtain for you and me. Once a person comes back, the curtain closes again and it becomes as it was. What happened to me in the time in-between is unknown to me, but I do know for sure, it is now reflected in my mind and life. It had to be good, but I really have no recollection other than that. Yet I do remember leaving from this side.

When we leave, there is no pain, no matter how we die, violent or peaceful, it is the same for everyone. When our body gives up, we leave peacefully and easily. You will have the best feeling you have ever experienced as you pull free of your body. Dying is the best feeling here on Earth, it really can't be described. You will pull free and look down at yourself. You will realize the value of life and accept what is next with no question or emotion, those are left here for us to worry about. You will know for absolute sure that everything you leave behind will be just fine.

It's is the strangest, yet most profound thing you will ever know. Then you will fade into the next. I had to come back, I hope you get what you've dreamed of, I *really, really* do. I know you deserve it, you've tried very hard."

He squeezed my hand and didn't stop until it felt like his muscles slowly quit squeezing. His lips moved a bit without sound. This was the last time I saw him move. He couldn't respond anymore, alive, but asleep.

Two days later holding his hand as he slept, he looked terrible, there was no way to recognize him anymore, he hadn't eaten in a week, emaciated and sallow.

"It's ok Grandpa, no need to stay, you can go now, you're finished here, I love you."

Twenty minutes later, while driving home I got the call.

My Grandfather left in the Summer of 2024. Although I tried to prepare myself for it, it was hard for me. With all our time together in the past few years, he had become my good friend. With all his life experience for me to ponder and all of my death experience that helped ease him towards his own, we became very close.
Always looking for ways to make each other smile.

I'm very glad he had someone that knew him well see him off. I'll miss him a lot.

Lucky S.O.B.

Epilogue

Writing all of this has been difficult, some might say cathartic. I'd like to think I'm past that kind of therapeutic relief by now but I am sure there is a bit of truth there.

To sit and think, forced to study things I haven't thought of in years, a lot of pain and stupidity. My past is an uncomfortable place. I've had to think through events and re-live them inch by inch, then explore the hows and whys; I've cried much. Several times I had to stop writing for weeks until the guilty thoughts subsided or I could hold it together long enough to finish that last section or paragraph. I am completely in touch now with the ramifications of these events. Many circumstances within have created repercussions and tendrils that expanded in other people's lives for a quite a while, some to this very day. I am really very sorry for that.

All of this anxiety manifested. Yet what you have read is merely an arc of causation for print with a few opposing anecdotes for softness. There is just as much and more which didn't make the final cut for this book.

I have consciously put most of what is in this book behind me, I'm not that person anymore. Who I once was, never thought about and didn't particularly appreciate the kind of person I am now, and now, the feeling is mutual. Plodding ever closer to the end, I am not who I was yesterday. Continually and consciously adjusting and refining my attitude for each day as it comes.

Love is hard to maintain, life is in the way, we must somehow endure. I am committed to endure.

Some might say the feeling of ludd which spurned me to move around to new places my whole life was my own fault, of my own creation. It was of course of my creation, *but fault?*

One might say it was the convention of the environments I was in I was railing against. If I had just chosen one environment and conformed to it like a good boy, perhaps I could have "made" something of myself. Perhaps I wouldn't have had as much drama, or pain, or excitement, or wonder, or knowledge, or skill...*or fun*. Maybe I could have relaxed in one place, raised a family and died happily ignorant of the world around me....

For some reason, many reasons, I have never been truly happy with my environment. Except for the first couple years in the Intentional Community in Arizona, all others have weighed on me until I felt I must get-out. Each start in a new place I can see the finer points and enjoy the new, fresh and exciting. Then after a while, sometimes a short while, I start to feel the ludd. Even though I'm now a bit older, I'm still ready for another Chapter. Now more than ever, I appreciate the slow, but still ready for the *Go*.

Not offering a comparison in any way other than mindful; Hemingway offers a fictional self in his writing. From his biography I think he and I had a similar affliction. I don't really appreciate fictional muse as much as perhaps I should. For me, the saving grace in his writing was the relevance of his sub-text. There are two things about Ernest Hemingway that have always stuck with me. One comes from like observation:

"Happiness in intelligent people is the rarest thing I know."

- From the Garden of Eden.

This is something I myself have noticed, yet, it does exist in the corners. The second is the fact that I won't be letting my Ego blow my head off with a shotgun for others to clean up the mess. Painful, drawn out or not, I'll try to fade away.

I've come to think most people pay no attention to the human part of life past the shell they've created around themselves. Most consider themselves people, not humans. At the end of their lives I wonder what they think of, do they take inventory of themselves? Do they ask themselves what have they learned which is actually true? Not their legacy or what they have accomplished, but something to carry on that says their Soul is worthy of something besides trudging around Earth trying to better everyone else. No matter how we win at life, we lose everything in the end. Held up next to everything on Earth, what have we learned about our life's experience which is undeniably true?

Being pushed forward a little faster than most, I have come to my life's pinnacle and true realizations a bit sooner than my last breath. Because I've come to this early, proven it to myself and still have some time left, I get to practice and example it, hopefully helping others come to similar realizations for themselves.

So I've come this far, after all this time, after all I've gone over;
What have I learned for myself?
Much easier would be; what haven't I learned.

The hardest, yet best lessons, are those seldom taught.

Seldom taught because few people actually know them, and when offered, even fewer are paying attention or giving them any weight. These are the lessons which make us successful humans. *Not* successful people, successful *Humans.* There are a lot fewer successful humans than people. As a matter of absolute fact, a successful person who is also a successful human, is one of the rarest things to be found. No one is looking in the corners.

It's not lost on me, I realize I've been charmed from birth.

For some reason, to me, it seems I started out on a higher stair, not fated to internal negativity. Even though born into it, even though immersed as a youth, even though I now know all the ways of negativity, I am separate.

Throughout my life, no matter what I've done or how it turned out, I've never done anything with malice. From a child, till this epiphany came to me. No matter if my actions created a bad situation for someone else, it was not my intent to do so. This pain I caused which others may have endured, was a result of my actions and I learned not to do that again, I never had evil or bad intent. I was never willing to purposefully hurt someone else to make myself feel better or obtain a thing, or status. When given a negative situation, I would actually feel bad and try to mitigate in some way if I could.

Through this, through positive intent, nothing negative stuck. Once I started noticing this, I more often and purposefully had good intent. Through this, not only are negative things held at bay, more good things move toward me.

Through this also, I have always been able to easily see the line between the dark side and good side of intent in everyone around me. I gauge intent. I know the possibilities of those around me based on the intent of the people involved. At some point, sometimes early, everyone shows their intent.

If we can all concentrate on this, we can purposefully intend good. We can try to only make others happy, wish only good things for them, help them, show them only Love and kindness. Give them the leg-up of taking nothing in return. Be altruistic in as much of life as possible. All of this comes back to us, none of this effort is wasted.

A secondary positive is this kind of personality attracts the same and pushes away the negatives.

With practice, soon life is 95% positive with only the uncontrollable unpleasant things remaining. The negative things which are there because of the dichotomy we are all fated to live within. If we can recognize and accept these things, we can push them away also, affect negated.

This has made me "Teflon," relatively invincible in this now small world. Nothing can really hurt me, I am aware of most situations and accept them, no more angst. I have become something most of the world is not, truly special, protected by others and my environment. In this way, I have become immortal, a spiritual human. A confidence I hope will permeate and transfer to others with example and time. Secretly, I now consider myself a white privilege Monk on an extended walking meditation.

Yet, most folks expect more.
Without knowing anything more, I am considered as anyone else. Yet, when people hear of my death experience they want to know more. It is natural to want to know of this, death is the one thing on Earth everyone is guaranteed, yet no one has any experience with. All we know is life.

I find people want validation of their lives and for their religions, but I can't give that. There simply is no validation for me to give. All I can really tell anyone is how the world around them actually works, this is all I have to offer. Mostly, this is not accepted since most people trudge through their life thinking what they are doing already works. Looking for the magic key to best both human nature and Mother nature. Yet neither will stand for that. We can learn to control one, but the other will not be bested. We can only hope to know, use and live with them.

Through every bit of what is previous in this book, I learned our intention is the only true measure, and our example, the only thing we have others pay any attention to.

I learned the ins-and-outs of human nature and how to control my own. But the most important thing I learned, after all is said and done, is how to live a truly successful human life.

I learned:
True human values are Love, compassion, empathy, caring and altruism. The control and material value most of us spend our lives immersed in, really has very little value.
The material heart can by nature, never know real Love.

I learned:
If I think only of you and your well-being, and you were to do the same for me, we both are perfectly taken care of.

Love and take care of those around you and they will Love and take care of you.
A *true* Circle of Life.

A full year after my Grandfather passed, I finished compartmentalizing all the events of previous years. While doing this I noticed a pattern of direction within my life. A subtext only noticeable when putting it all together as a long row of dominoes.
It was a validation of what I dared previously not speculate on.

I am one Lucky Son of a Bitch.

The End

It is not death a man should fear,
but never beginning to live.
~ Marcus Aurelius

If you enjoyed this book, please leave a review on Amazon, Goodreads or Smashbooks.

Then...

Look for similar books of interest by Michael McNaney

www.ingramcontent.com/pod-product-compliance
Lightning Source LLC
LaVergne TN
LVHW090550110826
845146LV00001B/96

* 9 7 9 8 2 1 8 9 2 1 3 0 9 *